T0354289

Two Wars and One Love

Front-Line Soldiers Remember World War II through the Battle of the Bulge and the Korean Conflict

Robert E. P. Moranda and George E. Moranda

iUniverse, Inc.
New York   Bloomington

Two Wars and One Love
Front-Line Soldiers Remember World War II through
the Battle of the Bulge and the Korean Conflict

iUniverse books may be ordered through booksellers or by contacting:

iUniverse
1663 Liberty Drive
Bloomington, IN 47403
www.iuniverse.com
1-800-Authors (1-800-288-4677)

Because of the dynamic nature of the Internet, any Web addresses or links contained in this book may have changed since publication and may no longer be valid.

ISBN: 978-1-4401-3934-5 (pbk)
ISBN: 978-1-4401-3935-2 (ebk)

Printed in the United States of America

iUniverse rev. date: 5/8/2009

To our family, friends, and all those who served with us during World War II and the Korean War

Contents

The Home Front

In Combat

Prisoner of War

After World War II

Preface

During World War II, I served in combat with the 7th Armored Division in Europe as an Infantry 2d Lieutenant. This is a story of my experiences during two wars, especially the Battle of the Bulge. Putting this down in writing creates quite a problem, for memory is not as good a friend as I would like. Names of those with whom I served have faded, unfortunately. But when a couple of my nephews asked me several years ago what I did in the war, I realized that I had kept all of the experiences within myself for these many decades, thinking that no one was interested in hearing about them. I had kept them silent in an attempt to forget most of them. About the same time I watched a documentary about the Ardennes Campaign in which there was no mention of St. Vith, and the viewer got the impression that the whole action revolved around the paratroopers in Bastogne and the famous "Nuts" statement. The 101st Airborne Division and several attached units did a great job there, but there was a lot more to the story of the Battle of the Bulge than that. So between the nephews' question and the film account, I started to write down what I could remember and began corresponding with former comrades in arms, attending reunions, and talking to others who were there with me.

I am disturbed by what I have read recently about the Ardennes Campaign. The Campaign was probably the biggest battle of the war, but there has been a great misunderstanding about what happened there. I saw the war through the eyes of a front line soldier—a guy who was drafted into the U.S. Army having almost no experience with guns or knowledge of military operations other than what I saw in such movies as "All Quiet on the Western Front" and "The Big Parade." I was a happy civilian, married with a young child, had a great family of five brothers and a sister, mother and dad, and, after struggling through a country-wide depression, finally was working in a permanent job that had what appeared to be a future. Perhaps my story will help in furthering the understanding of what so many of us went through during those days and help to improve the perspective about the actions that went on during the Battle of the Bulge.

My war experiences didn't end there, for my country called me and Brother George to serve in Korea during that conflict which again disrupted our lives. Perhaps this story will provide some understanding of what many of us experienced during that period of our national history.

Robert E. P. Moranda

Acknowledgements

We wish to express our appreciation to the individuals who helped with this story. First, thanks go to my nephews Theodore Waite Moranda and Steven Moranda, who pushed and prodded until the story was started. Additionally, those who were there in action with the 7th Armored Division helped read drafts and provided information to fill some of the gaps: Glenn Fackler, Ed Curtin, Maurice Conover, James P. Totoni, Carl Mattocks, and Gen. William A. Knowlton. Col. and Mrs. Donald P. Boyer assisted greatly and gave us permission to use much of Col. Boyer's material. Several others provided pictures and accounts, such as Mrs. Maurice Conover and her children Bret and Denise. Brother Theodore N. Moranda assisted significantly with advice and encouragement, as did Brother Walter B. "Bill" Moranda and our friend Mary Mackie. To get this ready for publication, we had capable and efficient help from Kathy Watts, Doug Dall, Janell Olson, and Anita Reiner. Finally, our thanks go to the men who fought at St. Vith but who never received the credit due to them for thwarting the German offensive at the Battle of the Bulge and to our comrades in Korea.

Robert E. P. Moranda

George E. Moranda

Introduction

Many of those who served in World War II are amazed at how little the younger generations know of that great episode in our country's history, of what sacrifices were made by people from all walks of life who enlisted or were drafted into the military services, or of what it means to them today. We are, at long last, learning more and more from those who participated in that vital struggle because of such popular and successful authors as Professor Stephen Ambrose, who opened a lot of eyes about many things that occurred during that war with his *Citizen Soldier*. Bob Moranda's story is an excellent contribution to our understanding, for he was a front-line soldier in one of the biggest and most significant battles of that war: the containment and defeat of Adolf Hitler's plan to split the Allied forces on the Western Front. Hitler's thrust through the Ardennes forest in Belgium has been appropriately named the Battle of the Bulge, although officially and more aptly titled the Ardennes Campaign, for it was a major part of the war that contained many, many battles.

When the Battle of the Bulge is mentioned during a conversation today, people less than fifty years of age either know nothing of that critical part of World War II or know only that "the Battered Bastards of Bastogne" performed heroically and that some general defied the German demand to surrender by responding, "Nuts." If St. Vith is mentioned, a blank stare is the response. Many television programs about the Ardennes Campaign never even mention St. Vith, which was the most significant part of the entire campaign in that bitter winter of 1944-45. The small group of soldiers who made a magnificent stand there is never mentioned. That group of soldiers was made up of a hodgepodge mixture of men separated from their units: a small group of engineer troops, several units of the 7th Armored Division's 23rd and 38th Armored Infantry Battalions, portions of its 87th Cavalry Reconnaissance Squadron, and a platoon with six vehicles of the 822d Tank Destroyer Battalion—some approximately 850 men formed into a task force. They were supported by artillery fire from a withdrawing corps unit whose commander had volunteered to do their job of firing artillery rounds—the 275th Field Artillery Battalion of 105mm howitzers. Leadership was provided by a young major who was left with that responsibility after his commanding officer decided he was unable to do the job and departed for a rear echelon. The success of this almost battalion-size group was a major factor in allowing General Eisenhower to shift forces to contain and defeat the German effort.

Even such a competent and popular historian as Stephen Ambrose failed to recognize the heroic stand of these American soldiers of the 7th Armored Division in and around St. Vith. When Ambrose wrote his landmark account titled *Citizen Soldiers,* he evoked a resentful outburst from retired General William "Bill" Knowlton, who was at St. Vith as a lieutenant in the 87th Armored Cavalry Reconnaissance Squadron. General Knowlton told his fellow survivors, "Don't buy this book." He will undoubtedly have the same recommendation for Ambrose's 1998 book *The Victors: Eisenhower and His Boys; The Men of World War II,* wherein St. Vith is not even mentioned once. Another historian's account, Professor Gerhard L. Weinberg's *A World at Arms,* praised the 81st Airborne for its brilliant defense at St. Vith—a unit that did not even exist.

Why are there such inaccuracies and inadequate interpretations? It may be that Professor Ambrose gave only a slight mention of the 7th Armored Division's performance in the Battle of the Bulge for reasons of space, lack of information, the need to be selective from the mass of material—written and oral—he had gathered, or plain oversight. Perhaps he singled out only a few of many separate battle-actions that made up the total scene. His treatment of the part soldiers of both sides played is outstanding and has been needed for a long time. It will probably open the door for many more accounts by active, front line participants in that struggle, such as the account of Bob Moranda's experiences. Ambrose's *Citizen Soldiers* is a welcome relief from the large number of biographical and personal accounts, many self-serving, by senior officers and officials who played prominent roles in World War II. As Ambrose pointed out in an article in *Newsweek* (July 13, 1998), it was "the kids who changed the world." Youngsters called into the service that had thrust upon them "ultimate responsibility. . . the kids accepted it, endured and prevailed. They were the sons of democracy, and they saved democracy. We owe them a debt we can never repay." However, there is no excuse for the historical revisionism in which Professor Weinberg engaged.

In Bob's story you will meet Maurice Conover, who was in Bob's outfit during the Battle of the Bulge. An article in *The Billings Gazette*, November 7, 1965, titled "From Bastogne to Broadview," told of Pfc. Conover's experiences during the war. Not once was his unit or St. Vith, where he fought and was captured, mentioned. The article ended: "Twenty-one years ago this Christmas he served with an outfit whose members were immortalized when fellow soldiers named them 'The Battlin' Bastards of Bastogne.'" Conover and his outfit were never in Bastogne. Such errors seem quite commonplace and raise questions about the accuracy of our historians who rely on reportorial coverage in published writings. Perhaps we need more of the participants—like Bob Moranda—telling what they experienced. We can learn much from such men about what went right and what went wrong. If we don't learn from them, mistakes will recur and retard the U. S. Army's ability to improve its efficiency.

Do such inaccurate accounts happen? Too often! Today's newspapers have errors of fact, warped interpretations, and false or fictional writing by inexperienced or self-seeking reporters. Yet these are the accounts that historians in future years will use in their research and writings. As for this critical battle during World War II and the impressions now in the minds of readers, perhaps a parallel might be found concerning the Battle of Gettysburg during our Civil War. Mention it and Pickett's Charge comes to the forefront in the knowledge of most people. Who knows about Generals Armistead, Pettigrew, and Trimble and their forces that played a much larger and more devastating role during that battle, or of Generals Meade and Hancock and a number of their subordinates who receive little praise or credit? We know of Pickett's Charge but little of Hancock's Defense. Professor Carol Reardon, in "Pickett's Charge in History and Memory" *(The Washington Post*

Magazine), points out that the dominant Richmond press celebrated with great fanfare the brave, albeit foolhardy, charge made by Pickett's all-Virginian force. The news of Pickett's Charge was then picked up by the Northern chroniclers who amplified the spin. Trimble's and Pettigrew's brigades consisted of soldiers from North Carolina, Tennessee, Alabama, and Mississippi, with only a few Virginians, and suffered much greater losses. Additionally, the Virginians ignored their Southern compatriots from other states and even went so far as to accuse them of cowardice and blame them for the losses suffered by Pickett as well as for the Confederate defeat.

True history is the accurate accounting of what events actually occurred. But historians usually base their writings on hearsay—reports of others, sometimes non-participants, of the events. This account is from Bob's memory and from the men who were there on the ground—they do not tell flowery or embellished stories, only what they remember.

The first-hand stories by the bloodied participants in the World War II struggles are important to our understanding of its history. Perhaps the true and accurate recounting of those stories, even after so many years have passed, will lead us to the truth. Those soldiers are passing from us at a steady rate. Bob is in his mid-nineties now, still with a keen mind and his great sense of humor. His memory of events is clear, but, like so many of his compatriots, he has forgotten names and minor incidents. After all, many of those men have spent decades trying to forget much of what they went through in order to put it behind them. Some have never been successful doing so, and Christmas comes every year to remind them what they were doing during those days more than fifty years ago. And I am in my early nineties.

When Bob asked me to look over his writings about his experiences during World War II, I was delighted, for his family had wanted him to do it for many, many years. Of the seven of our parents' children who served in the several services during that war, Bob was the only one whose duties involved actual front line combat. For decades after the war he avoided the subject whenever it came up, and we didn't press him. As an example, I was stationed for duty in the Pentagon when the Office of the Chief of Military History published the volume of its World War II series entitled *U.S. Army in World War II, European Theater of Operations, The Ardennes: Battle of the Bulge,* by Hugh M. Cole. I purchased a copy and arranged to meet with General Bruce Clarke, then retired and living in Arlington, Virginia, who kindly inscribed the book to Bob, and I sent it to him. General Clarke commanded the first units of the 7th Armored Division that were ordered to the scene of the German breakthrough that became the Bulge. A couple of years later when visiting Bob, I noticed the volume on his bookshelf and asked what he thought of it. His reply was that he hadn't read it and probably wouldn't, but he did appreciate my getting General Clarke to acknowledge his service. That was more than twenty years after the Bulge! And it wasn't until many years later that he responded to his grandchildren and nephews by recounting some of his experiences, and then began to get in touch with several of his comrades in arms. It has been just in the last couple of years that he started to put his memories down on paper.

In order for me to do the job, I was forced to get into the various accounts written about the Ardennes Campaign, and my interest increased with each article and book I read about it. The Battle of the Bulge was a campaign critical to the success of the Allies against the German war machine and for the demise of Hitler and the Nazis. I thought Bob's story should be told within the events of history as they occurred. For that reason, notes are interwoven throughout, italicized and inserted in appropriate places to give the reader a better understanding of the historical events surrounding his story. In addition, Explanatory Notes briefly explain the U. S. Army structure during World War II, along with some of the military nomenclature and acronyms. The chapter "Conclusions," presents my opinions and discussion of the events to provide a better perspective of the Ardennes Campaign and a better appreciation of the role of the 7th Armored Division. This chapter also includes an extension of the previously published *Bob's Story, Memories of Love and War,* published by Writer Club Press in 2001, and I have added some of my experiences in the Korean Conflict.

George E. Moranda
Colonel, U. S. Army, Retired

The Home Front

Hueneme

[Probably no other man had such a large and powerful impact on most of the world during the period of the 1930s and 1940s as Adolf Hitler. With his rise to power in 1933 and his marshaling a country and military forces to conquer by ruse, wile, threats, and pressure the neighboring countries of Austria and Czechoslovakia (1938-39), he triggered the war we know as World War II. When he invaded Poland on September 1, 1939, Europe was immediately divided into two opposing forces in an open conflict that eventually drew in the United States. He ruthlessly exploited and controlled his German subjects and those of his allies. His deeds affected the lives of almost everyone living in the world during that period.]

Tolstoy wrote of War and Peace. Not me! This is a story of War and Love—of a young man and a beautiful girl. It begins at the first meeting of the two, which happened at the local assembly point of the kids of our small town of Hueneme (Port was added to the name shortly after the harbor there was completed in 1939). The local tennis court was located at the Woman's Improvement Club—one old cement court which the whole town had to share. I was playing doubles, and I happened to look up and see two young, pretty girls standing outside of the fence. They were watching the action on the tennis court. I knew that I had to meet the older girl, so I yelled to one of the other boys who was standing around waiting to play and asked him to take my place. When that change was made, I walked outside the court and approached the two girls and introduced myself.

"Hi, I'm Bob."

1

The two girls smiled and introduced themselves. The oldest said, "I am Amelia and this is my sister Rozeel Swain. We recently moved here from the San Fernando Valley and live nearby— next to the Glen Dewar's, if you know where that is."

I knew where that was, and after we talked for some time, they excused themselves and left. I continued playing tennis for some time. But I was smitten—and my mind was not on the game. I knew that I had to find out more about Amelia.

The next day the weather was drizzly. I walked over to the house near the Glen Dewar's and knocked on the door. Amelia opened the door and invited me in. Her mother was doing some work in the kitchen. After some chit chat with her mother and the girls and clucking at a cute little girl, the youngest child Shirley, I asked Amelia and Rozeel if they would like to go for a walk in the rain. Both agreed, so we departed and walked for some time. During the walk, I discovered that Amelia was going steady and was serious about another young man in our town. That knocked me for a loop, but I still enjoyed the walk and the talk. The younger sister and I had an instant rapport, and the three of us had a good time. After the walk, I returned home. I felt that my quest was over. The girl of my dreams was already spoken for, and at that time I was without a job so any further pursuit was out of the question. But I had been impressed with the girls. Rozeel was small (her nickname was Tiny) and young, but I was taken with her forwardness and knew that the two of us were going to be good friends forever. As for Amelia, I wished that she was available, but at that time it wasn't to be. In the way she talked and smiled, her beauty would stay with me forever. I know that I could never describe her as she really was but only as I saw her: a cameo face below beautiful hair that would glint when the sun shone through it. When she walked, her carriage was straight with an air of stateliness.

Moranda family about 1938. Left to right with year of birth: George (1918), Paul (1920), Theodore (Ted) (1921), Walter (Bill) (1915), Maye (1910), Robert (Bob) (1913), Dad (Lawrence) 1884, Earle (1908), Mother (Nona) (1889)

After a few years of doing odd jobs such as cutting sugar at the sugar factory in Oxnard, picking lemons, and swinging a sledge hammer for the railroad and the Santa Rosa Farms, I survived but never had enough money to do much. The highest pay during that time varied from twenty-seven cents per hour to higher paying jobs of forty cents per hour working at the sugar factory. The Depression was still in effect. The steadiest job I had in those days was the time I spent working for Mr. J. E. Dewar in his grocery store. After working there a few months, I could see that soon the Dewar's were going to have their son Glen take over the business, so I left. The pay was eighteen dollars a week. The Dewars took most of the first months of my pay to apply to our family grocery bill that had soared during my dad's sickness.

I'll not dwell on all the good and the bad about the different jobs except to say that I was surviving. I certainly was not happy about lacking a good job with a future, but during those days people were living day by day, doing anything to survive. I even went on a mining expedition with my friends Norman Nichols and Bud Valentine. Norm had gone to the University of Colorado and had become a mining engineer. He had found a mine in the desert near Death Valley that he could work as a partner with the owner, a prospector Carl Mingle. Norm came to town and got the two of us to go with him on the venture. To participate, I was required to put two hundred dollars into a fund for the operation. Mom came up with the money by borrowing on her life insurance policy, so I could have a chance to go into the venture. The mine was in the Mojave Desert near Randsburg. Everything went fairly well until the mine caved in on me. I scratched and fought my way out from under a pile of rock that was covering me. I was hauled out and driven home in the back of a pickup. I felt every bounce on the trip until we finally got home, where I was taken to the doctor's office and bound up with tape and turned loose. I never went back. I knew then I was not a miner, and the danger was too great. But the experience was something I'll never forget.

In 1937, my friend John Moore asked me if I would help him, his brother Hobart (Buck), and their father in their restaurant, the Yellow Jacket Café, on Oxnard Boulevard in Oxnard, about five miles from home in Hueneme. John said I would be the combination dishwasher and counterman. As I was not working at the time, I agreed. A week after I started work, the night cook didn't show up for the 2:00 a.m. shift. Buck, the second shift cook, asked me if I could handle the shift from 2:00 a.m. until John could get there in the morning. I said I would try. He showed me the recipe for the hot cake batter and how to fry eggs, so I covered the shift. I liked the job, and after a short time I became quite proficient at it.

So I had a job. I worked the graveyard shift from 2:00 a.m. until 10:00 a.m. every day. I didn't have a day off for quite a while and really didn't want one as I was making 50 cents per hour and got my meals, too. Hell, I was rolling in dough! I got so rich that I went down to A. J. Dingman's Ford agency and bought a used 1931 Model A roadster. It cost me almost $200, and I soon named it the "Blue Goose." What a great car! Everyone loved it. Brothers George, Ted, and Paul borrowed it on occasion, so the car didn't rest much; but it was always ready for a romp around the town. All it wanted was to be loved and to receive an occasional pat and a compliment such as, "Good car."

Each day after work I went home and slept until about 7:00 p.m., and then got up and went to Oxnard and either played softball for one of the local teams or visited various people. The previous year, after working at the sugar factory, I had gone back to Salt Lake City with my brother Earle so that he could visit with his then girlfriend, Donna Rudd. He had met her at the home of our next door neighbors, the John Trehers; she was the niece of Mrs. Treher. I went along with Earle to share the driving and expenses, and I was going to get reacquainted with some friends I had met in Spanish Fork, Utah, a couple of years before when I had gone back there with Gerald "Shorty" Lykins to work with his grandparents. I had become friends with a couple of boys and a girl there and thought it to be a good opportunity to see them again. When we got to Spanish Fork, they were not able to entertain me so I went on with Earle. I wondered why the two boys couldn't accept me when I came to visit, but a year is a long time and things do change. The same thing happened with the young lady. She was somewhat glad to see me, but she could put me up at her house. There was nothing else to do but go on with Earle and hope Donna could find a bed for two instead of one. She did.

At the Rudd's home I met Donna's sister Flora. She was a beautiful girl but was going steady and about to marry a fellow she had been going with for some time. When Flora came home from her date and I was sitting in the living room reading and playing the piano, we became acquainted. Every night when she came home we would sit and talk. When Earle and I left she asked me to write which I did. For some reason my words impressed her, and soon she came out to see me on her way to San Francisco where she was going to live and work for a relative. She stayed for a week or so. Mom liked her as did the rest of the family. After she left, we continued to write and Mom wrote to her, too. But the idea of my marrying on my salary of four dollars a day was out of the question. On one of my few weekends off, Tom Murphy and I drove to San Francisco to visit with her. I noted something wrong because she didn't invite me to her house.

When Tom and I drove home from San Francisco, we went through the heaviest fog I had ever encountered. Going through one town, I had my head out of the window following the white line. Suddenly a red light came on, and I was pulled over by a police car. He asked how fast I was going, and I told him slow because of the fog. He asked for my driver's license, and somehow I couldn't find my wallet. Because I had recently purchased the Ford, I couldn't show him a bill of sale. The police hauled us into the jail as they thought we had stolen the car. I was about ready to call home when Tom brought out his wallet, and the policeman noted that Tom was a member of the Elks Lodge. That was enough for him. He dismissed us with a ticket and told me to send proof that I owned the car when I got home. I forgot about the damned thing until one day as I was sitting in Dad's Justice of the Peace office, I looked in my wallet and there was the citation. I asked Dad what I should do, and he said he would write a letter explaining everything. He instructed me to include a twenty dollar bill in the letter to pay for the fine, which he estimated would be enough. He also had me indicate that if the fine was more to let him know and the money would be sent post haste. I never heard from them again.

In about two months I got a letter from Flora asking me to quit writing as she had met a new friend and was soon going to marry. She remained a friend of my mother's for the rest of Mother's life. She was a great girl, pretty and intelligent, but it wasn't to be for the two of us.

The place to be on a Saturday night in our county was a dance hall, the Green Mill, in Ventura. On one of the Saturdays, I went to the dance hoping to pick up a date. Most of the time the boys went stag and met the girls inside the hall. The ladies weren't charged for admittance. As I was dancing I looked along the side of the dance hall, and I saw Amelia Swain sitting alone. After the tune ended, I walked over to her and we started to talk. I asked her if she would dance with me, and she stated that she didn't know how, that she had come to the dance with a couple of her friends just to watch. What I had seen on my first encounter with her was still there. She was beautiful! We talked quite a bit, and I asked if she would go home with me. She said no as she had come with friends, and they expected her to ride home with them. I remember how great it was to talk to her, but I thought she was still not too sold on me, although she seemed to radiate warmth. I could listen to her talk with enjoyment. Yes, I was smitten.

A few weeks later I drove into Oxnard early in the evening, and after visiting with the gang at the Yellow Jacket Cafe, I decided I would take in a movie. I walked to the theater and there in the booth selling the tickets was Amelia. She smiled and we exchanged a few words, and I went in and sat in the back. In about an hour Amelia came to where I was sitting and asked if she could sit beside me. You never saw anyone move so fast getting up to allow her to get to the seat beside me. We didn't say much during the movie, but it was a comfortable feeling being beside her.

When the show was over we walked out together, and I asked if I could take her home in the Ford. She said she only lived a few blocks away. I then said, "I'll walk you home." We talked all the way to her house. I found out that she and her old boyfriend had broken up quite sometime ago. We talked about everything people usually talk about when first meeting. When we walked up to the front door of her house I said to her, "Miss Swain, I am going to marry you." She didn't say no, nor did she say yes. She just smiled.

That encounter changed my way of living and entertaining. Nightly, I worked until 10:00 a.m. and then drove home and slept until about eight in the evening. At 10:00 p.m. I drove into town, stopped by the theater, picked up Amelia, and we would go some place, to Ventura or Santa Barbara, or stay for the second show at the movie. But we would do something. On one of the days when we were together at the Swain house, Amelia Habib was there. Amelia Habib said to my Amelia, "Remember when we called you 'Amolia' in Spanish class?" When I heard that I exclaimed, "That's it! From now on I am going to call you Molly." And the name stuck. The only ones who continued to call her Amelia were her mother and father and my mother.

For the first year we went together, her mother, Isabelle, and I became good friends but her father remained aloof. However, I was there so much, he finally got used to seeing me and finally accepted me. Isabelle, as everyone called her, was a joy. She was a devout Christian Scientist, as was Molly. Together they would read the lesson daily and go to the church on religious days. Molly was a better Christian than anyone I had ever met. She really believed. She had never been to a doctor, though at times she had a hard time breathing due to a form of asthma. But medication was taboo to her and her mother. It concerned me, but I had little or no knowledge of Mary Baker Eddy and her teachings. However, after watching the healings I became more and more interested and finally accepted that if a person really believed, it was the only way he could live. I remember so well the two of them singing the hymns of the church. Their favorite song was, "Shepherd Show me, How Go O'er the Hill Side Steep, How to Gather, How to Sow, How to Feed Thy Sheep." Molly sang in her pleasant voice and Isabelle sang in her rolling contralto, complete with a slight waver.

One of the things that I loved about our relationship was talking to Molly. I don't know how else to describe the chatter except cute. Her phrasing and interests were continually making me chuckle. When she and her mother talked while I was around, they often would not finish their conversation. All of a sudden the topic would change. As I was interested in what they were talking about, I would ask what the rest of the story was. Their answer was always the same, "Oh, she already knew the rest of the story." And that was it. No more embellishing on a subject when the answer was known.

Isabelle loved to hear funny stories. Daily she would walk down a couple of blocks to the grocery store owned by the Fulton brothers. There they would exchange stories. One day I had heard the story of the man who was entering the hospital. As he was walking down one of the halls, suddenly one of the doors flew open and a man in his hospital gown started to run down the hall. Running right behind him was a nurse, and in her hand was a pair of surgical scissors. Behind the nurse the doctor appeared to find out what the commotion was all about, sized up the situation, and called to the nurse, "Nurse, nurse! I told you to slip off his spectacles." Isabelle enjoyed the story and said she would tell that to the boys at the market tomorrow. The next day when I stopped in at the Swains,' Isabelle came to me and asked how the story went again. She said she had told the story to the boys and they didn't laugh. I asked her to retell the story so I could know what she had said. She told everything well until she came to the punch line, which was, "And the doctor came right behind the nurse yelling, 'Nurse, you misunderstood me. I said to take off his glasses!'"

The father, Henry Roe Swain, was a small man physically but strong when it came to being in control of his family. He didn't say much, but by his actions or inactions a person knew immediately how it affected him. Everyone called him Roe and that is what he wanted. He hated the name of Henry. One day I asked if I could call him Hank. He didn't answer so that's what I called him from then on. In fact, almost everyone started calling him that. and he enjoyed the name more and more.

When I was working at the Yellow Jacket Café, I would stop by the Swain house to see Molly. If she wanted the car, she would take me home and come get me at the cafe before she had to go to work at the theater. The old Blue Goose was a great car; it would go and go and go without much maintenance or gasoline. Sometimes we would do something during the day, and then I'd get some sleep in the evening. I saw Molly almost every day. We became very close, and it was apparent that we were an item. But to get married on four dollars a day was impossible. Even so, it surely didn't stop our relationship. We were in love and were willing to wait. We started to save for the day. We weren't able to save much, but every bit of change I received on a purchase that was in silver I gave to Molly. She saved it first in small jars and then in much larger containers. When Molly told her friends that we were saving for our marriage, the word got around and most of the cashiers in town made sure that I got a lot of change. After having a coke or something and I had to pay with a five-dollar bill, the change would all be in silver. "Oh sure," they would say, "I am sorry I don't happen to have any ones."

One Saturday night I came into Oxnard early and, as the stores were still open, I went into the A. E. Little's Jewelry Store. I worked out an arrangement with Mr. Little that allowed me to pick out the ring I wanted and to pay for it so much a week. So, with the ring in my pocket, I walked to the theater where Molly was selling tickets and said to her, "Hi Molly, will you marry me?" And with that I shoved the ring through the opening of the kiosk. She opened the box and with a smile that I will never forget, she said, "Yes, I love you." She then continued, "But I won't put the ring on until you ask my father and get his blessing." That I agreed to.

On the next day, Sunday, after I got off work, I drove to the Swain house. Hank was out mowing the front lawn. I said hello to him, then sat on the porch step, and talked to him as he worked. I could see he really didn't want to talk to me as he knew what I was there for. I waited. The thought of losing his daughter was something he did not want to face. I waited until he finished. When he walked close to where I was sitting, I stood up and approached him and said, "Hank, you know that I love your daughter very much and we would like to get married one day soon. We would like your blessing." He looked at me, and with tears in his eyes he replied very sincerely, "I knew it would soon happen and I am glad that it will."

I looked up at the front door and there stood Molly, Isabelle, Shirley, and Rozeel listening to the conversation. They had been standing in the doorway all the time I was waiting to talk to him. They were all happy and came out and gave us hugs and kisses. It was then I formally placed the ring on Molly's finger, and again there were hugs and kisses.

The town soon knew about the engagement. We did not set a date as we knew I had to have a better job before we could take the big step. We continued to see each other almost every day, but I could never get her to go to a dance with me—which I liked to do. Even so, our courtship was wonderful. We were in love and everyone could see it. We went everywhere together in the 1931 Ford. Because it was a roadster and some of the nights were cold, I purchased a long overcoat from Al Rodaway at the Wineman's Men's Store. It was part of the costume with a hat, a coat, and the Blue Goose—the open roadster. Molly's father used to kid me about the overcoat because when I came in to pick up Molly I wouldn't take the coat off. He asked why I wore the coat, but I am sure if he rode around in the Blue Goose he too would have dressed warmly. We were married a few months later. After the marriage, Molly decided we should have an enclosed sedan. I teased her that she couldn't stand the cold after the marriage. She would smile and say, "You no longer have to wear an overcoat to keep us warm."

Oxnard

Not long after our engagement I was offered a job as the truck driver for the Railway Express. I worked for Bob Barriclaw, who was the Railway Express agent. I worked for him as an agent and not for the Express Company. Had the job been directly for the company, I would have stayed with them for my working career as I enjoyed the job. My salary was about a $100 a month.

Later I was approached by a friend, Archie Petre, with another opportunity. The year before I had been playing baseball for the Hueneme team, and we had a pretty good team. I had a good batting average and hit the occasional long ball. Archie was the manager of the Shell Oil team though he worked for Standard Stations, Inc., at the station located at 3rd and Oxnard Boulevard. He asked me, "How would you like to work for Standard? If you will play for me and the Shell Oil team, I think I can get you my job. I am leaving Standard to take over one of their stations in Camarillo." It didn't take me long to say yes. Archie set up a time for me to see Bill Haydock, the station manager, for an approval. Bill and I hit it off right away, and he arranged for me to go to Pasadena to see about my going to work for them.

I drove to the office of Standard Stations, Incorporated (it is now Chevron Oil). I was first interviewed by Mr. H. S. Nottingham and after his approval, I was led into the office of Mr. P. J. Sullivan. I passed but not without his telling me I was getting a great break because I was the first man hired who didn't have at least two years of college. Then he told me that I would have to drive to Pasadena and go through a week of training at their school before I could work for the company. (We laugh about such a deal now as service station personnel would certainly not be one of the greatest starting jobs.) He also informed me that even if I were to make it through the school, I would be on probation for at least a month while working at my first assignment. I understand that in today's world it is hard to appreciate why it was so difficult to get a job of any type then. But to be able to work for a leading company then was a great break.

I made it through the school. The main man would come down and watch us as we waited on customers to see if we were treating the customers well. Mr. Sullivan graduated us with a promise he would be watching our progress with interest. I then purchased my uniforms and went back home. I had been away from Molly for a week and soon we were together, talking and planning our lives together. We knew if I could get over the probation period, we could soon marry.

I remember the type of uniforms I had to wear—three white and two brown. When I waited on the customers in the front at the gas pumps, I had to wear the white, and when I was assigned to the lubrication bay, I had to wear the other uniform. Both uniforms required black shoes, bow tie, and a belt that had no buckle (as the company didn't want any scratches on the customers' cars when the attendant leaned over). And no outfit was complete without the small whisk broom in the back pocket, used to clean the pump block. When a customer wanted the tires checked, I would ask them to drive to the air and water tower away from the pump block. I was also supposed to put an air chuck in the air hose and blow the dirt out of the car when I had time.

One day a lady drove into the pump block when one of our salesmen was using the air chuck out at the air tower. He was cleaning out a car that had been serviced in the lubrication bay. The lady got out of the car and asked for the restroom. The attendant thought she asked for a whisk broom. With that he yelled at the lady, "If you will drive over here, I will blow it out for you."

After a month or so at work, Bill Haydock got me promoted to full time. My monthly salary was to be $80 plus commissions, which usually came to about $30. I had to buy and have my uniforms laundered. But I was happy—I had a job with a future.

At first, the job called for me to work three days in Oxnard and the balance of the week in Ojai. I had to drive about fifty miles a day when working in Ojai, but I did it with pleasure. On those days I would work ten-hour days. That lasted for about three months, and by then we had built up the station business in Oxnard so I had a full shift there. Everything was going great. Then one day Bill Haydock had an accident. As there was no one around but me, I had to work long hours opening and closing the station. I did the job. There was no such thing as overtime or extra pay—we just worked.

Shortly after that an auditor came in to check on how we were doing at the station. He asked about the manager, where he was, and how come no one had relieved me for a week or so. I didn't have an answer and let it go. He then noted I had not been paid mileage for the many trips that I had made to Ojai. He asked why not? I said I didn't know I was supposed to be paid for that. He said he couldn't do much about the overtime but he could on the mileage. So I suddenly had an extra few bucks that Molly and I had not planned to have, and we pushed forward the marriage date.

Every night that I had to work, I would call Molly at the theater. We had a free phone we could use in the service bay. We answered the phone for the local Standard Oil Co. when they were not in their plant. That number was 320. The pay phone in the station office was our number, 811. Molly's number at the theater was 81. There was no dialing: we had to go through the operator, and we all knew the operators who worked the switch board at the phone company.

One night about nine o'clock, I decided to call Molly and tell her I would be along right after work and to wait for me at the theater. So I picked up the free phone, and the operator said, "Number please?"

"811, please."

The phone rang in the office. I said, "Damn," hung up, ran out the service bay and into the office, picked up the phone and answered, "Standard Stations, Moranda speaking." No answer.

I went back to the phone in the service bay, picked up the phone and the operator came on again, "Number please?"

"811, please."

The office phone rang again, and I ran out the service bay and grabbed the receiver and again said into the mouthpiece, "Standard

13

Stations, Moranda speaking." Again a dead phone. I cursed a few times under my breath and went back to the phone in the service bay. This time, when I picked up the receiver and the operator asked, "Number please," I asked the operator, "Hey, Lottie, who in the hell is trying to get me on the phone?"

"You are. I kept ringing you to see how fast you really were." Lottie knew where I worked; in fact she traded with us at the station and knew the phone setup. Needless to say we had a lot of laughs over my trying to call myself. When I called Molly and told her about what happened, she had a laugh. And of course the story got around the family and other friends, so we all had a good time about it.

When the date was announced to the family, there were many little showers and parties for Molly. Of course my brothers made sure that they gave me a shower with all kinds of dumb presents. They were excited about the marriage. They all loved Molly. One thing they appreciated about her was how loyal she was to anyone she loved and respected. At ball games, when the brothers were playing, no one could say anything negative about us or she would tear into him and tell him off.

Soon after we announced the date, our superintendent, R. O. Berryman, drove up from Pasadena to make a contact at the station. Bill Haydock advised him I was going to get married soon. Berryman called me over and asked, "How many hours did you work overtime taking care of the station when Bill was off?" When he heard the amount, he told Bill I was to have a week off with pay to cover the overtime I had worked. So the honeymoon time was paid for.

In planning the wedding, I asked a good friend of mine who traded at the station, Reverend W. Don Brown of the Episcopalian Church, to conduct the ceremony. The ritual was to be performed at the home of the Swains. The biggest problem my family had was to get Brother Paul to shave his beard. It was not my idea he shave, but Mom said, "You shave or you can't go to the wedding!!"

We were married on a bright June day. The front room of the Swains' home was crowded with all of our gathered family. We stood before Reverend Brown—Molly was so beautiful in her wedding dress. As we stood there Molly reached over and squeezed my hand. She was calm and collected, but I was very nervous and almost fainted. Tears filled my eyes as I looked at her.

The ceremony began. Henry responded to Reverend Brown's question, "Who gives this bride away?" in a strong voice: "I do." I was getting a bit queasy and was glad when the Reverend had us kneel on a couple of cushions and prayed over us asking the Lord for His blessing on our marriage. After that he introduced us to our families. "I now present to you Mr. and Mrs. Robert Moranda."

I was still so nervous, but with the usual ribbing from my brothers and the hugs and kisses from the rest of the family, I soon recovered. With all the people in the small room it was quite hot, and I'm sure the rest of the people there also felt it. But it did give the brothers something to kid me about for years after.

After the ceremony and while food was being served, Mother gave me my first and only talk about the birds and the bees. She asked me to come out on the porch so she and Dad could talk to me. So we slipped away from the party and went outside. Mom came up to me and said, very seriously and quietly, "Bob, I want you to remember that Amelia is a girl." (Mom and Mother Swain were the only ones who never used the name Molly as long as they lived.) Dad listened in on the message, and with a smile on his face he shook my hand. As he did so I felt something, which I discovered to be a bill for a large amount. I have always looked back at that little episode with love and respect for my folks; for they wanted me to love and care for my new wife and to be sure that I had enough money for the honeymoon.

When we left on our honeymoon, we fooled all of my friends who were lying in wait for me. I don't know what they had planned to do, but I guessed they were going to form a line of cars and escort us out of town. Brother Bill had suggested that we take his brand new car, so Molly and I sneaked out of the house, got into Bill's car, and drove off. No one spotted us, so we made it!

The boys, I understood, were betting on how far the two of us would get before stopping for the night. Camarillo and Ventura were the best guesses they could come up with, as they thought ten miles was about as far as I could go before consummating our marriage. We drove to Studio City and found a very nice motel and spent a wonderful night getting acquainted. I can still see Molly as she came out of the bathroom dressed in her beautiful gown. She was so pretty and desirable. The next morning when we awakened I looked over at my bride and said to her, "And how are you this morning, Miss Swain." She laughed and corrected me by reminding me that we had waited until marriage before sleeping together, so why should she be called "Miss Swain." She did not forget the incident as she told both our mothers when we got home from our honeymoon.

As I look back, I realize that I didn't know much about what a groom should do. As I was the first one of our family to get married, I didn't have a big brother to tell me the ins and outs of that part of life. Later I realized I should have arranged for a hotel room and prepared it with finery and flowers. It was part of life's education that I missed. We were two people really in love, and that made up for all the social graces that I had not learned.

When we returned from our short honeymoon, we moved into our first little home. It was a small house in back of a home on G Street in Oxnard. We moved everything we had in a couple of loads in the Ford. We were there for only a few months. One of the highlights of our stay there was the night the boys—Brothers Paul, George, Ted, and Wannie Woods (who was as close to us as a brother)—came to dinner. We invited them to the first meal Molly had cooked for guests. She bought eight pounds of hamburger with which she made a large meat loaf. The other items were mashed potatoes, all the trimmings, plus dessert. Those guys enjoyed the food—they ate it all. After a few minutes of visiting following supper, the boys decided they should get on with their life and left. We later asked what they did and learned they went to Rolly's Café and had hamburgers!

The boys would drop in at the house after they had been out on the town. They would knock and come in, and it didn't matter that we were in bed. Molly loved them and put up with them. The first thing they would do was to go to the refrigerator to see what they could find to eat. That's when they named me the "Big Bear," because I would try to get rid of them and get some sleep, but Molly always had so much fun talking to them that I didn't have a chance.

We didn't live in that small house for very long, as it was too small even for the two of us, especially when company came to see us. We had not been married for very long when we had an interesting visit. We had gone to bed and were sound asleep, but were awakened when we heard a disturbance outside of our window. Someone was pounding on the back door. I dragged myself to the door to see what the problem was. There stood the Blackwell's softball team members and their wives. They came with food and gifts for the newlyweds. But first we had to earn the rewards, so they loaded us into one of their pickup trucks and drove us to the main street in town. There we got out of the truck, and I had to carry Molly to a wheelbarrow, place her in it, and push her down the main street of Oxnard—she in her negligee and I in my robe. Following the wheelbarrow were the rest of the men and wives in their cars, honking their horns. Even the police came by and, when they saw who it was and what we were celebrating, they joined the ranks and followed with their sirens shrieking. When we finally reached the corner of 5th and Oxnard Boulevard, the parade was over. They all came back to the house, even one police car with two officers—about twenty people in all, and brought in food and gifts and we celebrated. It was then, after the gang left, we decided we had better move to a larger place.

We soon moved to a duplex on the corner of F and 5th streets. It only had one bedroom, but the place had a large living room and a huge kitchen. We made this move in a borrowed van. We accomplished our first move in the two-door Ford. By the second move, we had accumulated quite a bit more and it took the full load of a van borrowed from one of my friends. Again, the brothers and Wannie would come and knock on the door any time of the night and get us up so they could raid the refrigerator. I would growl, but Molly was always a great hostess and loved the company.

I remember we ran a grocery bill at Ditchfield's. I had said I would never run a grocery bill because of the large ones Mom and Dad had been forced to run up during the time that Dad was down sick. I realized then how difficult it was to pay for something that was no longer around. But we watched the bill very closely and never ran over a two week period. The good part was that Ditchy would deliver the groceries. Ditchy was the catcher and a teammate on the Blackwell's baseball team.

We were so happy. We had a good home with good neighbors, the Atkissons: Fay, Mildred, and baby. And we also were given a dog, a little Scotty. I gave it the name of Trouble, and the dog lived up to its name. Later, after we had our child, the dog bit the baby on the face below her eye. The baby had played with the dog all the time. This time the dog was eating and the baby came up and tried to pet the dog at the wrong time. We couldn't keep the dog then so I found it a good home and reluctantly gave it away. The baby was fine, but the bite left a small scar under her eye. I should not have given the dog the name of Trouble.

Everything seemed to be going the way we wanted. My life was busy and things were going along swimmingly. What went on in the world was of little concern to me. Hell, I was on cloud nine. The war in Europe was of no interest to me. Other than in family discussions, I hardly talked about Hitler and what he was doing, in spite of the attempts by President Roosevelt to try to alert the country to pending problems for us and other countries. My job at the station was going great: Bill Haydock and I had built the station from a "D" to a "B." I got automatic raises and was in line for a promotion.

At that time my father, who had been treated for tuberculosis until it was arrested and was also diabetic, was having a lot of trouble with a wound that would not heal on his right foot. He tried everything but finally he went to the doctor and found out that his toe was going have to be removed. Dad entered the St. John's Hospital in Oxnard. Our family doctor, Dr. Korts, attempted the operation, and during the procedure Dad's heart stopped. After they revived him, the doctor quit the operation and brought him out of the ether. Dr. Korts told my mother and me about the failed surgery and that she should take him to Santa Barbara to the Sansum Clinic for further treatment.

It was then that Mr. Sullivan from Pasadena came up and offered me a job as an assistant manager of the training station in Santa Barbara. I had to turn the promotion down as I was the blood donor for my dad. He smiled and said he understood and, further, when I was free for a promotion, to call him at his office in Pasadena.

A few months later, Dad was operated on at the Sansum Clinic. Dr. Saint was the doctor in charge. All went well this time and soon Dad was able to go home. Under the good care of Mom, he recovered. He wasn't the best patient as he was very restless and impatient with himself, and he took it out on her. I am sure at times Mom would have loved to leave for a time, but the one thing my mother had above all else was her strong sense of duty to the family. She never said anything to anyone about how miserable she really was.

Soon after that, the district superintendent of Standard Stations came into our station. He greeted us, made the usual inspection of the station, and pointed out some things he would like to have corrected. When he was about ready to leave, I asked him to call Mr. Sullivan and advise him I could now accept the promotion. The superintendent looked at me rather funny and said in so many words that he would not. So I said to him, "Then I will call him. But I asked you to do it while you are here so you won't think I am going behind your back. I was told by Mr. Sullivan that I should call him when I was in a position to accept a promotion." With that the superintendent did go to the phone and called Mr. Sullivan. When he hung up, he came out to me and said, "How would you like to be Station Manager of the Standard Station on State and Islay in Santa Barbara?" What great news!

War Approaches

[Not to be outdone, soon after the German invasion of Poland in September 1939, Stalin saw an opportunity to extend his country's control. He joined with Germany in taking the eastern part of Poland and then moved Soviet troops into the Baltic states of Lithuania, Latvia, and Estonia. An attempt at the same ruse in Finland failed, so Stalin started the invasion of its northern neighbor. Meanwhile the French and British forces faced the Germans. For different reasons, both sides stared at each other—the Germans behind the Siegfried Line and the French in their Maginot Line battlements. Concerned that the Anglo-French Alliance might prevent Swedish iron ore from going into Germany and that they might send aid to Finland through the Scandinavian countries, Hitler ordered the invasion of Norway in January, 1940.]

Although our local paper, *The Oxnard Courier*, carried little national and international news, we got some information from *The Los Angeles Times* and from radio, especially Roosevelt's Fireside Chats. But there seemed to be little concern about what was going on in the world. Even when the local National Guard unit was called in for Federal service, I never dreamed any of us would be affected. We continued our regular daily routines.

In the fall of 1940, the Selective Service Act was passed by Congress, which called for eligible men to register for the draft. That meant that the Moranda family had six men eligible for duty. None of us had any children, so we all could be called. The oldest, Earle, had applied for a job in Washington, D.C., working for the government as a civil servant. Walter (Bill) was working hauling lemons from the groves to packing houses. George and Paul were attending Fresno State College. And the youngest, Theodore "Ted", was going to Ventura Junior College. Our only sister, Maye, was working at Desmonds, a clothing store in Los Angeles. After she learned that her brothers might be going off to serve in the military forces, she quit her job and began training to become an Army nurse.

In April 1941, George received notice that he was to be drafted. The officials at Fresno State College obtained a deferment for him so he could graduate in June. Things seemed to be more serious, and people were more involved. One of the lads who worked for us at the Oxnard station was Charles Porter. He became a pilot in the Air Corps and his mother, who traded at our service station, kept us informed of his progress. It was a real thrill to see him come into the station one day in his uniform with the gold bars of a second lieutenant on his shoulders. (Charles was killed very early in the war.)

[Having come to an arrangement with Stalin, Hitler then turned his attention to the west, and in the spring of 1940, the Blitzkrieg through the Low Countries successfully drove the British out through Dunkirk, decimated the French forces, reached Paris, and effectively controlled France both directly and through a puppet government. The German Navy, with marauding surface and undersea vessels, was operating throughout the Atlantic, Mediterranean, and Baltic waters against shipping to prevent supplies and raw material from reaching its enemies' lands. By the end of 1941, Germany had extended its control over most of central Europe, Greece, and North Africa, was fighting in Yugoslavia and Egypt, and was heavily engaged in Russia, having started that invasion in June. By then Japan had bombed Pearl Harbor, which brought the United States into active war against the German, Italian, and Japanese Axis.]

On December 7, 1941, I was working at the station. It was a Sunday, and I had listened to the Catholic church's bell ringing. It was a beautiful, clear day. I had opened the station, so I was there alone when one of our regular customers came in to fill his tank. I gave the customary greeting and he responded, "The Japanese have bombed Pearl Harbor." I didn't even know where Pearl Harbor was, and I don't think he did either. I was filling his tank when I noticed a soldier hitchhiking out in front of the station. I called to the soldier and asked him where he was going. He said, "I have to get back to San Francisco to my base." I then asked the customer his destination, which was Santa Barbara, and he agreed to take the man that far. Molly called shortly after that and was upset, and I tried to calm her down but couldn't tell her much because I didn't know.

After that things changed for the country. Everyone knew we were all going to be involved in some way. I never knew what my mother thought on that day, but she must have been very worried.

I came home one evening after work and was met by Molly at the door dressed in her sexiest outfit, and she announced that she wanted a baby. We had almost decided not to have children because of Molly's health problems. But she was willing, wanted one, and sure enough she became pregnant.

We were transferred to Santa Barbara soon afterwards for a couple of months, and then to a station in Ventura. I had even been offered one in Pasadena, but asked Mr. Sullivan to let me stay closer to our parents for the time being. I was pleased that I was making progress up the ladder in the company. Besides, I could play ball for our softball team, which I was doing very well, hitting with a batting average over .500. Molly was happy too, for she was near her folks, her practitioner, and her doctor during her pregnancy

Molly had a difficult time giving birth to Tomilyn Robin Moranda. The labor was a 48-hour ordeal. The doctor knew she was due. Molly knew she was due. I knew she was due. Tomi (as I called her when she became older) didn't think she was due. She was warm and comfortable where she was. So we all waited and waited. I sat in the room with Molly, helped her by timing the contractions, and kept her company. The contractions remained at the same spacing for sixteen hours. I was worried because Molly was not strong, but she was a good patient and ready for the grand experience. She always had high blood pressure, but as a good Christian Scientist she wasn't about to take medication. We had alerted her practitioner, Mrs. Reedy, and Molly had called her a couple of times while we were waiting. But the contractions were coming too slowly. Finally they increased and were severe so the nurse called the doctor and told him she was ready. The nurse, and a dear friend, Sister Alexine, said to me, "Now we take over." I was sent to the waiting room. I paced. I walked the halls. I prayed. I talked to everyone who would listen. Finally at 6:00 p.m., the nurse came and said, "Come in and see your daughter." The baby was born, and I was relieved and happy, for Molly had wanted a girl. She came out loudly, not wanting to leave that warm cozy place where she had been living for the past nine months. Molly had been given a shot of medication, over her protestations, so she was not alert, but she knew the baby had been born. The birthing system there used what was called "twilight sleep," a method developed by local doctors, Drs. Swift and Livingston. It was a popular procedure then for child birthing.

Molly had spent some time writing different combinations of names. Molly's brother Tommy was in the Navy on a Destroyer somewhere in the Pacific. He had been the family's concern for some time, so she had come up with the name of Tomilyn. I suppose to make me feel good, the middle name was to be Robin. Even today I can close my eyes and still hear Molly singing the baby's name, Tomilyn Robin Moranda, over and over again.

I walked into the delivery room where the baby was on a table, and the nurses and doctor were cleaning her. She was beautiful. I watched as they cleaned her, and they placed Molly in a room. Then Sister Alexine said, "You had better go get something to eat and tell the families. Your wife will be out of it for at least two hours." This was the first grandchild on both sides of our families. Our parents and our brothers and sisters had been very interested in Molly's pregnancy, especially my youngest brother Ted who, when around Molly, would ask her if he could listen to the baby or put his hand on her tummy to feel the movement inside. I called Molly's folks and Mother Isabelle answered. I told her the news. I knew that all during the birthing she had been sitting and praying for Molly and the baby. Father Henry was also very pleased. I knew that Isabelle would tell all the rest of the Swain family, so I got in our car, an old Studebaker, and drove to Hueneme where I told Mom and Dad about the birth. As they were eating their supper, I sat down and joined them. They were very happy as were the Swains.

We started to call the rest of the family, but in between calls I had a call from the hospital. It was Sister Alexine who said, "Come back right away. Molly is having a problem." I rushed out, drove the five miles to the St. John's Hospital, and ran up the stairs to Molly's room where I found her crying. Actually she was a bit out of it, being still under the twilight sleep medication. She cried out to me, "Tell me, Bob, is the baby alive?" I reassured her that the baby was beautiful, healthy, and when last I saw her she was crying and moving her arms and legs. I then asked the nurse to please bring in the baby to reassure Molly. She did and the baby was placed in Molly's arms. What a wonderful sight: a young, beautiful mother holding her new born baby. She checked Tomi from head to foot. Now Molly believed. There was instant bonding. Both Molly and the babe relaxed and enjoyed each other. In but a few minutes both were ready for some rest, so the baby was taken to the nursery and Molly went to sleep. With that, I drove home to Ventura and went to bed. Sleep didn't come easily but it finally came. What a couple of days and nights, but it was worth the wait.

Molly was in the hospital for three days. Every day she had visitors. Mom went at the first opportunity she had. Molly loved the role of mother; she loved to show off her daughter. It bothered her that she was unable to nurse Tomi; she tried but had no success, so Tomi became a "bottle baby." Thankfully she had no problem with the formula. After being released from the hospital, they were taken to her mother's house, where we stayed for a few days. The house was full of love for the new arrival.

Bob and Molly   *Molly and Tomi*

The baby and Molly soon came home to Ventura. The bonding with the baby was so great. Since she was a bit fussy at night, Molly and I would take turns holding her. At night it was my job to quiet the baby so I would place her on my chest and she would quiet down almost at once. Perhaps it was the beat of my heart that reminded her of the sound or feeling she had when she was in her personal incubator. For the next six weeks I, too, got to bond with my "Pumpkin." I don't know of a greater feeling than for a father to hold his newborn baby on his chest while the baby sleeps.

One thing on my mind throughout the birthing was I had not heard from the Draft Board regarding my application for the Volunteer Officers Corps. Before Molly went into the hospital, I had received my notice from the Draft Board that I was to report in December. I had read and had investigated that men in my category could volunteer to become officers. To be eligible the men had to volunteer before the Draft Board called them up. As I wasn't 1A, I had thought I would be able to get into the program. I hurried to the Draft Board in Oxnard and talked to Mrs. Ed Brown, who encouraged me to apply for Volunteer Officer School. If accepted, the men would go into the army, take basic training, and, if they passed that phase, would go directly to the Officers Training School. If a person failed along the way, then the individual would be returned to civilian life. Mrs. Brown, the Draft Board secretary and a personal friend of Molly, helped me fill out the forms for the V.O.C. in either the Quartermaster Corp or the Transportation Corp. To do this, the Draft Board had to change my draft classification from 3A to 1A. Soon after that I received my notification to report for duty, not into the V.O.C. but into the Army. I went to see the Draft Board, and Mrs. Brown told me that when my name came up before the board the President of the Draft Board, "Hap" Maxwell, a personal friend of mine (I thought) said, "I know Bob Moranda personally. Go ahead and draft him. He will become an officer without going to that V.O.C. outfit."

[Germany and Italy began the defensive after being stopped near Moscow and Stalingrad during the winter of 1941-42 and in North Africa at el-Alamein. In the Pacific, American naval and military forces also started to force the Japanese into a defensive posture. In November 1942, American

and British forces invaded North Africa. The 7th Armored Division was activated at Camp Polk, Louisiana, on March 1, 1942.]

With that notice, I called my boss at Standard Stations, Inc., Mr. Pat Sullivan, who was sad that I was going to leave, but he told me to call my superintendent, Mr. George O'Brien, and give him my termination notice. I was sorry to be leaving. I liked my station at the corner of Meta and California in Ventura. It was my first large service station, and we had built up a good clientele. I loved my little house and really loved my girls. I hated to leave Molly because she was not strong. Her blood pressure was still high, and her asthma was still active. And the beautiful baby! But everyone was sacrificing. By this time every able-bodied man knew that he would soon have to go, so I was not too surprised by the action of the Draft Board.

Molly and I called her parents and asked if Molly and the baby could move back to their home. The answer was an emphatic, "Yes." We moved back to the house on 4th Street in Oxnard. The house was full with Molly's parents and sister Shirley still at home. But there was plenty of love in the house so we were comfortable. I remember watching Tomi's first bath at the Swain house: Molly, Isabelle, and Molly's best friend, Amelia Habib all hovered over the baby on the bassinet they had placed on the sink. They took turns trying to bathe the eight pounds of flesh. Tomi held them at bay, and the ladies were so afraid of so many things happening that never did: "Are we hurting her? Is the water too hot?" There was so much jabbering and fussing, but somehow Tomi survived and probably thought, "I sure hope they get better at this job."

I have always had a deep appreciation for the home folks who rallied around for their children and loved ones during such times of crises, and I've thanked God for the care and help for the families of those who were in the service during the war. So many of us were so fortunate our parents willingly sacrificed for their children and took them in and supported them. The pay in the Army was certainly not enough to keep a family going. The most I could send home was about $30 month for the first few months. As I was promoted, the money was not much more.

The December date for me to report soon came. At 4:00 a.m. on December 7, 1942, the first anniversary of the Pearl Harbor attack, I woke up when the alarm went off. Molly got up also, as did Henry and Mother Swain. It was tough on all of us. I sure didn't want to show tears. I felt I must be strong and show my manliness and not give them cause to break down. I gave our baby a kiss, hugged Isabelle, shook hands with Henry, and then held my darling close, kissed her, told her I loved her, and went out the door. I had a flow of tears as I walked to A and 5th Streets. Our assembly point was an abandoned store next to the Levy Bank building. The bus that was to carry the draftees to San Pedro was idling in front of the building. Inside the building were the 40 draftees with their families, the Draft Board, a reporter from the newspaper, friends, and a few onlookers. Coffee and doughnuts were available and served by Red Cross people. I had a cup of coffee, talked with some people, and met some of the men being called up along with me. I was called to the table where Mrs. Brown and "Hap" Maxwell and others on the Draft Board were standing. Mrs. Brown handed me a list of the draftees and told me I was the acting Corporal and responsible for the group. When the time came, I called out the names on the list and the group entered the bus as their names were called. We all were relieved to get away from the people. They were dear, friendly people but were making it difficult for us to remain dry-eyed.

The ride to San Pedro took about two and a half hours. There wasn't much conversation among the group as most of us were wondering about what would happen, where we would be assigned, what branch of service, whether they would recognize our desires and skills. We worried about our families. I was worried about my folks too. Dad, a diabetic, had had his leg removed. There were no males in the family left in Hueneme to drive my folks to needed places. Somehow, deep down I knew things would work out.

Fort MacArthur

When the bus pulled into Fort MacArthur, the San Pedro Army base, we were met by two acting sergeants. I debarked and gave the roster to one of the acting sergeants. It was then that I made my first discovery: I was a nobody. My first "promotion" to corporal (temporary) had only lasted a little over two hours. They started to yell at us even before we got off the bus. They had only one way to talk and that was with a loud scream. Any kind of error on our part, we were threatened, would be the cause for a court martial. Hell, none of us knew what they were talking about.

We were taken to a nearby barracks, and each of us was assigned a bunk—a double-decker for two of us. The other soldier and I flipped a coin and I lost, so the lower bunk was mine. We were then herded to another building to be issued the supplies that would convert us civilians to soldiers. The term was "issued" but "thrown at" was more appropriate. First, we got a duffel bag into which we put the rest of the stuff as it came at us. After some guy looked at us and yelled out a size, the men behind a counter grabbed items from shelves and threw them at us: shoes (2 pair), fatigues, blouse, pants, socks, mess kit, utensils, underwear (brown), and so on. At the shoe counter they had me put my feet in a foot measurer. Then the soldier yelled out, "11C." I told him I had never worn anything larger than a 9B. That made no difference. He replied, "That's it soldier, you'll grow into them. Next man." After receiving the clothes and stuff, we were taken back to our barracks. There we took off our civvies and put on our uniforms. We were told we could either ship our clothes home or give them to a charity outfit. Before coming I had heard what to expect and had worn old clothes, so

I flung mine on the pile for charity. I sure didn't want Molly to have to unpack the old clothes and give her another chance to cry.

We were marched to another large building. There we were told to take off our shirts and form a long line. We moved along slowly, and the horror stories started about the pending shots. To hear some of them, anyone who got through the series was really a man, but many fainted when they got them. As each man entered the door, he was suddenly attacked; a man on each side hit each arm. A couple of guys did faint, but I'll never forget the sadistic look on the faces of the needle pushers. When we were finished we waited outside with all of us rubbing our arms. The only one that bothered me was the tetanus shot.

We were then herded into a large hall. We were given a short briefing and then a quick physical, namely a "short arm" inspection. A short arm inspection is nothing more than a medical officer sitting in a chair looking at each man's penis, to check for any venereal disease, as the man walked by. Short arm inspections were done regularly—about once a month—as long as a man was in the Army. (Later in my career one of the men instead of taking his penis out of his pants, stuck one of his fingers through the fly of his shorts. The inspector didn't crack a smile when the man passed. He looked up and said, "Your penis needs a manicure.")

After that sequence, I sat on my bunk and thought about all that had happened to me during the day so far. I was already homesick, and for the first time it dawned on me that I was not going home that night and for many more to come. About that time and after a few minutes of rest, the "commanding officer" (another corporal) came in and told us that anyone who lived in the area could go home for the night. No one took him up on the offer. Here we were at a camp, ten miles from nowhere, so how could we get home and back? Some of us, though, after being dressed in our new uniforms, decided to walk to the Post Exchange. When we got there the stock was depleted except for some dry cookies. So we each bought a box and went back to the barracks.

Night came and we went to bed. Sleep came easy to most of us. I listened to the various noises others were making while sleeping—moaners, gaspers, talkers, whistlers, and so on. It didn't take me long to fall asleep.

At the end of the day I was Private Moranda, serial number 39548092.

Morning came too soon, awakened in the Army manner with the bugle call reveille. The routine now started and remained so throughout my career in the Army. Get up, walk to the latrine, and do your ablutions. Every barracks had a latrine equipped with a line of toilets and a line of wash basins—no walls or partitions. You sat on the throne and the world could see you strain in getting relief. It didn't take long though to get used to the audience as you sat down to play. Then you went back to your bunk where you dressed in your new outfit. The next job was to make your bunk in the military manner—as they said "high and tight, like Saturday night." It took me quite awhile to do the job correctly the first time. One of the men who had been there a day longer than I had came by and showed me the correct way to get the blankets on so tight that when the inspector came by and threw a quarter on the top blanket, it would bounce.

When the bugle sounded, we went through the routine and then were called out by the same loud-mouthed corporal. We lined up in formation, did a right face and a forward march, and we were off. About ten yards later we heard the command for double-time march. The leading men had never done double-time, so they started to run. The men in the rear were soon sprinting. By the time we reached where we were going, everything was confused. The first two ranks were in formation, but the last ranks were scattered. We didn't look like any Army formation that I had seen in the movies or newsreels.

We went into a building with a large room and desks. The people in charge started our testing. First we took an aptitude test and then others, including an I.Q. test. They didn't tell us the results, but I guess I passed. One of the tests was on communications—to determine whether we could understand the difference between a dot and a dash coming in over a wire or radio. I knew the Morse code as over the years Dad used to practice at home using whatever was around—a knife, fork, spoon, or pencil. During his early days with the Southern Pacific Railroad, Dad had been a telegrapher before he became a station agent. The tests took all morning and a part of the afternoon. Then we went back to the barracks for what we thought would be a rest. No way!

Part of the men was sent out to "police" the area around the camp, and others were given similar busy work duties. Three of us were taken to the mess hall to do KP. I was assigned to vegetables. As I was cleaning them, the mess sergeant came and watched me work. He said, "You have done that before. How would you like to join the mess crew?" At that time I was not against the idea, but I was never given the chance. That was the only time that I worked in an Army mess.

The next day we were herded to a large room with desks and chairs. Behind them sat soldiers conducting interviews. My interviewer was a young man from Oxnard, Corp. Herb Wasserman. I knew his father well as he was the manager of the Oxnard Savings and Loan, the firm that held the mortgage on my parent's house in Port Hueneme. My first reaction was, "great—someone will listen and help," but I was wrong. He asked my background. I told him my occupation of working for Standard Stations, Inc., and one of my main jobs was the maintenance and care of automobiles and trucks. I had also worked for the Railway Express and was aware of waybills and schedules of railroads, which was my reason for volunteering for the Quartermaster Corp or the Transportation Corp when I applied for the Volunteer Officer Corp. Wasserman listened. Nothing was done. He listened but that is all he could do. My fate had already been decided before I arrived at the camp. As we went back to the barracks, rumors started about places we would be sent. One rumor we heard even went so far as to say that we would be sent to England directly and be trained there as replacements for the European operations.

So much for the Army classification system. I don't think it would have made any difference whether I was a Mensa or a dull ignoramus, or whether I had been a plumber, lawyer, or field hand. The Army apparently needed infantrymen at that time, and the orders came at about 3:00 p.m. the next day. I recalled when Brother George was drafted immediately after graduating from Fresno State College with a degree in political science, he was sent to Camp Leonard Wood for training with the Corps of Engineers! All the people drafted with me had orders for various places, but none knew where at the time. We had two hours to be ready to move out, so we packed our duffel bags and sat on them waiting. At five o'clock they called us out and we were marched to a waiting train. It was then I got my first sack lunch—two dry sandwiches, one cheese and the other jam.

Training in Texas

Everything was Top Secret in those days when it came to movement of troops. We all wondered where we were going as we loaded aboard the passenger cars. No one knew except the officers of our group and the crew of the train. Because my father was a railroader, I knew a lot of rail people, so I looked for an old acquaintance but found none. As we went along, we found out we were going to Texas to a brand new training facility near Fort Worth named Camp Howze. The next day I learned that I had orders assigning me to the 84th Infantry Division, which was being formed.

We were in Pullman cars, but it wasn't that great. I had to sleep with a total stranger. To conserve space, the Army assigned three men to a section, two for the lower berth and one in the upper. My bunk mate was a man named Morph from Los Angeles. He was a real nice guy and was honored by being named commander of our car. He didn't know what that job entailed and never did find out. We all figured he would soon become a non-commissioned officer, but as far as I know he never was more than a private in his whole career. For the moment he was king.

We were proud as we were going through towns and people waved at us with friendly hellos. We stood a bit taller and waved as heroes should. We tried to look like soldiers, but I know the people weren't fooled; they were being patriotic and friendly. It was a long ride but finally we came to Kansas City where we detrained for a short time. They gave us a hot meal, not good, but we ate it gladly. We weren't allowed to leave the station proper, but I roamed around a bit. There was a group of townspeople in the station serving coffee and doughnuts.

It was a labor of love for them, and they came out and met every train that passed through. We had some wonderful people in our country.

We were loaded again on the train, this time with a different crew, and headed south through Oklahoma and into Texas. We pulled into a siding near a small town called Gainesville near the Oklahoma border. I overheard someone say Camp Howze—the name of the place we were headed for our training. The Army must have a sadistic general whose only job is to fly over the United States to find enough space in the most unlivable location and report to Washington D.C. that he had found a spot with no other use and that was a miserable place in which to live. He would then recommend that this was a great place to train our soldiers. And for that he gets another ribbon or medal to wear on his uniform. That had to be true, for Camp Howze fits the description. The weather was terrible, and if you didn't like it, it would change for the worse in a minute.

We debarked at the camp and were met at the railroad siding by a group of officers. On a nearby level spot, tables had been set up and the officers interviewed each man. Again I was hopeful. These were officers and non-commissioned officers who were the cadre for the new division. As we approached the tables, we were instructed to salute, state our name, rank, and serial number. We were questioned about our civilian backgrounds. I gave them the spiel about my job with Standard Stations—maintenance and care of vehicles. The officer said, "Great, we have need for people like you who know how to service vehicles. We have a great many vehicles of all types in this division. I am sure you will be assigned to a job that the Army can take advantage of your background." I was then assigned to the 333rd Infantry Regiment.

At my next stop, via truck, I was again interviewed by people in the 333rd Infantry Regiment and I repeated my background story. The reply I got again was, "Good, we have a need as we have many trucks and no one knows how to service them. We sure need you."

The next stop, again by truck, was to the 3rd Battalion, 333rd Infantry Regiment, where I was greeted by the new battalion commander. He helped conduct the interview with the same questions. "My name is Colonel Barrett, welcome to the 3rd Battalion. What did you do in civilian life?" Again I told my story and this time I was assured by the lieutenant colonel that his outfit needed men with my training, "Great, we need you in our motor pool." I told myself, maybe this time they listened. I was then marched with a group led by an old soldier, Sgt. Hand. He announced: "I am the First Sergeant of Company M of the 3rd Battalion of the 333rd Infantry Regiment, of the 84th Infantry Division. I will now take you to meet your new Company Commander, Capt. DeFriend." He called us to attention and marched us to our new company area. There I was interviewed by Capt. DeFriend. "Now Moranda, what did you do in civilian life?" I repeated my background and interests, to which he replied, "Good we need you, we have 24 vehicles and no one who knows anything about vehicles and we don't even have a sergeant who is capable of handling a motor pool." I never rode in, much less serviced, one of those vehicles nor did I ever have the opportunity to ride in one of the 24 jeeps. Throughout my Army career, I never served in anything involving the servicing of vehicles.

The first few days we did not do much except police the area and do some physical training. I had plenty of time to write home and tell the folks all about the new world that I was in. It was interesting, but I was homesick. I was not alone as most of the men were in the same predicament.

We were issued our rifles (mine was #18367) and bedding—which consisted of a mattress cover and two blankets—and other necessities. One new item that we were given was a pair of leggings. These were heavy canvas leg coverings that were something like spats except they went higher up the leg. They were worn over the shoes and had to be laced up, using the hooks on the outside of the leggings. I remember the first time that we were to assemble when we were going to have to wear them. I figured it was easier to lace them on the inside. I looked around at the other men and saw they were as confused as I and none of them knew how to wear them. I took the easiest way and laced them up on the inside. When the first call whistle blew I got up and started to run toward the front door. The hooks caught and I went down on my face. Several others did too. The old first sergeant got his laugh and then showed us how to lace them. I think that the training cadre knew that some of us would lace them the wrong way and wanted to have a good laugh, for the officers and NCOs were all there to see the falling soldiers.

That problem didn't last very long, for in a couple of weeks each man was issued two new combat boots to replace the shoes and leggings. When we received them it had been raining, so our sergeant told us to put them on and to go outside and stand in a puddle of water and get them thoroughly soaked, then leave them on and let them dry on our feet. That way the boots would be broken in and would never give a person any trouble wearing them. It worked for me as I never had a blister or any problems with my shoes all the time I wore them.

We were assigned our barracks. This time we had single beds. For the first couple of days we were kept busy policing the area and doing a few exercises. On day two the first sergeant called us out and said we looked like we were in poor shape and he was going to remedy that. He said, "Now you men will follow me and we will jog until you all fall out from exhaustion. Now here I am an old man going to show you how out of shape you are." He was going to show us up and he did. That man could jog forever. He kept going and going. One by one the draftees fell out. Soon there were only a couple of us left so he called it off and he wasn't even breathing hard. I lasted but I was beat.

On the first day with M Company, we were called into our first formation. Our first sergeant called out our names. Capt. Defrient talked about what was expected of us. Sgt. Hand then called out our assignments in the new platoons. I was sent to the .30 caliber Heavy Machine Gun platoon as acting corporal in a sergeant's position. Our platoon sergeant was Clary Mercer, a tall southern man. Our platoon commander was Lt. Babb.

When we were in our new platoon, Lt. Babb gave us his message. Our platoon would be the best. No one would ever fall out on a march unless he fell on his chin. No one would ever say he was so tired he couldn't march. I immediately took a liking to Lt. Babb—he was young, good looking, had a dark complexion, curly hair, and stood six feet tall with a good build. He was going to be a good man, I thought.

Lt. Babb then called, "Moranda."

"Yes, Sir," I answered loudly.

"Step forward."

That I did, and then he asked, "Ever do any drilling or marching?"

"No, Sir. But when my brother came home on leave from his basic training he called out four of his brothers and gave us a few minutes of drilling. We were armed only with a stick, two brooms, and a yard stick. We weren't very good, but we did do the command 'fall out' very well, but did have a few minutes of practicing close order. And I marched in the school band."

He smiled and said: "Come out and see what you can do in drilling the platoon."

I moved to the command position and called the platoon to attention. I did that in a professional manner. I got the unit to turn by issuing the order "right face." Then with the command "forward march," we moved along the company street in a fine fashion. Before long I must have given the next command on the wrong foot because things got a bit mixed up. I got them halted. The CO then took over and restored the ranks by giving the proper commands. He dismissed me, but my performance must have put me in his good graces because I was soon made an acting sergeant and never served as a private (except at the pay table). I didn't know what I was doing, but the men understood me and I always had good relations with them.

Placing me in a sergeant's position was putting someone in charge who didn't know what being a leader of a section of heavy machine guns meant. The only guns that I had ever fired were an air rifle and once a shotgun. I was lost in that leadership spot for a time, but proved to be a quick learner and the men didn't seem to mind my lack of knowledge. The first few days we didn't do much except get acquainted with our fellow soldiers. Every day, a few more came in. As they were assigned, we early birds gave them the dope on what we had been doing and questioned them about their backgrounds and about where they came from. To keep us busy we were given a lot of make-work jobs. That's when we learned the Army term A & E—ass holes and elbows. When they called for us to go out and do A & E work, we knew it meant we were to walk the area and pick up anything lying around: paper, cigarette butts, and other things. We soon learned to "field strip" our cigarettes—splitting the butts, dropping the remaining tobacco on the ground, and rolling the paper into a small ball before throwing it away.

Our platoon sergeant was part of the cadre that came from Georgia. All the enlisted men of the cadre came from the same division, and most spoke with a drawl. Many were regular army people. Coming from California, I needed some time before I could understand accents such as: "You peeple, I am goin to make it hoard for you. We are goin to march a couple of moles and then y'all will fol out and some of you will go on gord. Tonight when you go to the winda y'all will see the CO inspecting the area so make shore your raffle is clean and roddy for inspecshun. So make me prod of y'all."

Lt. Babb seemed to have good leadership qualities. In his first speech to us, he stood in front of our platoon and said in a quiet but authoritative manner what he stood for and how we would become the finest machine gun platoon in the Division. No one was ever to fall out on a march. But if he did he had better fall on his chin and be out of it because that's the only excuse he would tolerate. In the months that passed, we never lost a man on a march even though we had to carry heavy machine guns with us on most of the marches. But one hot, hot, muggy day when we were on a fifteen mile march, Lt. Babb fell out—fell on his chin. He had followed his own orders.

The Platoon Sergeant Clary Mercer was a quiet man. He never asked a man to do something that he hadn't done. He wasn't loud, but he got the job done. He walked with a lope, one short step and his next step long, and he could walk forever. When we came in from an all-day march, he would shower, dress and take off for town, drink a bit, and come back in the early hours of the morning, go to bed, catch a couple hours sleep, and rise at reveille with the rest of us ready for the day, and it never seemed to bother him.

The other two platoon leaders were two 2nd lieutenants fresh out of officer's school. The machine gun platoon was commanded by 2nd Lt. Brown, a big, good-looking young man. He was quiet, but a capable, dedicated officer who carried himself well. He was steadfast in his ways and his men seemed very happy with him as their boss. The mortar platoon leader was 2nd Lt. Zavala. He was full of fun with a great sense of humor, a bit overweight, but carried himself well. The other lieutenants seemed to enjoy picking on him but never got him to change his way of life. His men all seemed to be happy with him too. The Executive Officer for the company was 1st Lt. Burns. He stayed with the unit throughout the training period and took over the company when our first commanding officer was promoted to major and reassigned.

The men in my section were from all parts of the country: Byrd, a man of about thirty from South Carolina, was the gunner of one machine gun; Ashworth, surely an Irishman, was an ammunition bearer; Salee, a young man from Kentucky, was assistant gunner and someone I would have liked to have as a life-long friend; Emiterio, a full-blooded Indian and Ashworth's drinking buddy, also an ammo bearer; Oberholster, a young man from Philadelphia, bunked with me when out in the field in tents; and old Bill Marshall, right out of the hills of Arkansas, was quite a character.

Bill always tried to look out for me. I think he was pleased that I placed him in a bunk near the front door and the pot-bellied stove. He took over the chore of making the fire every morning, and those Texas mornings were cold. He always had a chaw of "tobaccer" in his mouth. At one of the first formations Bill was standing at attention. The captain stopped and asked Bill, "Marshall, do you have a chew of tobacco in your mouth?"

"Yassuh."

"Do you always have a chew in your mouth?"

"Yassuh."

"Even at night?"

"Yassuh, even when I go to sleep, I go to sleep with a chaw in my mouth."

With that, the CO took his spot in front of the company and made the announcement: "Private Bill Marshall is the only man who can have a chew of tobacco at all times. None of the rest of you will have the same privilege."

Bill had a very limited education. He noticed that I wrote to Molly and the family almost every day. He tried to write a couple of times but it was clear he was having trouble and it was a real chore. After we had been together about a month, he came to me one day and asked if I would write to his folks for him. I agreed and got out some writing paper and asked him what he wanted to say. He replied to tell them what we do and that I am fine. So I wrote them a long letter in my best penmanship. Bill thanked me and mailed it off to his folks in Mountain View, Arkansas. About a month went by and Bill got a reply to his letter in which the message was, "Dear Bill. Thanx fer the letter that you had rote. That feller can really rite reel good. Don have him rite no more. We had to take it to town to have someone read the letter to usun." So my job as a public stenographer was over—but Bill and I were still friends.

The company spanned the ethnic spectrum. We had northerners, southerners, easterners, and westerners. We had a prince, Jake the Fink, college graduates, and the almost illiterate. We had Italians, Prussians, Mexicans, American Indians, Irishmen, and a group of "Duke mixtures." But there were no Blacks and I wondered why.

We also had in our barracks Rod Munday, a well-known golf pro. I knew that he wouldn't serve long with us, for too many of the officers knew of him. They even gave him time off to play a tournament being held in Texas. He left our company right after we completed basic training.

And then there was Jake the Fink. He advised his bunk mates he would soon be out of the Army. He claimed he could not use his right arm, and kept his hand in his pocket all the time. If someone forced him to take his hand out, he would let his arm and hand dangle by his side. When he was told to pick something up, it was quite a show. He was about ready to be discharged when one day, while the rest of the platoon was out; he was left in camp as barracks guard. After we had been gone for a short while, the CO and the 1st Sgt. went into the barracks and found Jake making up his bunk with his bad arm. He was right—he didn't stay long in our outfit.

One of the best guys in our unit was a young man from Utah by the name of Udall. He was groomed to be an officer from the time he came in, and he left right after basic training for Officer Training School and got his commission as an officer. After he graduated he was assigned to a training unit in Texas. While he was giving his first lecture to his troops, a bolt of lightning struck and killed him.

Others in the outfit were Botto from San Francisco, Dave McDvani, who claimed to be a Georgian prince from Russia, whose family was related by marriage to Barbara Hutton, the Woolworth heiress, and Esteridge, a sharp young man who had been made an acting non-com. Frank Ledesma was a street-smart Mexican lad from Los Angeles. He was small and wiry, unafraid of others, and always had stories to tell of his exploits while growing up in L.A. He became our barber. When the supply sergeant found out he could cut hair, he gave him clippers and equipment for haircuts and he kept us shorn.

One day when the company had been on a long march with full field packs, and it was a hot day not very conducive to marching, Ledesma was bitching about the weather and the Army, and claimed he was tired and couldn't finish the march. It was customary in our company that, as we neared camp, we would halt and take a ten minute break, spruce up, and go in looking pretty good. Our colonel and his staff always were in front of his office to review the troops as they passed. When Lt. Babb halted us and told us to "Take ten," we could see the camp hospital about 500 yards away. Frank was bitching by then, claiming he could never make it the rest of the way. We had our packs on, so Frank sank heavily to the ground. He sat there beefing and moaning and after a couple of minutes he jumped up with his pack still on his back yelling that he had been stung by a scorpion. He took off running toward the hospital and didn't slow down until he charged into it for treatment. Lt. Babb watched the fleeing soldier as he reached the hospital, then turned to us and said, "See, I told you that a person can go farther than he thinks."

Hugh West was my best friend in the 84th Division. He was from Richmond, Virginia. We had been inducted into the Army on the same day. We made private first class on the same day, corporals and sergeants on the same day, were interviewed for Officer Candidate School and became 2nd lieutenants on the same day. When we graduated, we were assigned to different outfits. I missed the guy. Six months later, when I reported to Fort Dix, New Jersey, there sitting in the office waiting to go overseas with me was Hugh West—and we went aboard the same troop transport and spent time together in England, after which we went different ways and never saw each other again. We exchanged Christmas cards for a few years, but how sad that we didn't make a better effort to keep in touch.

While in the service, like most others, I looked forward to news from home. Molly was very good about writing. Sister Maye was sure to write at least every two weeks. Mom had a lot of letters to write to all her children away from home and she too did a good job. All of us were worried about Dad, so she kept us posted about the news of the town and family. Mom was the hub of the wheel. To name the spokes of the wheel: Earle was in the Army and stationed in Texas going through basic training. Maye was in nurses training in Los Angeles becoming an Army nurse. Bill (Walter) was in Hawaii in the Marines. George was a lieutenant in the Corps of Engineers. Paul was going to school to become a Naval officer, and Theodore was in the Air Transport Command learning to be a radio operator for the C 47s that the Army Air Corps delivered all over the world.

Our training had been tough. We went from early morning until late at night. That training molded us into a unit starting from untrained, raw civilians. I feel that our unit was better trained than any that I came across later in my service. The first six weeks were essentially for the individual, to get each one in shape mentally and physically and to learn his weapon. I can still remember my rifle serial number—I carried it, slept with it, and cleaned it every day but Sunday. It was an M1. I had never handled a gun before, but I took good care of my M1. I always thought the weapon originally issued to a soldier should stay with him throughout his career, but it wasn't to be. I wasn't fortunate enough to go overseas with a unit, but I learned later that when the division left for the European Theater of Operations, the men were all issued new rifles. Before getting the rifles, we were initially taught the .22 caliber. On the short range, my grouping of shots on the target was good. Then with the M1 and carbine I made Expert on the regular range. When the CO saw my results, he asked me to "zero in" all the rifles in the company. I did, but at the end of the day my arm was sore.

Two of my men were the best of buddies: Ashworth, the Irishman, and Emeterio, the American Indian. Every Sunday they would head for the PX and see if they could drink all the beer in the place. At times they did get enough down to get a good buzz on—and I'm sure they must have spiked it. On one of the Sundays I was sitting on my bunk with my writing material, putting together a letter to Molly, when I heard a lot of swearing and noise coming from the front end of our barracks. I looked up and there was Ashworth running as fast as he could and Emeterio yelling as he chased Ashworth: "I'm going to kill you, you dirty Irish bastard." Ashworth ran out of the other end of the barracks. As Emeterio approached my bunk, I saw he was swinging an entrenching tool and looked as though he was going to scalp Ashworth. So I tackled him and took the tool away from him. Both men were drunk. Emeterio calmed down and I got the story. It seemed that they had gotten into a serious argument and were kicked out of the PX. The argument continued as they were coming back to the barracks, and along the way, Ashworth called Emeterio a drunken S.O.B of an Indian. Emeterio got hold of an entrenching tool and took out after him. Things calmed down, and I had Ashworth assigned to an adjacent barracks. It wasn't long before the two drinking buddies were back at the PX guzzling beer again, but it's a good bet the Irishman never again called the Indian a term of disrespect.

One hot day we were on a fifteen-mile march when the cheeks of my "arse" became chaffed from too much rubbing together as I walked. It was almost impossible to continue the march. When it was almost unbearable, I remembered a pair of socks I always carried with me in the arm pits of the sleeves of my jacket. At the first break I took one of the socks and folded it and put it between my cheeks, and that saved the day as I didn't want to fall out. In my next letter home I told of the experience, and that I now knew how women felt wearing Kotex. The next letter from Sister Maye told me to wear one for a week and then I'd get the feeling. I got the message.

In February I received a letter from Molly saying that she had received a large check from Standard Stations, Inc. That helped as I was unable to send any money to her, except the allowance. It was a fine gesture by my old company. Others in the outfit were also in financial straits.

43

Another field march, this time for twenty miles, was supposed to be a tactical march. We carried our weapons and full field packs. When we arrived at our objective, we halted and dug foxholes. As we started to pitch our tents, we were attacked by the Aggressor Forces (our troops in enemy uniforms) firing blank cartridges and dummy hand grenades. After much yelling, confusion, and pretending to fire our weapons, the tactical problem was called off. We had passed the test. We then were fed and slept the night. The next day we returned to camp. When we got to the barracks we flopped on our bunks, as we were tired from the march back. Suddenly the front door opened and in came one of the aggressors still dressed in his enemy uniform. He came in to have some fun with his best buddy. He raised his rifle that was still loaded with a blank cartridge and fired. His friend fell over. We all rushed over to see what had happened. The fallen guy was dead. The blank shell had wadding in it that kept the powder inside the cartridge. The wadding had pierced his friend's heart. There was a hearing. I testified what I observed, as did others. The judgment was that it was accidental. The GI had not been informed about the wadding and the danger of firing at close range. The lad was transferred to another unit and we never saw him again. I felt sorry for the guy as well as the victim.

Basic training of six weeks was about to come to an end and we became eligible for weekend passes. I was proud of my unit. We had progressed to a point where the men were feeling they were at their best. They wouldn't back down to any other unit. The most angry that I ever remember getting was the time we had to lend our two machine guns to K Company. They were running a tactical problem and needed machine guns to provide some overhead firing. We didn't want to lend the guns, and I so advised the Company Commander. He said we had to follow the order. Our guns were absolutely spotless. The men in my outfit cleaned and polished them every day. When the guns went to K Company, it happened. It rained, and K Company left our guns out in the rain overnight. Hell, the guns weren't theirs, so why should they worry? They returned the weapons to our supply room and not to us. When my men saw the condition of the weapons, they were ready to have a brawl with K Company. I felt the blame belonged to the officers in charge, not the men.

It was Friday afternoon and soon the company commander and the first sergeant would be making their weekly inspection. They wanted to see if we could be given weekend passes. We worked on our machine guns all afternoon. The rust had become embedded in the metal and was not coming off. The CO came in, looked at the machine guns, scowled, and said to me, "Your outfit will be confined to camp until your weapons can pass the inspection." I told the CO what had happened, but that is not the way the Army works. So we polished for over an hour. I could see the rust was deeply embedded into the metal, and there was no way were we ever going to get the guns ready for inspection unless we took some different action. I told the first sergeant what I was going to do. He smiled and said, "You're learning."

So to the supply room I went, obtained a small can of army green paint, went back to the barracks, and within an hour we were again ready for inspection. The captain came in and again looked at the weapons. With a smile on his face, he turned to the first sergeant and said we passed. He knew what we had done and also knew it was the only way to fix the problem, so it would pass. The sad part was we were never able to get the weapons back into the prime condition they were before K Company used them.

Unit Training

After basic training, we went into unit training where we learned how our platoon fit together with the rest of the company, battalion, and regiment. The triangular infantry division that fought the war was comprised of three infantry regiments: division artillery of three 105 mm howitzer battalions with twelve tubes (designed for each one to support an infantry regiment) and one 155 mm howitzer battalion with twelve tubes to give general fire support, an engineer battalion, a cavalry reconnaissance troop, and division service troops—with a strength of 14,043 men. Each infantry regiment was, in turn, made up of three infantry battalions and a headquarters and service company. Each battalion had three companies, each with three platoons made up of three squads, plus a weapons and a mortar platoon. The weapons platoon is a direct support unit to provide additional and protective fire for the rifle platoons.

When basic training was over, we seemed to have more time on weekends. Hugh West and I got a pass and headed for Fort Worth, about 40 miles from Gainesville. I didn't have much spare cash, so we tried our luck at hitchhiking. We were almost instantly successful and were picked up by an elderly couple who happened to be going to Fort Worth. When we got out of the car, we walked to the main part of the town, looked around, went to the USO, and at evening time decided to look for a room. We went to a downtown hotel, registered, and as there wasn't much of a lobby—only a few chairs, a table, and an old lamp, we went up to our room. It had two beds and an overhead light dangling from the ceiling. The bath was down the hall. We each flopped on our bed. Soon there came a knock on the door, and Hugh opened it and two women in flimsy outfits that revealed about everything they had, which wasn't very attractive, walked in. They then asked if we wanted to "play around." I replied, "What do you mean? Bridge? Hearts? Or what do you have in mind?" They then approached each of us, and we told them in no uncertain terms that they should get their fannies out of there. Hugh said he guessed we should have expected such in a hotel with the name The Roan Hotel. They were unquestionably a couple of the most unattractive women I've ever seen and met the criteria of the Lee sisters—Ugh and Gast.

The next day we got up and went to a nearby café for breakfast, and after visiting for an hour or so, Hugh said, "There is a church, the same as mine at home. I think I'll go." He did, so I went back to the highway and thumbed a ride back to camp. Later when Hugh got back he said that after the service he had been invited by an elderly couple to their home for dinner. He teased me because I had missed a delicious home cooked meal. And I had the usual Sunday night meal at the mess hall—cold cuts.

One night when we were on an overnight exercise, we set up our tents and were ready for chow. As it was a tactical problem, we had to wait for nightfall. That night was cloudy and dark and it was hard to find our way around the area. One of my men got lost so we all had to look for him without making any loud noise or talking. We finally found the man, and after chow we bunked down. Soon we were awakened and told to move out. Rolling up the tents and getting all our equipment together was a problem, but we finally made it. The exercise was our first large field maneuver as part of the entire 333rd Infantry Regiment. We were supposed to provide support for a rifle company. I found out how difficult, if not impossible, it is to control men at night. We had radio contact but that was not enough. It was a good lesson, for I knew it would be worse in combat. From then on I took extra precautions when moving about in the dark.

Early the next day the tactical problem continued. My section was assigned to guard the battalion headquarters. After I placed my two squads in position, I moved a bit closer to the battalion commander. The lieutenant colonel was trying to run his companies from his position on a hill and to use a walkie-talkie. He seemed to think that the louder he talked into the radio, the more information he would

47

receive. During one sequence he was yelling into the set: "S3 [Battalion Operations Officer], come in! What is your position?"

"Right behind you, Sir."

"Give me your position again."

"Right behind you, Sir."

"Where? What are your coordinates?"

"I am standing right behind you." With that he reached out and touched the CO.

The colonel turned and continued talking to the S3 over the radio. It was a strange scene, giving orders over the radio to a man standing a few feet from him. The S3 shrugged his shoulders, said, "Yes, Sir," and left to follow the instructions he had received.

I wondered then how that battalion commander would do in combat. After the war, I learned from friends about the confusion with the same people when the 84th went into action in Holland and Germany. Some of the officers above the rank of major were commissioned through the ROTC system, or came up from enlisted ranks of the regular army, or were regulars who were trying to stay in long enough to get pensions; they were inexperienced at commanding troops and were not equal to the weight they tried to throw around. For all the bad, there were enough good ones. After all, the American Army was essentially a civilian army that defeated one of the greatest armies ever assembled. I remember one day when the temperature was about twenty-seven degrees, a horrible one to be doing anything but resting in the barracks. Thankfully, before I fell out in the morning I had put fatigues over my ODs. I was warm in my body, but my hands, feet, and face were cold. The training mission that day was to lead my machine gun section on a drill to learn how to creep and crawl dragging the machine guns along with our weapons and ammunition boxes. We were supposed to stay along the ground at all times and keep below the horizon so the "enemy" couldn't see us. That was the toughest exercise that I ever had to do. We made it to the spot where we set up the machine guns while remaining in the prone position—doing everything without standing or kneeling. We couldn't raise our heads except to fire either our rifles or the machine guns. It was a good lesson on the limitation of maneuverability with heavy guns, but a miserable day otherwise.

Molly found out about the weekend passes and asked if she could come and visit me at Gainesville. Gainesville was not a place for a young lady. I said no, but that I would contact my dear Aunt Annie Forney Newton and see if Molly could stay with her in Little Rock, Arkansas. Annie Forney said she would welcome her. So Molly took the train to Little Rock. I arranged for a three-day pass and went to Fort Worth and took the train, "The Rocket," to Little Rock.

How wonderful it was to see Molly. We spent two days together with Annie Forney. She arranged for us to meet our cousins, Alice and Anale, and took us around to meet our future sister-in-law, Nancy Dowell. What a beautiful girl. The only problem with the weekend was that Molly had an attack of the asthma. Nothing any one could do for her except to watch her suffer. Annie Forney found a Christian Science practitioner and drove us there. Molly stayed in with the practitioner for some time. When she came out she was breathing much better. Excitement always seemed to bring on the attacks.

While I was visiting in Little Rock, I had a history lesson from our Aunt Annie Forney. I was relating that in our barracks about half of the soldiers were from the South and the rest from the North with a few from California. I was laughing about how I would sit on my bunk at night and get the group going about the Civil War. I said that after they got arguing and fussing with each other, I would lie back on my bunk and laugh at them. It was then Annie Forney told me that we had relatives who fought on the side of the South during the war.

During the last night Molly and I stayed close together holding each other. We spent most of the night just talking. She told me of her fears and how she was making it, living with the Swains and Mother Moranda. She enjoyed staying with them, and our daughter was doing well. She gave me news of our families and friends. Letters are fine but talking is the better way to learn about all the fears and things that were on our minds. The next day we were driven to the railroad station and I departed. As I pulled out of the station I saw the tears in Molly's eyes. With Molly were Annie Forney and Nancy. They all waved. And with tears in my eyes I waved back.

Molly stayed another day in Little Rock. She was wined and dined by our relatives and Nancy and her folks, the Albert Dowells. Molly took the train home without any problems. She said she had a good seat all the way.

Not long after that trip I was again invited to Little Rock. There was to be a wedding, and I was invited to be the best man for my brother George. Nancy Dowell had said yes, and she and George were to marry. I wanted to go back, but it was not possible. I asked the CO if I could again have a few days off, and the answer came back with a resounding no! The reason given was that we were in the middle of the tests for the company and they didn't want anyone to be gone at that time. I was saddened, but there wasn't much I could do about it. George forgave me when I called him to advise him. He understood.

During this unit training the squads and platoons were taken to the field and given simulated problems. I was leading my section on a simulation problem one day, and my outfit was in support of a rifle company. We set up our machine guns to be able to provide the support. After a time I was to go ahead to reconnoiter the place where the rifle company had moved forward. Then I was to bring up my men to place them in a new position to provide support in the new location so we could continue with the problem. All went well—the timing was good and the positions I selected were perfect. Watching the exercise were officers who were the judges checking on how well we did the job. After we had finished the problem I heard, "Sergeant, what's your name?" I stood and reported to a full bird colonel.

"Sergeant Moranda, Sir."

"Good job. You are going to go to Officers Training School."

Not, "Do you want to go to OCS?" It was a command. So as a good soldier does, I said, "Yes, Sir!"

It was only a few days later that I was called to the regimental headquarters and appeared before the OCS Board. Again they wanted know what I did in my civilian life. I went through the whole thing again, but I knew it was a waste of time. I knew the Army needed infantry officers, so why fight it.

Camp Polk

Soon after my meeting with the OCS board, our outfit was sent to Camp Polk, Louisiana. There we were trained further in tactics. The training was mostly unit training for the benefit of the officers on how to control troops in the field. It is easy to control a small unit, but working with those the size of companies and battalions is much more difficult. If the Army had a weakness, it was leadership of troops in combat. The time I spent in Camp Polk was confusing most of the time. Communication is bad at its best, but in the field it seemed to me no one knew what was going on.

Before we left Texas, to get away from camp, Hugh and I went to Fort Worth a couple of more times. On one of our trips, I met my brother Earle at a GI hangout. We sat in a bar and talked of home and what each of us had been doing. Earle was in training in Texas at Camp Hood. He looked good. It was great to see him. Also while in Camp Howze I saw my cousin, Leonard "Billy" Edwards. He was stationed across the post from where I was located. He seemed to be doing well. One other man from home was Jack Fulkerson from Somis. We had gone to high school together. He soon left the 84th, and I lost track of him.

Other people left our company for various reasons. Rod Munday, the golfer, was placed in Special Services. Dave MDvani, the Georgian prince, was allowed to leave. He tried but he was too old to become an infantryman. Two others were Jake the Fink and one more enlisted man who refused to shower. The men who slept in the same barracks took him to the shower and gave him a good bath using GI soap and a lot of elbow grease. He went over the hill. When he was caught, they brought him back to camp and the Army gave him a dishonorable discharge.

American officers above the rank of captain needed the field training at Camp Polk. In my opinion real leadership was rarely shown during actual combat. I am not speaking of company grade officers, most of whom did their jobs exceedingly well—they didn't last long enough in combat.

To quote from the book about Company K, of the 84th Division, reporting on their action in World War II, a company that lost 60 percent of their personnel in their first battle including all their officers but one: "During our first battle no officer above the rank of lieutenant ever came to see how we were doing. The battalion officers were trying to run the battle from their command post. They had no concept of what was going on. When the front line people needed guidance, they could not get it from their headquarters. The only field grade officer they saw was a British officer who happened to come by to see if his unit could help. He saw that they needed help, so he got a tank from his unit and assisted the troops in getting out of a horrible situation."

We thought Texas was bad, but Louisiana was worse. It seemed to rain every day. It poured down day and night. Did the commanders ever call off the tactical problem? No way. It seemed our platoon was forever being attached to some rifle company, and the CO didn't know what to do with us. On one occasion they placed two of us guarding a road and ordered to stay there until relieved. Well, they forgot about us. We stayed at our post until the exercise was over and no one came for us. Finally when they took a check of the men, we were missing and they came for us late at night. They had nothing left in the mess tent for us to eat except six hard boiled eggs for each of us. That with a slice of dry bread was our supper. That night in our pup tent the air was blue from the smell of rotten egg flatulence. My buddy Oberholster was ready to move me out.

On the subject of chow, we didn't have a good field mess. After one of the worst meals, one of my buddies said, "Let's explore and see what we can find." We did. We came to an old shack, the home of a black family. We asked if we could buy anything in the food line. The lady of the house said, "I can make you a pan of corn bread." We said great and soon we had a large pan of the best corn bread I have ever eaten. The cost was two dollars. The lady was happy and said come back anytime and I'll cook for you. So we had discovered a source.

Our company roamed over all of the hills and swamps around the Camp Claiborne area. We were broken up into gun sections and then attached to a rifle company. The CO of the rifle company was to use our weapons to give his company more fire power. That was what we were there to learn. In all the times that these attachments were tried, none was done correctly. (Machine guns were rarely used correctly, even in combat.)

During this time I got a letter from Molly telling me that there had been a fire and we lost some furniture and other things. One thing was irreplaceable—my stamp collection. It had been one of my main hobbies before entering the Army. A mother of a friend, Ken Winslow, had given me a bag of stamps that were old and valuable. I had taken them home and looked them up in Scott's Stamp Catalog and discovered that they were of exceptional value, after which I took them back to the Winslows to return them. I told them of their worth, as I knew it, and suggested they take them to an expert for his evaluation. However, they insisted that I take some of them as a reward for being honest, which I did. I wrote Molly back and told her not to worry about the loss and that we could replace most of the things in time. But I was sad about the loss of the stamps.

There is one night I remember vividly. It was payday. We were in our bivouac area, after chow time. I heard a young male voice singing a sad western song. You know the type, a love song about the woman he had left behind, how he missed the girl of his dreams. A full moon was out. I followed the sound. The moon shining through the branches made my walk through the trees something special. The wet grass with the reflection of the moon shining on the dew made it seem like I was walking on diamonds. I followed the sound of singing to a group of men who were listening to a young soldier who had his guitar and was strumming and singing. What a beautiful voice. The men were laid back and thinking of home, some lying on the ground, others with their backs against the trees, and all had that far away look in their eyes.

I joined the group and thought of home. I soon had diamonds in my eyes—tears from thinking of home.

Going back to my tent, I heard more voices from different groups of men from three different places. Each group was sitting around a blanket spread on the ground. The first group was our company officers who were playing poker for nickels and dimes. I watched for a short time and then I walked to where the non-coms were playing blackjack. This time the bets were of paper money. I watched Hugh West try to win a few bucks. I soon left and went to the third group. This time it was the privates with the same setup. Only this time the game was craps, and the bets were high. One lad said as he threw down a large amount of money, "Shoot the works, what the hell. They feed us and clothe us so what in the hell do I need money for out here in the pucker brush."

Blackjack was the destruction of our 1st Sgt. Hand. When we first got to camp on paydays, he would come to our barracks and get in a game of blackjack. As he had a lot of money he would "tap" the dealer. He had enough money so he could double up his bet until the dealer would go broke. One night shortly before we left for Louisiana, he came to our barracks only this time his luck ran out. One of the men, Esteridge, was lucky and broke the sergeant. He was never able to bluff his way in a game again. It wasn't long after that our CO discovered the sergeant had been selling weekend passes and also lending money illegally. For example, he would lend five dollars on the first days of the month for ten dollars on payday. Later in the month, the rate would be less. On the 20th of the month, the rate would be seven for ten. The sergeant couldn't lose as he was a member of the paying group, so when the soldier was paid the sergeant would have his hand out to collect. It was an old-time caper in the Army, and no one complained. The CO saw the action at the pay table and asked what was going on. Then he found out the sergeant was also selling weekend passes. That was the last of the Old Man, Sgt. U.G. Hand. Better known as Sergeant Ugh!

It was about this time that I found out cousin Billy Edwards had been in a wreck. He was in the back of a truck that was involved in an accident and was badly injured. They placed him in the hospital at Camp Claiborne where he was kept for a long time. Later, he was reassigned to the Military Police for the duration of the war.

The chow we had in the field was very bad. It was bad enough having to eat from our mess kits with all the food thrown together, but the preparation was never good. To make the situation even worse, our meals were served as follows: breakfast was before daylight; at noon we were handed our lunch, which normally consisted of two dry sandwiches made from stale Army baked hand-sliced bread. Only three types of sandwiches were served, a peanut butter and jam, a dry bologna Army style that the GIs called "donkey cock," and the infamous dry cheese. When we were eating our lunch we would sing: "Won't you try a donkey cock or a cheese and a jam. It's the driest that ever was in the land." The bread was always sliced unevenly so that one side of the sandwich was too big to bite. We had to break off half the bread to get it in our mouths. To make things even worse, we were only allowed one canteen of water for the day. Dry sandwiches, hot weather, and limited water certainly weren't like dining on the Riviera. The evening meal was served after dark. It didn't matter because it was bad, and we ate sparingly. But we had found where we could get corn bread at any time, so we knew we were going to survive in spite of the mess.

Fort Benning

My stay in Louisiana was short. One day the company commander came into the field in his jeep and picked up Hugh West and me. We were given orders to go to OCS at the Infantry School at Fort Benning in Columbus, Georgia, with a short delay in route. As soon as I could, I called home and told them that I would soon be home for a week before reporting to the school. The family was happy with the news.

The ride home on the train was not the easiest as the train was full, and I had to stand or sit either on the floor or on the edge of one of the seats. Finally, I was so tired that I lay on the floor and got a couple of hours sleep. What a couple of days! The toilets wouldn't work. We didn't have enough water, and they ran out of food. On the second day I finally found a seat, so the rest of the ride into the station in Los Angeles was better. I had called Molly, and she was to meet me in Los Angeles. She was excited with the news and said she would ask Uncle Bill Cummings and Aunt Marie to take her to the station. Bill had a source for gasoline. What a great aunt and uncle! During the war, they were always willing to drive the family around and help whenever problems arose.

As we approached the station in Los Angeles, I looked at myself. I was a mess. My uniform was black from sleeping on the floor and being on the train, I needed a shave, my hands and face were dirty. I then made a decision that the people meeting me were not going to see me in this condition. As we came in to the station, I grabbed my duffel bag and found the way to a restroom where I changed my uniform. I hurriedly shaved and washed. It took a few minutes so when I got to the ramp where Mom, Molly, Tomilyn, Aunt Marie, and Uncle Bill were waiting, I found them wondering why I was not coming up the ramp with the rest of the people from the train. But with a lot of hugs and kisses, all was well with the world.

I was home for a week. It was great! I saw friends around Oxnard and Port Hueneme. They were interested in what I was doing, and I was willing to talk. I even went by the Draft Board and saw Mrs. Brown and the people who had drafted me. They were pleased that I was going to the officer's school. Mrs. Brown felt bad that they had not been able to send me to the school that I had applied for before being drafted. She was glad I had made it on my own.

I soon had to leave. But this time the trip would be faster and better. I had a ticket to fly from Los Angeles to Atlanta, Georgia. The flight was uneventful. We stopped a couple of times along the way for refueling so I was able to get out and stretch. We arrived in Atlanta early enough, and I was able of catch an Army bus to Fort Benning located on the outskirts of Columbus.

I remember the ride into Fort Benning, an old established Army station with red brick buildings on the Main Post. Every rock was in its proper place and painted white. I was impressed. But we didn't stop at the pretty brick buildings; but kept going until we reached a group of wooden two-story frame buildings. I got out and reported to the company office, where the company clerk told me to report to the Officer of the Day.

I walked into the adjoining office and stood in front of the officer's desk and saluted, "Sergeant Moranda reporting for duty, Sir!"

"At ease, tell me about your last assignment. My name is Lieutenant Jacobs."

I told him about the training I had been through for the past nine months. He listened well. He told me the school was tough, but he was sure if I really tried I would make it through the course. He said he would be the Tactical Officer for the platoon I had been assigned to. He seemed interested in me and asked about my family and background.

With that I went to the supply building and picked up all the supplies I would need during the next four months. From there I found my way to the building where I found my bunk. In the next bunk to me was Ted Ranger. He was a short, stocky man. I could see that he was in good shape. He too was a sergeant. He had been with the division being trained in Colorado and wanted to go back to his unit if and when he graduated. It sounded good to me, and I said that I thought that I would like that kind of a unit. He and I became good friends.

Soon the rest of the new company of candidates filled the barracks. We were bunked alphabetically. My neighbors around my end of the barracks were Ted Ranger, a young man by the name of Morf, an older man, Sgt. McFarland, Sgts. Meece and Meisner from New England, Lassiter from Georgia, Pippen and Lebow from Pennsylvania, and Hogan Lang from California. When everyone had reported in, I discovered that most of the candidates were ROTC men and had just graduated from college. It seemed that half of them were from Pennsylvania University and the other half from southern colleges.

I looked around at the men in the unit and could see the competition would be tough. But somehow I didn't worry about the school, for I knew if I tried I would make it through.

As we were sitting around getting to know each other, over the intercom I heard, "Moranda, report to the company headquarters."

I wondered what was going on, but it didn't take long to find out the reason for the call.

I reported to Lt. Jacobs. "Moranda," he ordered, "you are to be the First Sergeant of the company for the first week of the training." Nothing more except that he told me the acting company commander would be Ted Ranger. No other information. I was dismissed.

I went back to the barracks and found Ranger. He and I got busy. By hook or by crook we found out who else had been selected for the rest of the positions needed to operate the student company. Ted and I then gathered them together. Then we set up where we were to form the company, how many platoons we would have, and so on. Ted and I marked off the spots where each platoon would stand and directed each platoon leader to mark their spots so they could easily find them in the morning.

The next morning all went well. The acting officers and non-coms found their spots. The formation was about perfect. I saw a smile come to the face of Lt. Jacobs. He watched as I called the company to attention and dressed the ranks. I then turned the company over to the acting company commander, Ted Ranger. As I stood at my post in the rear of the troops, I saw Lt. Jacobs look at the commanding officer of the training company and give him thumbs up. The gesture was returned to Jacobs. I served one week in that job.

A few days later I was summoned to the headquarters. I reported to Lt. Jacobs. He gave me a mission that didn't please me, but I didn't know how to refuse it. I was told my job was to watch two candidates in our company who were of German descent. I was to report anything they would do that wasn't in the interests of our government. I wanted to say, "Why me?" But how does one say no? I asked why they were being watched but didn't get an answer. I soon found out the two men, if they graduated, were to be assigned to U.S. Army Intelligence. The two men were Meisner and Hogan Lang. Both men were bunking near me. As I walked back to my barracks, I thought about the only thing good about the assignment: Lt. Jacobs obviously thought I was going to make it through the school.

The assignment made me change my way of going out on my free time. I always tried to go with the two men. Both were good men. Hogan was from Laguna, California, so we had some things in common. I learned to like them very much. As so many things happen in the service, the three of us were separated; so I was unable to continue our friendship. I never did find anything bad about them. They were good, loyal Americans.

In December I became very sick. Only by dragging myself out of bed and going through the day was I able to make it. I should have gone to sick call, but I was not going to give the officers in charge a chance to wash me out. As I look back on it all, I wonder why I was so intense about finishing the school. For two days I forced myself to carry on. On the second day as we finished up training, I suddenly felt stronger. From then on everything went well. I had a cough for a few days, but the fever was gone.

In January, I heard from Molly. Her dad was doing well in the service station that he had purchased in Hueneme. Molly and Shirley helped him as much as they could, but he was without real help. Her dad was getting tired of the station and was looking with keen interest at some property in Lancaster. I was not surprised about his tiring of the station because all the labor force normally available for such work was gone. Those men were either in the service or at some better paying job in the defense industry. Soon after a letter came telling of Henry and Isabelle Swain going into a business arrangement with their daughter and son-in-law, Rozeel and Eddie Gabbert, to raise turkeys and chickens. They had purchased a small ranch of twenty acres in Lancaster that had two houses and other buildings already in place.

The main entertainment for us while in school was going into Columbus. Our favorite place was a famous steak house called Patterson's. Their menu specialty was steak of any size or shape. One item was a large steak; if you could eat it all at one sitting you didn't have to pay. I saw a couple of men try, but unsuccessfully. That steak was tremendous. The trimmings that went with the steaks weren't stinted in size either. After the meal we would walk around town for a short time and then go back to the Fort.

We all liked to get packages from home. When the package was brought upstairs where we were staying, the receiver suddenly had his bunk surrounded with people hoping for a home treat. I well remember the day I got one of Molly's famous cakes. I opened the package and passed the cake around. A couple of the men decided they would write to Molly and thank her. They did. And it worked because it wasn't long before another cake came in the mail.

For me, the school was a four-month rest. The studies were easy and so was the physical part. The young men from the ROTC units were in good shape, and they helped me keep in shape, especially a young man by the name of Lebow. He would challenge me to do one hundred sit-ups and push-ups nightly. I could do them easily. One of our tests was to run the 400-yard dash. I did it easily—which surprised me. We burned the midnight oil before an examination. The men would test each other to make sure that we could all pass the written tests.

I have always wondered why some of the men were treated better than others. I assume the tactical officers saw something in their overall appearance to make them good officers, even if the candidates would do some dumb things. We had two such men in our barracks: Kirk and Lassiter. Both men were good looking, but were slow in grasping the different subjects. They had trouble in every part of the course, especially in learning the mechanical functions of weapons. For example, Kirk never learned how to detail-strip his rifle. Twice when the tactical officer came to him on an inspection, the officer would grab the rifle from Kirk. When he opened the magazine, the parts would come flying out. Both of them would be on the ground picking up the parts with the tactical officer apologizing to Kirk. The rest of us in ranks would do our best not to laugh. When Kirk graduated, the Army placed him in the gunnery section of the school. His assignment was to instruct the candidates on the functioning of the M1 rifle.

Lassiter was slow in many ways, but he looked good in his uniform. He, too, passed and became an instructor at the school. Both of these men, when I heard from them later, said they were able to instruct on the things they had problems with when in the school.

Every week some of the men were dropped out of the school. One of the first was Morf. He had the bunk next to mine. He was a slob and lazy. He would not mop under his bunk nor get his clothes laid out neatly or his shoes shined. What washed him out was his performance in the field when we were on a training exercise learning the .81 mm mortar. He was the loader, the man who dropped the shell in the tube. Ted Ranger was on one side of the tube and I was on the other. The shell didn't slip down the tube correctly. One of the instructors told Morf to tap the tube on the side. Not Morf, he reared back and kicked the tube violently. The shell was live, and the tube started to fall with the opening of the tube aimed at the watchers. In the audience, in addition to our Lt. Jacobs were our commanding officer and his guests who scattered and ducked. Ted and I were able to catch the tube before it fell completely. We were able to hold the tube and aim it down the range. When the shell exploded, everyone breathed a sigh of relief. When we got back to our barracks, Morf was called to the headquarters. The next day he left for his next assignment.

The next man the Army let go was a good friend, Sgt. McFarland. I didn't understand why he flunked out. He was a good man. He was one of the men who would go with our group on Saturdays to eat at Patterson's. He seemed to do everything correctly but something happened that I didn't know about. He may have asked to be let out. The reason I say that is when I was coming home from Europe, I ran into him while I was in Italy. He was coming out of the USO. I spoke to him for a few minutes. He was with some men, so we didn't talk long, but he said that he was happy about leaving OCS. He got his job back in his old outfit. The job he had was safe from combat. I wished him well.

The lecture I remember the most was given by an officer who had earned the Congressional Medal of Honor. He read the citations of a few of the men and officers who had earned the award. He read his last. He received the Medal of Honor when he led his men through a mine field, and, after saving a couple of his men, then went on to wipe out an enemy machine gun nest. He had been severely wounded but carried on. I don't know why his award impressed me so much. Maybe it was his almost apologetic attitude as he read the citation.

On November 28, I received a long letter from sister Maye telling me about the seriousness of Dad's illness. In it she told of how crazy Dad was about Molly and the baby, and appreciated so much the visits we made with him which kept his spirits up. I was proud of Maye, too, for taking the time off from her nurse's training to be with Dad and hoped it wouldn't jeopardize her progress with the schooling.

One day as we were forming to march to our next assignment, Lt. Jacobs called out and said, "Moranda, you are the guidon bearer today." I went to the front of the formation, got the guidon, and took my position. I was standing tall. "Right face" was the command. I did, and when the next command came, "Forward march," I began to march. We marched about a hundred yards when Lt. Jacobs told the candidate in charge to halt the troops. He did. Lt. Jacobs relieved me of my job as guidon bearer. His comment was that I rolled when I marched, and no matter how I tried when I stood at attention I always looked at ease. He was smiling so I knew that I wasn't being condemned, only that it was not in my make up to be rigidly at attention. He always teased me about my way of walking. I told him that I walked like my father so guessed it was hereditary.

[By May 1943, the German and Italian forces had been driven from North Africa, and the Allies started to prepare for an invasion of Sicily and the

Italian peninsula; the invasion began that fall. Russia had turned from a defensive posture and began to take the offensive. The Americans were becoming battle tested and casualties were mounting, requiring a great increase in replacements to fill the vacancies created. Germany began to strengthen forces in the West, preparing for an invasion of the British Isles as well as to preserve the sites for the V-Bombs they rained on England. In August, Sicily was overrun, and the bulk of German forces evacuated to the mainland and took charge of the Italian campaign after the fall of Mussolini.]

I was called to the office one day and handed a telegram from Mom. It said, "Expect the worst. Dad is dying." I was devastated. What was I to do? Lt. Jacobs happened to be in the office when I opened the telegram. He came out from behind his desk and asked what the problem was. I handed the telegram to him. He was very sympathetic and told me to go to see the chaplain.

Before going to see the chaplain, I went to a telephone and called Mom. She said Dad had just died. The funeral would be in a couple of days. Mom was very calm. No tears or emotional outbreaks. She knew death was coming and so had steeled herself to cope. She also said my sister Maye was with Dad when he died. Maye said Dad really didn't want to die but went easily after the priest came and gave him the last rites. Dad had been raised a Catholic, but had married a daughter of a Methodist minister. After the family moved to Hueneme in 1924, he became a member and official of the Community Presbyterian Church there.

With that I went back to the headquarters and discussed the situation with Lt. Jacobs. He spelled it out. He could get me time off to go home, but I would have to join another company and take some of the training over again. When I talked to the chaplain, he said the same thing. He further said, "Your dad is gone. You would see your mom, but she must have plenty of help there now."

I then walked to the phone and again called home. I told Mom I had decided that I was going to stay and the reason. She said, "Good, that is what your dad would have wanted you to do." I went back to the barracks where Ted Ranger and the men all came to me and expressed their sympathy.

The next day we were going to the range to fire our primary weapon, the M1. I was in a blue funk, and on the way said to myself, "I'm going to dedicate my day to my dad." I did. I had one of the highest scores the Army ever had at this range. When we were at the 500-yard mark firing from the prone position, I maxed the score. All shots were perfect. I looked around when Ted Ranger said, "My man, you have quite an audience." I looked around and saw a large group watching to see if I could make it through the 500-yard series with perfect hits. I did. "That's for you, Dad!" At the next formation the company commander announced that I had broken the school record at the rifle range. I was pleased with the honor especially since in my mind the day belonged to my father.

All the next days, Dad was in my thoughts. As I was growing up, I never knew what he wanted in life. I wondered if any of the seven of us ever stopped and said to him, "I love you, Dad. Thanks for doing for us all your life, and without much thanks from any of us including Mom. From you I learned to accept what is dealt and accept it with calm and, if necessary, bravery. When you were young, what did you really want out of life?" There were many things that I would like to have known about Dad. How did he feel when his father was killed? So many thoughts of the past came to me. I remembered when Tomilyn was born, and Dad would hold her and play with her. You could see that he loved babies.

A few days later I was called into the office and informed that I was to be the company commander of the "Infantry company in the attack," a tactical problem. It was an honor as the role went to someone in the top of the class. The next day we ran the tactical problem, and it was a challenge. I remembered how difficult it was to communicate during our Louisiana tactical maneuvers, and I relearned how hard it is with troops especially when they are under your command. There was noise from the weapons going off. The acting officers of the company were on the radio calling for instructions. With the help of my Acting Executive Officer, Rosensweig, we finished the exercise. The umpires said they were pleased with our company problem. I certainly was not satisfied and thought I should have had more control of the men. This was a lesson learned that I never forgot.

Only about a week later Mom surprised me. I had thought it would be later, but she called me from the railroad station saying she was in Columbus to visit me. Her arrival was on a Wednesday. I think Mom thought I could get off any time to come to see her. I told her I had not reserved a room but had talked to the USO about renting a room. I told her to go to the Travelers Aid, and they would let her know where she could find a room and I would be there as soon as I could get away. I went to see Lt. Jacobs and told him the situation. He said take off tomorrow afternoon early. I picked Mom up and took her for a ride on the bus to see where I was located and showed her the rest of the camp. She was impressed. I told her that I would not be able to come into town until Saturday. Then we would have some time together. She said she was going to try to look up some of her distant relatives, the Edmondsons. From her report later, she said they were not very hospitable, so she wasted no more time trying to get to know them. While she was in Columbus, she stayed in the room the Travelers Aid had obtained for her. She said it was comfortable, and she enjoyed the other women at the house. I was tied up most of the time she was here, but was able to visit and learn what she was going to do now that Dad was gone.

She told me she was going to sell the old house. My first reaction was why? But she said she didn't want to roam around in it with no one else there. I could understand that. She said she would sell the house and live on the interest from the money she would get from the sale. I smiled as I did the calculations. She also said that she would move in with the girls at 331 4th Street, the house where the Swains lived for years that was now occupied by Molly, Jeannette, and Lorraine. I was glad she had all the answers. She also said she would work at Dad's office until they found someone to take over for him. Mom had reservations to go to her next stop to see brothers Earle and George in the Washington, D.C. area on Sunday.

I had wished she could stay, but there was no way I could spend any more time with her. I was in the middle of purchasing my uniforms, going back and forth between the fittings, as well as completing the course work. I had received $250 allowance to buy the uniforms. The local merchants had set up a large warehouse full of the clothing that a new 2nd lieutenant would need. I bought the necessities, and my bill came to $200. I had one dress uniform of "pinks and greens" tailored because of my long waist, and the uniform fit well. I also had to arrange to get my tickets so I could fly home. I couldn't fly all the way home, but I could get as far as Dallas. From there I would have to catch the train. Paying for the tickets was difficult as they wanted cash. I had a money order which for some reason the ticket seller would not take. Mom offered to pay, but I said that she was going to need all her cash. I went back to camp and cashed the check then went back to town and bought the tickets. I said goodbye to Mom as she was leaving that day, too.

The next day we dressed in our new officer's uniforms and walked to the auditorium where we were to attend the ceremony of having bars pinned on. I was number two in the class. There was no money for the honor, but it was nice that I was chosen.

After the ceremony we walked back to the barracks to pick up our Val Packs and head for the airport to go home. On the way I passed the first enlisted man I encountered since getting my bars. When he saluted me, I gave him a dollar bill. That was the custom, and I did enjoy it.

From there I went to the airport. We were loaded on the plane and took off. One of my friends was on the same plane—Billy Reinhardt, who had played football and was one of the big names at the University of California. He was in our class. I enjoyed talking with him as we flew together to Dallas. We then got on an overcrowded train and made it the rest of the way to California. When we arrived in L.A., somehow he took my Val Pac while I took his. Thankfully he remembered my name and where I lived so he was able to track me down. The next day I drove with Molly to Los Angeles where Reinhardt and I exchanged bags. That was the last time I saw him during the war. After the war we met at the football camp where he was trying out for a professional football team, the Los Angeles Dons, and we told war stories to each other.

Again the same routine: we went around the town and saw the family and friends. I went by the Draft Board and saw Mrs. Brown and Hap Maxwell. He was pleased that I had made it as an officer. I had proved his prediction.

I would soon be heading for my first assignment. When I graduated, the Army assigned me to serve with the 176th Richmond Blues at Fort Benning. They were the school troops, which did demonstrations for the classes at the OCS. To serve with that outfit was an honor. They claimed to be the oldest National Guard unit in the USA and were then commanded by a Col. Cox.

Molly was to go with me to Fort Benning. We loaded our old 1937 Studebaker with clothes and things we would need while living in Georgia. Baby's clothes and supplies take up a lot of the space, but we got it all in the car. By packing a lot of items in the back seat, we were able to place the baby's mattress on top of the boxes and make a place where she could spend her time. Tomilyn didn't know me at this time and tried her best to ignore me. With patience and persistence, I finally won her over. But for a few days it was up to Molly to care for her. This made it tough on Molly, as I couldn't help in the job of tending Tomi because she would cry up a storm whenever I tried to take over.

Off we went, 50 mph all the way. We only stopped long enough to eat and relieve ourselves, and then on we would go. I didn't have much time to get to my new assignment so we had to drive almost continuously. Besides, we had to find a place to stay when we got there. It was a long, tedious, boring drive! Molly could climb over the front seat and get some rest with the baby on the mattress. I drove and drove and drove. I didn't think we would ever get through Texas, but we finally arrived in Columbus.

The first thing I did was go to the Travelers Aid. They were helpful in finding us a room in a private home. No private bath and no cooking. Molly was able to fix the baby's formula, but we had to go out for every meal.

We ate at the same place almost every day: a Greek restaurant. The owner of the place took a liking to Tomilyn. The two of them hit it off. He would come by our booth and take Tomi for a tour of the restaurant. He introduced her to his family and the customers. When we were finished, he would bring her back to us. It was a nice thing for the owner to do as it gave us a little break.

Everyday, Molly would take me to the base and then go looking for a place to rent. About the fourth day of looking around the town, she decided to take a country road. After driving a few miles on the new route, she saw a small house that had a rental sign posted. She slammed on the brakes, stopped, and went to the house next door to find out about the house which had the sign in front of it. Thanks to Tomilyn, the lady of the house took an instant shine to her and rented the house to Molly.

What a break. It was a two-bedroom place. The rent was inexpensive, but there was a condition attached to the rental. I had to mow lawns of both houses, and the area was big. It took me a couple of hours a week to mow both places, but I didn't mind. I had my family with me. The neighbors loved taking care of Tomilyn, so Molly and I could go out on the town or go to the Officers Club at Benning. We met some nice couples from the 176th Infantry that I was assigned to, so we had a social life. Our landlords encouraged us to make a garden, which I immediately planted. Our landlady also asked of Molly if she would take her to the store a couple of times a week. Of course Molly did so gladly. They also had a piano and asked me to play and liked the few songs I knew. Sometimes in the evening we would spend some enjoyable hours with them.

When I reported to the 176th Infantry, I got the surprise of my Army career. I was assigned as the Motor Officer for the regiment. I went to the motor pool and met the men. I was very happy with my assignment. I went home and told Molly that at last I was assigned to a job that I was well suited for. The assignment lasted for only two days. I was then called into the headquarters and Col. Cox said that he had been watching me during the past two days. During the noon hour the officers would play a volleyball game. Col. Cox was always there and watched the games and decided I would be wasted in the motor pool. I was assigned to Company B, 1st Battalion, and 176th Infantry.

My first assignment at B Company was to be the platoon leader in the demonstration for the OCS of "The Platoon in the Attack." The men of the company had staged the attack problem many times. All I had to do was be a role player and do what the sergeant advised me to do. We rehearsed the problem a few times with the instructor from the OCS board. I was ready for our first run through for a live audience, but I was called into the office again and was given another assignment. I was to become the Commander of Company B. The Army had a sudden need for company grade officers in the pending operations overseas, which turned out to be D-day! The only reason I was not shipped out along with some of the others was that I had been an officer for only a couple of months. I knew it soon would be my turn to go. It wasn't long before we got word the 176th was to be broken up.

[Postponed from May "Operation Overlord," the Allied long-debated invasion of Northern France, took place on June 6, 1944. This was the war's celebrated D-day when 156,000 men were landed at the beaches of Normandy: 83,000 British and Canadian troops on the eastern beaches and 73,000 Americans on the western. By 9:00 a.m. the coastal defenses were generally breached, but Caen in the British sector, timed to fall on D-day and the hinge of the Allied advance, held out until July 9. Though the heavy fighting in the Caen area attracted most of the German reserves, the U.S. forces in the westernmost sector likewise met very stubborn resistance. Not until June 26 did they take Cherbourg and proceed to clear the rest of the Cotentin peninsula. On D-day the 7th Armored Division sailed on the Queen Mary from New York harbor for Greenock, Scotland.]

The job of CO was easy. The hardest job I had was spending the company fund. The former CO had allowed the fund to build up to a large figure. The Army wanted it spent before the unit was broken up. I asked advice from the headquarters on how I could spend the money. Their only advice was to spend it for the benefit of all the enlisted soldiers in the unit. It was then the First Sergeant and I came up with an idea. Why not hold a banquet for the soldiers, their wives, and sweethearts. We formed a committee. The men were to go into town, find a very nice place, and arrange for a banquet. As I was a part of the committee, I went along. The place was selected. The subject of cost came up in finalizing the night on the town. The amount of money that we had to spend was told to the owner. We made an agreement: the menu and the price were to be the exact amount of the money in the company fund. All was agreed.

The night on the town was a fine one: corsages for the ladies, a special menu, and a band to play later for a dance. Everything went well. The men of the company enjoyed the evening with their wives and girlfriends. Molly and I had a good time. Our good neighbors took Tomi to their house where she stayed the night. With no baby to worry about, Molly and I had a romantic night. At night's end, the company fund had a zero balance.

In Combat

Overseas

It was only a few days later that I was called into the office and given my orders to report to Fort Meade, Maryland. I asked about the rule that a 2nd lieutenant was supposed to have a minimum of six months duty as an officer before he could be sent overseas. The answer I got was, "Oh, you will have it by the time you ship out."

How I hated to go home and tell Molly I was going overseas. I knew she would be upset, and she was. But Molly was always stronger than I gave her credit for. We had been so happy being together in the little house with the wonderful landlords next door who loved Tomi and Molly and with all of our new friends with whom we had so many good times. Those few months were some of the happiest times of our marriage. We kept in touch with those friends for years after the war.

With great sorrow we again packed the old Studebaker. This time we were better at packing as we had learned from our first journey across the country. The sad part was saying goodbye to our friends next door. Tomi would have been glad to stay with them. The car was serviced, and we left for California. The speed limit was still 50 mph, so I knew it was going to take us a long time to get across the country.

I drove from Columbus to Texas and only stopped to eat and gas up. The baby rode well especially with Molly playing with her and talking to her whenever she was awake. I don't remember how many times I heard "See the cow," or "See the horsy."

When we were approaching Dallas, I had to get some rest so I asked Molly to drive and I sat next to her and dropped off to sleep for a few minutes. I awoke as we were going through the main part of Dallas. Molly had the car in the right lane. Ahead was a street car. The street car stopped at the intersection. A black woman leaped off the street car, across the loading zone, and right into the hood of the car. Molly stopped the car immediately. I saw that the lady had made it to sidewalk. I told Molly to drive across the street to get the car out of the intersection. I got out of the car and applied pressure to the gash on the lady's head. Her glasses were broken, but otherwise she seemed to be OK. All the time Molly was in the car. She was really broken up about the accident. The police came and questioned Molly and me about what happened. We told them what we saw. They talked to the lady and she said the same thing. They asked me where we were going. I told them we were going back to California and then I was going overseas. With that an officer said something that I sure didn't like: "Go on, she is just a nigger." We gave the lady and the police our address. Later, we had our friend Attorney Mark Durley in Oxnard arrange to pay for the lady's new glasses and the cost of her doctor.

Marine Sgt. Bill and Bob

Morandas during World War II

Lt. Earle

Lt. George and Sgt. Bill

Seaman Paul, Cadet
Nurse Maye, and Bob

Airman Ted in Naples

Molly would not drive again as she was so upset. The driving was mine to do. Those miles were long and tedious as we slowly crept across the country. One time we stopped in a small town in Texas to eat at a restaurant that was full of people with large hats and cowboy boots who were out with their families for dinner. We were tired and the baby was fussing. Our food had been served.

Suddenly, the baby up-chucked all over the table and our food. The owner and the waitress were really asses. They made such a fuss about the mess. I was embarrassed, but surely they had seen babies vomit before. I was about ready to pop the owner in the kisser, but instead I went back to the kitchen and got the mop and a couple of wet rags. I told Molly to go out and get in the car. I didn't want her to take any more guff from that staff. After I had cleaned the mess, I went to the restroom and cleaned myself. I returned the mops and rags, and then made my reappearance at the cashier's station. There I proceeded to tell the owner how I felt about him and his staff raving and ranting about the incident. I threw the money for the meals on the counter and walked out. As I left the people applauded my actions. A couple of them tried to give me money, but I sure didn't want that. I am certain most of those people had seen babies get sick before.

From there all the way home I drove and drove, only stopping for food or to relieve ourselves. I got so tired I had to stop once for a couple of hours and sleep by the side of the road. Finally we reached the California border and in a few more hours we drove into Oxnard, California. Man, oh man, I was certainly glad to see familiar sights. For two days I visited family and friends who were glad to see us again. They also knew I was going overseas, so they were very solicitous. They wished me well and sympathized with Molly and Mom.

After the few days at home, it was time for me to leave my family again, this time for Fort Meade, Maryland, where I would be processed for overseas duty. D-day had happened and the Army had a great need for cannon fodder—better known as first and second lieutenants in the infantry. I really didn't believe any lieutenant in the infantry who fought in the war for any length of time escaped either being killed, captured, or wounded. I thought I knew what I was getting into. But I also knew the family was placing me in God's care, and I would have plenty of prayers going on for me. When I left Molly, she said to me that she would ask God to place me within a shield of love. Molly also had a Christian Scientist practitioner, a Mrs. Reedy, work (pray) for me all the time I was overseas. And I prayed for the same thing.

This time I went on a plane so I didn't have to drive across the country again. We stopped a couple of times flying over the states and landed in Washington, D.C., where I was the guest of my older brother Earle. He took me around the city to see the sights and where he worked. We talked baseball and went to a game, for at that time in our lives we followed the baseball "stats" closely. He was addicted to baseball. I remember his discussions about baseball with his barber as I sat and watched him get a haircut and listened to the two of them tell each other what the Washington Senators should do to improve their team.

Washington was a city of haste. Everyone was in a hurry. The war effort was at its height. Everyone had someone in the service, so it seemed they were looking, listening, talking, and praying for a quick victory. Brother George was stationed at the Engineer School at Fort Belvoir on the faculty teaching officer candidates and living in nearby Alexandria, Virginia, with his wife Nancy and their newborn son. I spent one afternoon with them and caught up on their news.

After a few days with Earle, it was time for me to report to Ft. Meade. Earle took me to the bus line. When I got to Fort Meade, I entered the headquarters building, reported to the Officer of the Day, and there, waiting in line ahead of me, was my enlisted buddy Hugh West. We were so glad to see each other. He had been sent to an Army unit in Texas. We were together for the next few days and later sailed on the same ship to cross the Atlantic.

They sent us to Camp Shanks, New York, located about an hour away from the Big City. We were there for a week, during which time Hugh and I went to see the sights. He took me to a night club where he knew the maitre d'hotel, who gave us a special table near the stage. The singer came to the table and asked if she could sing us a special song. We thanked her and she honored our requests.

We had to take a variety of modes of transportation to get to the city. First an Army truck, then a bus, and finally the rails. I was fascinated with the underground system. Hugh and I got pretty good at getting around the town. On one of my trips, I was hustled by a woman. She wanted me to get off at the next stop for a good time. I thanked her and she cursed me, "What's the matter with you. Don't you want a freebie?" That was my first time experiencing the neighborliness of New York.

Everyone in New York seemed in a hurry. If you asked directions from a person walking in the opposite direction, he would give you the instructions as he walked away from you. As the distance got farther between the asker and the responder, the voices got louder. In a few minutes, the two people would be yelling at each other. I'm sure the people around were certain there was bad blood between the two when they were only being friendly.

At the end of the week it was time for us to depart from Camp Shanks for the harbor and load onto the ship taking us overseas. They trucked us to the Hudson River. There we were loaded onto a river barge that took us down to the New York harbor. After sailing for an hour, we arrived, unloaded, and after milling around for a few minutes on the pier, marched to the waiting ship and boarded the HMS Mataroa, an old English passenger ship converted into a troop ship. Hugh and I were in quarters with a group of officers, all of them company grade officers heading for the war.

England

On board, we were quite comfortable. We had a steward who took care of our bunks and kept us abreast of the happenings aboard the ship. He would wake us in the morning and as he did he would announce in his British accent what was on the menu. It seemed that the breakfast on most of the days was kippers. Kippers are fish, but fish for breakfast? No way! When the menu was announced, there was always a groan, and most of the men would stay in their bunks. We soon learned that if we didn't eat kippers for breakfast, we would get them later at another meal.

The only way we could bathe was with salt water. A tub was filled with warm salt water. After we soaped with a special soap and rinsed with the salt water, our orderly would bring us a basin with unsalted water for a final rinsing. As we had no way to exercise, we didn't have to bathe every day.

Daily, Hugh and I went to the salon, found a table and comfortable chairs, and spent most of the day playing gin rummy. I didn't know how to play the game when we first started the voyage, but I soon learned. The stakes were 25 cents a box and 50 cents a game. We played hundreds of games. As we were within a convoy, it took us a long time to get to England. When we debarked, Hugh paid me two dollars—we were almost evenly matched.

The convoy was made up of a large number of freighters. Our ship was in the middle of the convoy, while on the outside of the convoy, destroyers from our Navy patrolled for submarines. We thought we were fairly safe with the U.S. Navy nearby, but we also knew the Germans had sunk many of our ships going to England. Our biggest danger came not from the Germans but from Old Mother Nature. Near Newfoundland our convoy had to fight through a scary storm with waves that seemed 50 feet high. I went to the upper deck and watched the waves break over the bow of the ship. What power! The ship's captain slowed down and sort of laid to by turning into the waves at reduced speed and held there while plowing ahead.

The ship never varied from its course. I learned later the convoy had lost a freighter during the storm. I am sure if a person ever went overboard during that storm there would be no way to rescue him. After that storm, the sailing was fine: smooth seas, fleecy clouds, and a friendly breeze.

The morning we arrived, the steward came into the cabin and announced that England was soon to be visible. We got up, ate breakfast, and took places at the rails where we could observe the coast line. There it was: green and pretty. Slowly we approached the harbor and soon docked in Bristol, a large, busy harbor. It wasn't long before Army personnel came aboard and welcomed us to England.

We debarked and were loaded on trucks which took us to Warminster Barracks located near Bath. This time there were no barracks for us. When they dumped us off, we were guided to our new homes—permanent tents. We soon were greeted by the commander of the base, who told us we would be in England for only a few days. The war was going great and that they wanted us to get there in time to participate in the victory. What a yuk! He was, in his way, trying to be cute. One of the officers in our ranks asked, "If it's so wonderful, how come you are still here in this camp?" No answer was forthcoming.

Our quarters were tents with Army cots, which never were comfortable but were adequate. Our toilet facilities were about fifty yards away from the tents. Maybe the Army wanted us to be so miserable that we would enjoy going into combat. Our group was made up of all 1st and 2nd lieutenants. The morning muster was a mess. Many of the officers would go to town, get a little drunk, and then at the morning call would not want to make muster. The captain in charge would not dismiss us until everyone was accounted for. He was forever saying, "Shape up or you will be sent overseas to combat." That didn't faze anyone in our group, as we knew we were already headed there.

The city of Bath was nearby. We would catch a ride into the town on an Army truck. It was easy to get into town but tough to get back to camp. Not many Army trucks would travel during blackouts. On the first day, one of the regular cadres told me there was a mail truck that came back to camp at 10 o'clock every night. He told me where to find the post office. So I would go to town and then come home on top of the mail bags containing letters from the wives, mothers, and sweethearts of the men in our camp.

One night I went into town and into one of the numerous pubs. I sat next to a family of three: Mom and Dad and a young girl about fifteen years old, a beautiful blonde girl. I found it was customary for families to go to their favorite pubs in the evening and visit. I talked to the family, telling them where I was from and about my family. We visited for quite awhile. I asked the young girl what she missed most because of the war. She thought for a short time and then said, "An orange. In my mind I can still smell the scent of an orange. It has been four years since I had an orange." I stayed there for some time visiting and watching the continuous game of darts and thinking to myself what a rotten thing wars is. The people who suffer most are the kids. It was not their fault a war was going on. I asked if she came to the pub every night. She said. "Yes, we come here nightly to visit with our friends."

When I got back to camp, I went to the mess sergeant to ask if I could get some oranges for the young lady. He gave me six of them. He smiled and said, "That is certainly a new story." I took the oranges to the girl the next night. I assumed she would wolf them down. But no, she just sat and took one of the oranges and smelled it. Never in my life was a gift I gave appreciated as much as those few oranges. Sadly, I never saw the young girl again. But this much I know, she will forever remember the American lieutenant who gave them to her.

My assignment for the next few days was one I didn't enjoy. I was assigned to teach a group of enlisted men the art of bayonet fighting. The night before I found the manual and brushed up on the proper way to teach the subject. Then I got Hugh West to practice with me. The men I had to train were prisoners who had been court-martialed and were in the guard house. They had been given the choice of going overseas and joining an Army outfit or staying in prison. Their choice was the guard house or combat. Those I was assigned to train had decided that they would take their chances in the war by going overseas and joining a combat unit.

The next morning the men were marched to the training area and the training began. The Military Police stayed around watching the training. I was glad they stayed. Some of the men were tough looking, and I wondered if I would ever get some of these men when I was in combat. The training went well, perhaps too well. When I went back to my quarters, I was called to the CO's headquarters. There I was informed I would be the officer in charge of the prisoners until they got to France and were turned over to the Replacement Center. The good part was I would have the weekend off.

Friday I went back to Bath. I sat in the pub and visited for a time with new friends. I was tired and decided that it was about time to get back to camp. I had to first make it back to the post office where I could find the mail truck. I went outside and darkness descended. The moon was not out, and clouds covered the stars or was it fog? Whatever it was I was having a difficult time finding my way. I knew it was a couple of blocks one way and then a couple blocks another way. So I bumped along the sidewalk keeping my body next to the walls. I stumbled into a couple doing their thing in the standing position—practicing the art of standing seduction—known in England as the "wall job." I said, "Sorry," and continued on my way. Finally my eyes became adjusted to the darkness and I found the post office. I paid the man the few shillings and climbed on top of all the mail sacks. There I relaxed until the truck arrived at our camp.

The next day I decided to go to London. I found the highway and used my thumb to hitchhike. I was soon picked up by a lady—I mean a real Lady driving an open roadster. She said to me, "I say there, would you like to ride with me for a while? I am going almost to London." I thanked her and came on board. She reminded me of Mrs. Richard Bard, a friend of our family's in Port Hueneme. She introduced herself as Lady So-and-so; I do not remember the name. She questioned me about where I was from and kept up banter until she came to the driveway where she lived. It was a manor. She said goodbye and told me where the best place was to pick up another ride. I got a ride and was soon in London.

When I arrived, I wandered about and came to a large park. On the lawn were hundreds of couples sitting on the grass listening to music. There were many GIs with English girls. Romance was in the air. I listened for a time, moved on, and ran into Hugh West. He was going to a party and asked me to go. I was soon aware that I was a fifth wheel, so I left and went back to the highway. It was only a few minutes before an Army truck picked me up and took me back to camp. My experience in London was not one to remember except for the friendliness of the people.

The day soon came when it was time to move out. The MPs marched the prisoners to waiting trucks and loaded them aboard. The MPs saluted and said, "All present and accounted for." My instant thought was I hope that I can say the same thing when we reach the shores of France and I turn my charges over to the replacement center.

France

The trip to the waiting ship didn't take long. I was in the first vehicle and saw where many of the ships had been loaded for the great invasion. The harbor was busy with ships loading men and supplies for the troops in France. We were driven to the loading area. The prisoners were unloaded, assembled, and counted and then taken aboard ship. My group was taken to an area where they could be guarded easily. The men were quiet and seemed to be thinking of their next assignment. Soon the blast from the ship's horn sounded and the tugs pushed us out. We were on the way across the English Channel.

There were various ships around us carrying supplies to the Allied Forces. Ours seemed to be the only one carrying troops. I thought of the time and planning that had gone into making the first attack on D-day. Most of the men were playing cards or writing letters. They were quiet, and there didn't seem to be much joy among the troops. I am sure they were impressed with this trip and were thinking of D-day. Some of the men became seasick and made trips to places where they then could relieve themselves. My time was spent watching and thinking of what was to come next, and I wrote letters to Molly and Mom.

The next morning we saw the shores of France. We were coming into the area of Utah Beach and could see the remains of the great battle. We were approached by LSTs. They came along the side of our ship. A net had been installed on the side, and our group was supposed to hold their duffel bags and climb down the net into the waiting LST. I now found out how brave some of the men were. They were afraid and didn't want to climb down. After trying persuasion, I decided I would show them how easy it was to take the trip. I grabbed the first man in line and made him place himself at the top of the net. Then I placed my body in position around his so he could not fall. Down the side we went. When we got into the waiting ship, I noted the rest of the men were following. I got quite a hand from the watching men. We were finally loaded and started toward the shore. I was thinking of what the men had gone through on D-day. We can read about them, but we cannot ever understand what they went through that day. We will never know of the many heroes because so few were left to write all the citations that were deserved. Each minute must have seemed forever. I wrote a poem about how I felt about the day:

Remembering D-day 1944

You see the waves

That flow toward the shore

You hear the music of the waves

As the tides flow and sands reach for more.

You hear songs

Of gulls that are screeching

You smell the sweet scents

From the tides and sands that are reaching.

I see red waves

Carrying the blood of the wounded and the dead

I hear the blasts of the guns

From ships behind and guns ahead.

I hear the moans

Of the wounded and the dying

I smell the Death

Of bodies floating, no longer crying

Those who were there remember

As thoughts blast through their minds

And bring tears

Not possible to leave behind.

I could see how the Allies suffered so many casualties. I visualized the carnage and the bravery of many of the participants. I could also see the many who would not move from a safe spot until someone booted them along. There were many, many heroes that day whose actions will remain unknown.

The Navy had blinkers working to guide our landing crafts to shore. At the landing area, each man reached down, hoisted his pack on his back, and moved onto the shores of France.

What we saw made me think more about the men who braved D-day. We could still see the burned out tanks, the gun emplacements, and the sunken landing craft. We had passed hundreds of underwater obstacles. We saw some Germans, but they were no longer fighters. Instead, they were prisoners under guard and some of them were loading trucks—which I thought was odd. They didn't seem to be under any stress; they seemed relieved.

We continued up the hill on hastily built roads. The place was busy with trucks being loaded with rations and other supplies. There were thousands of Jerry cans filled with gasoline waiting for someone to load them into trucks. I wondered what a German airplane could do with machine-gun strafing. Thank God that the Allies had the upper hand in the air war. Then I learned that the Army had run out of gasoline and that had stopped their drive. After the war, many hours and words were spent discussing what the outcome would have been had the supply of gasoline kept up with the charge across France.

I followed signs to the replacement center. When we arrived, I halted the group of prisoners and said to the officer in charge, "All present and accounted for." I said to myself, "You and the two sergeants did a good job." I turned to the two sergeants and said, "Thanks for a good job." That reminds me of a situation that happened in Texas. We were in the field when the colonel in charge said to one of his officers, "Get that platoon to come over here." The officer yelled at the platoon leader, "Please bring your platoon over here." The colonel chewed out the officer and told him, "You never say please or thank you in an Army command." So I broke the rules, but I was not sorry. Those men had had some tough days, and I appreciated their effort.

[In July 1944, the American Army on the Allies' right, newly supported by the landing of the Third Army under Lt. Gen. Patton, broke through the German defenses at Avranches, the gateway from Normandy into Brittany. Though some of the U.S. Forces were swung southward in the hope of seizing the Breton ports, others were wheeled eastward to trap in the Falaise "pocket," a large part of the German forces retreating southward from the pressure of the Allied left at Caen.

Meanwhile, more and more Allied troops were being landed in Normandy. On August 1, two Army Groups were constituted: the 21st (comprising the British and Canadian Armies) under General Montgomery, and the 12th (American) under General Bradley. General Montgomery was given operational control of both groups until General Eisenhower arrived in France. From August 10 to14, the 7th Armored Division landed at Utah and Omaha Beaches in Normandy and was made part of the XX Corps, commanded by Major General Walton Walker, part of General Patton's Third Army. The 7th spearheaded the XX Corps drive from Chartres to Metz between August 14 and September 25.

By the middle of August, an eastern wheel wider than the one that cut off the Falaise pocket, had brought the Americans to Argentan, level with the 21st Army Group on the left front so that a concerted effort could be launched eastward. On August 19, a U.S. division crossed the Seine. Orleans was taken on August 1, and after the French Resistance-led uprising in Paris, the capitol city was entered by General LeClerc's French force on August 24.

The U.S. 7th Army under General Patch and the French 1st Army under General de Tassigny landed on the French Riviera on August15, advanced rapidly up the Rhone valley, and joined the Americans north of Lyons early in September.]

When I landed in France, the front lines were almost to the German border. The lead units were near Verdun. I remembered that name from World War I. A large battle was fought there—trench warfare at its worst. Being so far from the front in Normandy, we were fairly safe from shellings. The only worry was an occasional fly-over by a German plane.

I reported to the headquarters of the Replacement Center. They said it would only be a couple of days before I was assigned to a unit at the front and that I could relax and enjoy the rest. I pitched my tent: first-class accommodations! I had plenty of company. Most of the officers I had come over with arrived about the same time. Lt. Kinnebrew was made the officer in charge of the officer group. Somewhere along the line, I was separated from my long-time buddy Hugh West. When we parted in England, it was the last time I ever saw him. The soldier who was also my friend and was on every promotion list with me from Private First Class to Second Lieutenant was gone. I don't know why I never tried to see him after the war.

While I was waiting for my number to come up, I took walks around the area, saw the remains of the war, watched the hustle and bustle of ships coming in and the cargo and men coming up the slopes—quite a sight. I saw small children hanging around the camp hoping for a candy bar or a cigarette. The French adults went about their daily lives. They were relieved to have the Germans gone, but I am sure they were unhappy, for their homes were destroyed. They appeared to be in shock. The battles of D-day and the subsequent actions for the territory must have scarred them for life.

At night we sat around, talked, and played cards. There was always a blackjack game going on in one of the tents if you can imagine five or six men in a small tent playing cards. I remember many types of money in the pot—a mixture of francs, pounds, and dollars. We soon learned the exchange values. The game was usually played by flashlight as blackout was ordered. Amounts grew in the pot when we were gambling with francs or English pounds. We knew the exchange rates but we didn't seem to mind losing foreign money. I was soon finished as I never seemed to have money to gamble. I hung around because the chatter was interesting, and I enjoyed watching the action.

One night two of us walked into a French bar. We each had a glass of wine from the owner's private stock. I was never a wine drinker, but have not tasted a better one since that day. I do not know all the things that good wines are supposed to have, but this wine had it. We tried to pay for it. The owner accepted a package of Chesterfields, but no cash.

We were advised one night that we were to leave at 0700 the next day. We would be going to the front. There we would join an infantry unit already in combat. When I heard the news, I got a twinge in my belly. Fear? I guess so. But the term "combat" seemed to be like a dreaded final exam. For two years we had been practicing, and now was the time to see how it would be. No longer would it be our own aggressor forces playing the enemy roles. This would be the real thing, where the enemy would try his best to kill. I soon cleared my mind and said, "Here we go. Dear God, I place you in charge."

The morning came. We were twenty infantry officers and two hundred enlisted men. The officer in charge was still Kinnebrew, the young man from Georgia. He was wise enough to see he had a group of men who would do what he wanted without having to play the role of tough guy. He told us what to do and we did it. After we had reached the point of our assignments, I wondered why no one out of the large group had disappeared. When the war was over, I heard that over ten thousand deserters had left combat and stayed in and around Paris for the duration. But I don't remember any mass court-martials for the deserters.

We were loaded into French railroad freight cars of the First World War vintage: the 40 and 8 cars. It was possible to get forty men or eight horses in the car. The engine pulled the cars easily. The tracks were somewhat smooth, so the ride was comfortable. We rode with the doors open so we could see the countryside. France was colorful with rich green and the other vivid colors. We saw the results of the drive of the armies that had preceded us by a few weeks. We got a look at the Hedge rows. I capitalize the "H" because they were a great defensive weapon. There was no way to fight against them except by the old World War I command, "Over the Top!" They were too steep for tanks, so tanks were rarely used. The infantry would be exposed for a hundred yards or so between rows. If the infantry tried to attack over the open ground, they would be mowed down by machine gun fire. The best way to overcome the problem was by mortar fire—both sides used their mortars effectively. With their high angle of fire, the shells would drop just over the row's edge and cause havoc.

During my train ride across France, I noticed the women working in the fields harvesting crops. While the Germans were in control, the French were reluctant to harvest any crops. We were told that if they had brought the crops in, the Germans would have taken most of them.

When we passed through a town or city, we noticed how few steeples were left standing. The tanks and artillery always zeroed in on the steeples as either army always assumed the enemy would be using them as observation posts.

Our route followed that of the allied forces as they crossed France. The one city that I remember was Chartres. In that town the steeple was still intact. The Americans knew the church was a treasure so they took pains not to knock it down. We didn't stop, but we had a good look at the city as we passed by.

Verdun

We crossed the Moselle River and the train came to a stop. We had arrived at the historic French town of Verdun. I remembered the stories told about the Battle of Verdun in World War I. For some reason, Mom had saved pictures of the great battles of World War I. I think she obtained the pictures from magazines. I remember reading about the trench warfare, and the trenches were still visible. The trenches stretched for miles during that war. Of course, the barbed wire was no longer in place. That war killed many on both sides by shells, bayonets, gangrene, and poison gas. The continuous bombardments by both sides lasted for months. And now I was at that historic place. I imagined I could hear the sounds of artillery in the distance. Was it still going on? Or was that the ghosts of war still practicing their arts? Why Mom of all people saved war pictures I cannot understand, for she was so against all wars. The only explanation I can think of is that her brother Basil Newton was in the Army, training in a camp in Texas, but he was never in combat; he was still in training when World War I ended. He became a prominent member of the Arkansas National Guard following the war and stayed with it until his death in 1941.

[In the north there was discord. Montgomery argued with the Supreme Allied Commander General Eisenhower for a single main thrust northeastward through Belgium into the heavily industrialized Ruhr valley—an area vital to the German war effort. The U.S. Generals wanted to continue the advance on a broad front in accordance with the pre-invasion plans. Eisenhower, by way of compromise, decided on August 23 that Montgomery's drive into Belgium should have the prior claim on resources until Antwerp was taken, but that thereafter the pre-invasion plans would be resumed.

Consequently, the British 2nd Army began its advance on August 29, entered Brussels on September 3, took Antwerp the next day, and went on to force its way to the Albert Kanaal. The U. S. First Army, supporting the British on the right, took Namur on the same day Antwerp was taken and was nearing Aachen. To the south, Patton's Third Army, having raced forward to take Verdun on August 31, was attacking to cross the Moselle River near Metz hoping to achieve a breakthrough into Germany's economically important Saarland.]

    We unloaded from the train, boarded Army trucks, and were taken to a field near the Verdun trenches. The two hundred infantrymen and the twenty officers would soon find out where each would be assigned. Naturally we were anxious. As soon as we were in the field and positioned in a semi-horseshoe formation, a jeep came on the scene. It brought the commanding general of the 7th Armored Division, Major General Silvester. He was a large man with gray hair—a good looking officer. Along with him were members of his staff. When the jeep was close to the troops, it stopped; the general stood in front of the troops and spoke to us.

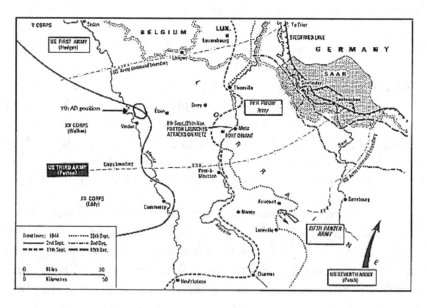

Bob joined the 7ᵗʰ Armored Division at Verdun

His talk went something like this: "Welcome to the 7th Armored Division. We have just come across France liberating the land that had long been in German hands. We are now preparing to move into Germany. Each of you will be assigned where you are needed." Then he turned to the twenty officers that were formed in a group at one end of the formation and continued, "As for you officers, you will be assigned to infantry companies. I want each of you to look to your right and to your left at the officers next to you. After the next battle there will only be a few of you left to carry on." I looked right and left and said to myself, "You unlucky bastards." And he was accurate. After the first serious battle, there were very few of us left; over half were lost in their first battle. I remember thinking when the general was talking, that is one hell of a way to greet inexperienced soldiers. We were all filled with anxiety and were concerned about what was going to happen. The odds quoted were not good for morale. As we stood there waiting, we heard a gun shot. Everybody ducked. Our eyes followed the sound, and we discovered that a soldier had shot himself in the foot, better known as a SIW or self-inflicted wound. I guess the speech by the general had made a deep impression. To cap off our introduction to the division, as we were waiting for the next thing to happen, a truck drove slowly past our position. Inside the truck was a load of bodies—American soldiers that had been killed in the last battle.

While we were standing around the area I first heard the far away rumblings of artillery fire. The sound, though not close, seemed to be a foreboding of things to come. From that day until the end of my experiences in the combat area, the rolling rumble was there. I do not know how many rounds of artillery and other explosives were used during the war on all sides, but it must have been tremendous.

After that the enlisted men were assigned. Their names were called and the men were loaded into waiting trucks. The trucks delayed as officers were assigned to the same groups. One by one the officers received their assignments and climbed aboard the trucks. There were only two officers left, Lt. French and myself. French had been a machine gun instructor at Camp Roberts for two years. I had worked at a service station for several years. There were two jobs left. A motor officer and a machine gun platoon leader. French had never had any experience in motors, while that had been my civilian job. So he became the motor officer, and I was assigned leader of the machine gun platoon of the Headquarters Company, 38th Armored Infantry Battalion.

Like most armored divisions, the division had three Combat Commands (CCA, CCB, and CCR), three Armored Infantry Battalions (23rd, 38th, and 48th AIBs), three Tank Battalions (17th, 31st, and 40th TBns), three Armored Artillery Battalions (434th, 440th, and 489th), a Cavalry Reconnaissance Squadron (87th), an Armored Engineer Battalion (33rd), an Armored Medical Battalion (77th), an Armored Ordnance Battalion (129th), a Signal Company (147th), a Band, a Military Police Platoon, and Division Trains (for maintenance and supply). They usually had one Antiaircraft Battalion and a Tank Destroyer Battalion. The AIBs were made up of three Infantry companies, a Headquarters Company, and a Service Company. The Headquarters Company, besides the Commanding Officer and his staff, contained a Reconnaissance Platoon, a Mortar Platoon, an Assault Gun Platoon, and a Heavy Machine Gun Platoon. I was assigned to command the Machine Gun Platoon.

The authorized strength of an armored division was 10,500 men and 168 medium tanks, 77 light tanks, 450 half-tracks, 54 self propelled 105 mm howitzers, 35 assault guns (105 mm), 54 armored cars, 1031 motor vehicles, and 8 light aircraft. In my machine gun platoon, I had four heavy machine guns organized into two gun sections. Our job was to have sections go out with Infantry units and provide fire support for specific operations.

7th Armored Division

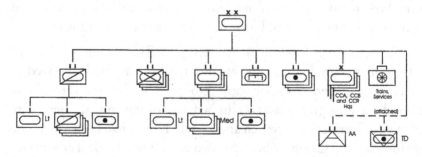

I was given background on the 7th Armored, which had come across France and made an excellent record and had not suffered many casualties. It was a rapid moving force and had been successful in exploiting the hole made in the German defense line. It was in XX Corps, commanded by Major General Walton Walker, and a part the General Patton's Third Army. It had liberated many towns and cities and must have thought this war was easy—you know, "bring on the Germans." Then gas supplies ran out, causing a wait of seven days. As they waited for supplies, the units had a short rest and caught up on maintenance and sleep. I learned that the largest battle the 7th Armored had fought going across France was the Battle of Chartres, which is located about sixty miles southwest of Paris. At that battle my new commanding officer, Capt. Carl M. "Rusty" Mattocks, distinguished himself. His unit had come across a company-sized German force that was apparently trying to get back to their own forces, and the two companies clashed. After a sharp fire fight, the Germans put up a white flag and Rusty's outfit won. Rusty and his men took 42 prisoners. For his gallantry in action, he was awarded the Silver Star.

From Chartres the 7th continued on the march and arrived at Verdun so fast that the Germans did not have time to blow out the bridge leading into the town. They captured the town intact. One of the soldiers who went looking around the town found a warehouse full of Wehrmacht cognac and other alcoholic beverages. The news didn't take long to get around the division, and soon cases of liquor were on almost every tank and half-track. It was issued to the units with the stipulation that it was only to be used during inclement weather and for snake bite. It must have rained a lot because no snakes were ever seen.

The division's next objective was to get across the Moselle River. One evening the mess sergeant, after imbibing a few drinks, decided that the crossing would be easy. He said, "You damn doughfeet don't know how to fight. I'll show you how to get across that damn river." He talked a cook into driving a half-track, on which he had mounted a .50 caliber machine gun—he was going to show the GIs how to get the Army moving again. Off they went toward the river, and as they came close to it, a German 88 opened up on them. After a near hit the sergeant quickly decided that the life of a front line soldier was much more dangerous than that in the kitchen, and crossing the river was not as easy as making a stew. So he hightailed it back.

When the gas supply finally got to the front, the attack commenced again. The 38th Armored Infantry made it across the Moselle at West Arnaville and later took over the town of Lorry. It cost the units many casualties, but they were successful. The Germans were getting tough. They knew the area and had every crossroad covered with mortar and artillery fire because they had been operating an artillery school nearby and had every key place plotted. The town of Arry was the next objective. The area was mostly hills and forests. On one day during the battle for Siligney, the 38th lost four battalion commanders—three were killed and one was seriously wounded and evacuated. When I heard of the loss of the battalion commanders, I wondered if they ever thought of moving their headquarters. It seemed to me that the Germans knew the position of the battalion command post and were playing, "Let's shoot the colonel." The surviving commander spent all his time in his foxhole digging it deeper. He was given another job after that fracas.

I learned that the lieutenant I was replacing had been captured. On his first combat mission in his new assignment, he was captured along with the commander of the headquarters company. It was apparent why the need for infantry officers was so great. Left in the headquarters company was Rusty Mattocks, recently promoted from lieutenant to captain. While I was getting acquainted with him, I wondered how I would be received by the men of my new weapons platoon. After meeting Mattocks and his staff, I asked where my new platoon was located. 1ˢᵗ Sgt. Alvie Davis pointed to a group of men with their half-tracks on a hillside about 500 yards away. I took my stuff out of the truck and started up the hill. It had been rainy for days, so with slipping and sliding I finally made it to where the platoon was located. I remember wondering why none of the men came to help me, but that is the way of war. I reminded myself that I was a new officer and the men were only testing me. I fooled them. I didn't ask for help nor did I give them hell for not helping. The immediate problem of a replacement officer was to prove himself. His new men would size him up quickly. The first experience in combat would do the proving and nothing else. I wondered how I would behave when the fighting was going on. We all would soon know.

A big sergeant stood up when I approached. He came forward, saluted, and said, "Sir, Sergeant Sicari reporting." I gave him my name; after a few minutes of conversation, he assembled the men and introduced me. They were men of all sizes and shapes and from all races except blacks. I took my bed roll and other baggage to my half-track, pitched my tent, and started around the area to get acquainted with the men: Sgts. Sicari, Simoneaux, Curtin, and others. My driver was Corp. Cox, who helped me get my stuff into the half-track. The next man I met was Maurice Conover, who was to be my runner and who proved to be a godsend for the rest of my time in combat. Conover was from the small town of Broadview, Montana, where he had a large wheat ranch. Most of the other names in the platoon have disappeared from my memory. I can see them vividly, but the names are gone.

After meeting with my men, I went back to see the other officers and enlisted men of the Headquarters Company. It was essentially a re-staffed unit with Capt. Mattocks as the Commanding Officer and Lts. Kinnebrew, French, and me as platoon leaders. Over a cup of coffee, Capt. Mattocks told us of his experiences during the race across France:

> The 7th's first mission was to seize the cathedral city of Chartres, about sixty kilometers southwest of Paris. The twin spires of the Cathedral were seen as we approached the city. The 38th AIB was assigned to by-pass the city to the north through the village of Leves and seize a small German airport on its northeast perimeter. A small task force made up of a reconnaissance platoon, an infantry platoon, and my assault guns (75 mm guns mounted on light tanks with an open turret) fought the first battle the 38th was in.
>
> As the task force took the east road from the center of the village, it came under direct machine gun fire from some place near a large church in the eastern side of the village. No casualties were sustained by the Recon Platoon; however, the platoon leader, Lt. Frederikson, became separated from his unit and took refuge with a group of nuns at the church. The infantry platoon leader was hit and had to be evacuated. I took command of the task force and deployed the assault guns in a wooded slope west of the town from where we could fire into the church area. First we demolished the brick wall, which

then allowed us a clear field of fir. A German armed with a *panzerfaust* (bazooka) came out from the ruins of the wall and became our first prisoner. I told the rifle platoon to move into town after my guns had finished shelling, which would be signaled by a smoke shell. The troops advanced and seized three of the four corners of the crossroads near the village center. However, the Germans in the fourth part were able to fire into the turret of one of the assault guns and wounded two of my men. I had moved with the infantry and was in a house looking eastward towards the burning church. While I was doing so, a lone German, unnoticed by me, came out of a building in the unoccupied fourth part of the town. He shot at me, striking the window frame, which got my complete attention, and I took him down with a quickly borrowed M-1 rifle.

The infantry advanced to the east side of the village to a point near the burning church, where we found a Renault car that the Germans had abandoned when they apparently withdrew through some heavy woods nearby. We proceeded east for approximately one-half a mile and then turned right, crossing an abandoned stone quarry that had probably been used during the construction of the church. We then approached the air strip and came under artillery fire from the southeast. We withdrew to a point overlooking the quarry, where we spent the night. We thought the artillery fire came from our own forces which were part of the pincer movement around the city.

That night we captured several Germans who were trying to break out to the east. After a burst from our ring-mounted .50 caliber machine guns, we heard the yell *Kamerad*. We didn't close the gap that day, but did on August 17.

Capt. John M____ and a platoon of riflemen were ambushed in the city. John abandoned his men, which didn't endear him to his men, but we were able to get the men back safely. I went back to where we had lost Frederikson. I found him as he was coming back to our lines after hiding out with the nuns in their domicile.

We had Col. Wellborn Griffith, the Operations Officer from XX Corps, monitoring our action. He came down into Leves to check things out after we had passed through. He was riding in a light tank; when he stuck his head out of the turret, it was promptly shot off by one of the many Germans we had by-passed.

Our next major engagement was at Melun, located on the Seine River about thirty kilometers upstream from Paris. We forced a crossing of the river on August 24 and sustained several casualties doing so.

Our advance took us northeast through the World War I cities of Soissons and Verdun. Our next assignment was at Reims in the champagne district of France. The city had been liberated by the 5th Infantry Division, working with the 7th Armored across France. Our outfit was located on the extreme right flank of the division. We seized a fort called De Brimont, which overlooked a small German airfield about three kilometers northeast of Reims. The Germans had stored a lot of planes in this underground fort—which we destroyed. While we were there, my assault guns intercepted and captured 42 Germans who were trying to make their way back to Germany. We hit them hard and our medics had quite a time treating their wounded.

From there and into Germany, we encountered heavier enemy resistance, especially as we neared the West Wall. At the town of St. Privat, we had a real donnybrook and lost quite a few men, including our S2 [Intelligence] officer. 1st Lt. John Cornel of Company C of the 38th won the Distinguished Service Cross there.

We crossed the Moselle River at Thionville in coordination with the 5th Division, but it proved untenable and we withdrew. We were in the Metz area which had twenty-six forts, some of which were nine stories underground. We again made a river crossing over a pontoon bridge at night with the rest of the combat command following. We ran over towns named Arry, Lorry, Marieullies, and Bouxiers-Froidmont.

My assault guns passed through Lorry and traveled to a small crossroad where they parked and turned off their engines. We heard noise in a nearby clump of bushes and threw a concussion grenade into them. We didn't hear any further noise after the explosion. As dawn arrived, we heard a groan from that area and found a German soldier with a *panzerfaust* who had been hit by the grenade and his testicles were hanging out by a shred of skin. We took him to the aid station, but he died shortly thereafter.

At daylight, a German short-barreled antitank on the edge of Marielles opened fire on our tanks. Every gun in the combat command brought fire down on the AT gun, and I saw Germans running to our lines, all crouched over, wanting to surrender. Throughout that day, September 18, our division engineers labored to clear a road through the dense forest located to our front. All that day we had received heavy shelling; one of the barrages seriously wounded my supply sergeant, Charles Schenk, who was so mangled it was impossible to identify him.

The next day, the 38th advanced to the eastern edge of the heavy woods after the road had been constructed. We received a new commander that day, Lt. Col. Henry Rosebro, who had been assigned previously to Division Trains. On a personal reconnaissance, he apparently discovered an 88 mm gun emplacement near a small crossroad on the eastern side of the village of Sillegny. He was shot through the head. Next our S3, Major Tom Wells, came forward and was immediately hit by a 150 mm shell. His body was also destroyed beyond recognition. Shortly thereafter, Lt. Col. Ted King arrived from division headquarters. He too was hit by a bullet through his helmet and evacuated. The next commander was Lt. Col. Robert Rhea. He, too, didn't last long. His main contribution was to return the remnants of the battalion from the woods which we had attacked that morning and to enlarge the slit trench he occupied. He was relieved at dusk. We then got our present commander, Lt. Col. William H. G. Fuller.

After hearing Rusty tell his experiences, I received my first assignment the next day. I was to take a section of men in one of our half-tracks, on which we mounted a machine gun, drive it to the Combat Command Reserve (CCR) headquarters, and meet the commanding general. At that time the 38th was with CCR. We arrived at its headquarters and were met by the aide. He showed me the vehicle the commander was going to ride in, which we were to guard. So on one of my first days I was able to see a lot of the division, as the commander wanted to visit with several of his units. It was a good quick introduction to my new outfit and was the first time I had ever been in a half-track. The job lasted for a couple of hours. When we were dismissed, we returned to our bivouac area. On the way back to our area, as we were driving through woods, I suddenly had an urge to relieve myself. I had the sudden "gripes" and I knew I had better take the time to do something about it. When our vehicle stopped, I got out and walked a short distance, stopped, and did the job. I stood up and started to pull my pants up when I spotted, deeper into the woods and on the ground about thirty yards away, a German soldier. I ducked behind a tree. I kept looking and the soldier didn't move. After a short time I decided the man was dead. I walked over and verified that he was dead. As I stood looking at him I wondered about the man. He was somebody's son or husband. I got back to the half-track and told the men about it. They asked if I had searched the body, and did he have a Luger pistol? I found out then that Lugers were a real prize and that I had goofed. I said no and that I would tell the graves registration officer about the body, which I did.

The next two days were spent doing our wash, cleaning our equipment, and, of course, writing home. I had continued to try to write every day, and suddenly it came to me that I was homesick, for I had not received a letter since I left home to come overseas. I knew there were letters in the mail pipeline, but no one knew where I was or where to send my mail. I wondered about the family. The only member of the family in harm's way at the time was my brother-in-law Tom Swain. I took comfort that the last I had heard everyone was okay.

The 7th Armored Division was decimated trying and finally making it across the bridge over the Moselle. When the division finally made it, the casualties were counted, and the powers that be in the Third

Army decided that it was necessary to bring the 7th back to strength. We were alerted and advised that we would soon move from the Third Army to another major command. I did not know much about other armies, but everyone had heard of General Patton. By hook or by crook, he was going to be the hero. I think the personnel of the 7th Armored Division were glad to leave his command.

Holland

The weather had been rainy for days. When we got the order to move out, we had a problem getting the half-tracks down the hill from where they had been parked. The half-tracks would slip and slide, but by skillful driving, Corp. Cox and the other drivers made it down. When we reached the road, we were met by Sgt. Curtin. During the night he had gone absent without leave exploring the area. He had been roaming around in the nearby town, had confiscated an old twelve-cylinder Packard, got it running, and wanted to join the convoy. He said one of the villagers had given the car to him. It didn't take me long to get him back into his half-track and leave his prized possession. I thought about breaking him back to private for going AWOL because he had gone without permission, but Sgt. Sicari talked me out of it. He said that Curtin was the best combat leader in the platoon. He would goof off when there was a lull, but he never missed a formation and was always there when needed. I decided then and there I would test Sicari. I told him that he was to talk to Curtin and tell him the next time he wandered off he would be broken back to private and that no one in the platoon was to leave without his permission. It worked out well. Sicari knew then and there he was to be the boss of his men.

West Front, 15 December 1944

[General Montgomery attempted a thrust to the Rhine at Arnheim. The British 1st Airborne Division and the U.S. 82d and 101st Airborne Divisions were dropped ahead to clear the way for the British 2d Army, but the Germans were able to check the thrust, thus isolating the airborne troops, many of whom were taken prisoner. By this time the German defense was rapidly stiffening as the Allies approached the German frontiers. The U.S. First Army spent a month grinding down the defenses at Aachen, which fell on October 20 (the first city of pre-war Germany to be captured by the Allies). The Canadian 1st Army, on the left of the British 2nd, did not clear the Scheldt estuary west of Antwerp, including Walcheren Island, until early November. Likewise, Patton's Third Army was held up before Metz. Regardless of the Allied advance of about 350 miles, the Germans in November still held both the Ruhr Valley and Saarland. On September 24, orders were received for the 7th AD to shift from the Third Army to the First Army in Holland.]

We were on the move. I had never been in an armored convoy. With the jeeps, half-tracks, assault vehicles, and tanks, the rattle of the vehicles could be heard for miles. Our route was through Belgium and a part of Holland. Little did we know that we were soon to return to Belgium for one of the most critical battles of the war. At every town we motored through the streets were full of people watching and waving. Some appeared to be happy to see us and others did not have a look of joy. For the most part, there was a look of happiness on their faces. The men in our half-tracks had their heads above the side plates. They were enjoying the sound and appearance of the people. Most of the men in my platoon had been on the break-out from Normandy after D-day and had participated in the march across France so they were not as excited as I was. Never had I seen so many friendly waves. I hadn't earned and didn't deserve the reward of these masses, but I enjoyed the reception by them. At one of the towns we were going through, the convoy for some reason came to an abrupt stop in the middle of the city. Standing on the corner was a beautiful blonde girl. She was waving an American flag and cheering. Sgt. Sicari was going nuts! He was yelling at me. I was in the lead half-track, and he was in the following one. He was shouting, "Hey, Lieutenant, how would you like to hold that girl close and love her? Isn't she beautiful?" and so on. He raved to me for about fifteen minutes how he had fallen in love with the girl. All the time the girl kept waving and smiling. Finally the convoy started again. As it began to roll the girl called out to Sicari in perfect English, "Why didn't you come over, Sergeant?" We laughed at the crestfallen look on the sergeant's face. We learned most of the people of Holland could speak the English language.

We came to our new area. The division was now a part of the First U.S. Army. Our new assignment was to clear out the Peel Swamp, west of the Meuse River. After we arrived in the area, I received my first combat duty. My platoon was to guard tanks during the night—tanks that were going to make an attack in the morning. The armor unit had moved close to the front lines waiting for dawn. I took the platoon to the area and placed the machine guns defensively where they could be used in case of an attack by the enemy. What struck me when I reported to the officer in charge was that the men in the tank were trying to see the terrain from their small openings. I began to understand why the infantry hated tanks: tanks are so vulnerable. They can't hide, they make a lot of noise, they attract artillery fire, and all it takes to stop them is one bazooka or antitank gun of any type. The night passed without incident, and we were relieved and returned to our area. Later that morning we were given a new task—to be a part of the combat team cleaning up an area where a disorganized group of Germans was supposedly ready to surrender. We got that kind of intelligence all the time, and most of the time the German ability to fight had not diminished very damned much. As I was leading my men and following the infantry unit my platoon was assigned to, I was aware of a glint of a bullet that whizzed past my head. It just missed me. Odd as it might seem, I knew right then I was going to make it through the war; that bullet had my name on it and it had missed. "Yea, though I walk through the valley of Death," came to my mind.

It struck me that there were not as many men in my platoon as there would have been in a regular platoon in an infantry company. By the time the driver and assistant driver remained with the half-track, I noted there were not very many ammunition bearers. I wondered about that at first but later understood that an armored infantry unit is not supposed to stay in the front lines as long as in an infantry division. Our infantry was supposed to follow the tanks and exploit their efforts. I soon learned it was designed to be that way, but it didn't work out.

When the tanks and the infantry took off toward the enemy, it wasn't long before the first tank was hit and exploded. Then the Germans hit the rear tank. One by one the tanks were knocked off. It was like a shooting gallery. In some cases the men got out of the tanks, but most of the men inside the tanks that were hit were killed by fire or by shell fragments. When a shell penetrates a tank, the shell tears the insides of the tank. Pieces of metal fly around causing fire and hitting all of the personnel. Rarely do any of the members of a tank crew survive a penetrating hit.

It was a shock to realize how easily our tanks were destroyed. For some reason I was under the impression that our tanks were almost indestructible. In talking to the tankers in our division, I found they were very unhappy to have to fight the German Panthers and Tigers, with their better guns and armor plating. The tankers had to beat them with numbers and by outmaneuvering. I discovered that the Allies had a number of weapons that were inferior to what the Germans had, such as the *panzerfaust* which was much more powerful than our bazooka. The German mortars were bigger and more effective, and their machine guns had a higher rate of fire. We had better rifles, the M-1 (Garand), and artillery. Our greatest assets, besides the quantity and superiority of our arms and equipment, were the leaders in the front lines: the captains, lieutenants, and noncommissioned officers—the guys who were pulled together from our population, given some training, and sent to fight a war with men who never knew each other before entering the army, who were drawn from all parts of the country and yet developed a closeness that is most difficult to describe.

The battle continued. Finally, our troops knocked out the antitank gun that had caused all of the problems. It was a rough situation for the infantry as the GIs had to cross an open field to reach the Germans. My platoon was committed, but we didn't have to do much firing as our fields of fire were full of our own men. But we were able to help on the flanks.

[Early on October 27, the German Army launched a vigorous attack against the 7th Armored Division, which was guarding the right flank of the British 2d Army in southeastern Holland. For three days two Panzer Divisions clashed with the 7th in an attempt to force a diversion from the Allied drive on the Scheldt Peninsula to the west, or to cut lines of communication and supply along the salient into Holland toward Arnhem. At that time, the 38th AIB was with CCA near the town of Meijel, Holland.]

The next engagement was the attack toward Meijel. I had to break up my platoon. Sgt. Sicari took one of the sections to support a combat team while I took the other section to a position in the small town of Nederwert. My mission was to protect the flank of the operation. We placed our guns. Then we found a tall building used for the storage of grain. We could see the surrounding area from the top floor of the warehouse. We were there for a couple of days and could see most of the terrain. I even called for some artillery fire from that observation post. We had heard the German mortars popping as they dropped shells in the tube. I don't think we hit the spot exactly, but we did silence the mortar firing from that position.

On the second day, I was called to one of the lookout windows. The men had spotted a German soldier about 500 yards away. He was either a forward observer or a sniper. The men had heard I had made expert on the M1 rifle. They challenged me to hit the man. How do you back down from that kind of challenge, especially from men who did not want to fire their weapons for fear their position would be given away? I set the sights on the weapon, squeezed off the round, and the man went down. He got up and then fell again. I knew I had wounded him. Soon the Germans came with a stretcher and carried the soldier away. I was looked on with more respect after that, but I have seen that German soldier fall every day since. Why only that one I do not know.

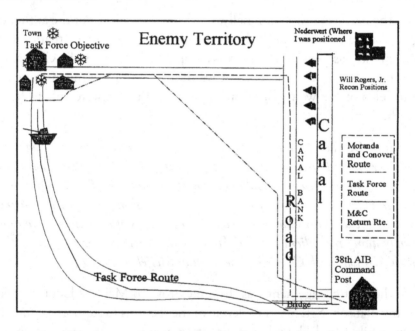

Enemy Territory

After three days, Capt. Mattocks came and told me to bring the men back to the headquarters. We packed and followed the captain's jeep back to battalion headquarters. I went in to see the maps on the wall of the S3 (Operations) room and asked where Sgt. Sicari's section was located. The S3 pointed out on the map where it was supporting a combat team outside a small town about a mile away. The town could be reached either by the road the combat team had been following, or by a shortcut I noticed that went along a road by a canal where it joined another road. I would have to take a left turn and go across a field about a thousand yards to the town. As the section had been following on foot, I knew they did not have K rations and were in need of some sustenance. I went out to my half-track, placed a case of K rations on my shoulder, and said to my runner Conover, "Let's go."

We started up the road by the canal. When we were halfway to the road we were going to take to the town, we took a shortcut across the field. When we reached the road, we took it toward the town. As we approached it, we heard a fire fight going on. We were almost to the town so we continued on. Conover, who was my eyes said, "Hey, Lieutenant, that's Sergeant Sicari waving his arms at us." Sicari was signaling us not to stay on the road but to go behind the town. The task force was still fighting for it. We took the circuitous route to enter the little town. There Sgt. Sicari took the rations from me. I checked to see how the men were and went close to the front, where the noise was coming from. The firing had quieted down, so I told my men I would see them later. Conover and I left taking the same route back. We walked the road rather than taking the shortcut across the field. As we got close to the canal, we could see American soldiers aiming their weapons at us, but we continued on and came to the canal. A lieutenant stood up. I recognized him. It was Will Rogers, Jr. He was the officer in charge of the men along the canal. He said, as he chewed on the end of a piece of straw, "Where have you been?" I told him where and why I was on the road. I asked why they were guarding the road and why he didn't stop us when we went across the first time. He said none of them had seen us. They must have been asleep as we sure didn't creep and crawl along the road. Rogers was a member of the Reconnaissance Company of the 7th Armored Division's 87th Cavalry Squadron.

I returned to the headquarters and told them there was no enemy along the area of the road. They didn't believe me because the combat team had been fighting to clear that area for some time. I told them Conover and I had walked the road, and I would be glad to show them again. Conover and I said later that we had freed more land with a case of K rations than the task force had done with all their combat team.

K rations! There were three types: one each for breakfast, dinner, and supper. I liked the one for breakfast best, for it had a can of eggs, some kind of meat, a couple of cracker biscuits, a bit of toilet paper, and about ten cigarettes. When we got a package that had Raleighs in them, we gave them away to civilians, but they were not even good trading material. The dinner ration had some kind of spread that we could put on our package of crackers, and the usual paper and cigarettes. It also contained a candy bar that no one could eat because it was so hard, but was saved for rainy days. The supper box was about the same as the dinner one, except it had more biscuits and the worst cheese ever concocted. But they kept us alive.

The battle continued. My platoon was again assigned to another task force consisting of tanks and an infantry company. This time the objective was some small towns. The name of one of the towns was something like Dork. The attack started at 0600. We knew there were enemy tanks in the towns ahead, as we had heard the WHOOMP of their 88 mm shells going by. No use ducking when you hear the WHOOMP because the shell has already passed, but scary it is. We had questioned an elderly couple who had just come from the town, and they confirmed seeing some tanks and *soldats* around. Most of the civilians had left the town and made their way through our lines when the Germans appeared on the scene. It seemed that everyone in the town had a bicycle, and those that could rode toward and through the Allies' lines.

We positioned our heavy machine guns to give maximum support to the attacking infantry. The attack started. First, the tanks sped ahead into the town. We watched the infantry take off across the open field ahead. I admired their guts, especially the leaders. They would yell at one man and the man would take off for a few yards flop on the ground, then the next man would take off, run and flop and fire toward the enemy. A mine exploded killing one of the men. The cry of "Medic!" rang out. The medic crawled out and looked at the man and saw there wasn't a thing he could do; he stuck the man's rifle in the ground and continued on. All this time I had my men in position behind a pile of dirt about two feet high and twenty feet long. The dirt covered a crop of sugar beets that had recently been harvested. Sgt. Simoneaux was next to me sitting with his back to the mound. We heard a splat and then the WHOOMP of an 88. Simoneaux quietly called to me, "Lieutenant, look." He pointed at a shell that had come to rest between his outstretched legs. It had not exploded. I said, "I don't know about you, but I am moving out. Pass it down to your men that a mine field is ahead. Follow me. Only step in my tracks or other footsteps that you can see. Don't panic. Carefully step around the unexploded shell. We must get through the mine field. The infantry got through it with only one casualty, so maybe we can get through safely."

I led off. The men followed. I could see they were carefully watching every step they took. Suddenly we began to get machine gun fire so we dropped to the ground. What a hell of a deal! Where was the damn gun located? I couldn't see the machine gun, but I knew the firing was coming from the left. I also knew that one of the tricks of the Jerries was to pin the troops down with machine gun fire and then lob mortar rounds into the pinned-down soldiers. I heard the horrible sound of the plop of the mortar round going into a tube. I yelled to the troops, "Let's go. No use staying here and getting killed. Run for the buildings ahead. Watch your step." With that I took off running toward the nearest building.

Those damned mines scared the hell out of me. Usually they were hidden and set to bounce high enough to clobber the victim. Usually, the damage was a very severe wound, which then required more personnel, especially medics, to care for the wounded. They were a very cruel weapon with tiny prongs that protrude slightly above the ground, and who has time to look? It must have looked odd to see us trying to run fast while attempting to step where the guy ahead had stepped before.

I took off running for the nearest building. As I came to the farm building, I saw an opening into the barn. I dove in and landed next to a sow's ass. She was lying on the ground grunting every time a shell landed. The mortars' rounds were coming in regularly and with every WHOMP of a shell the pigs' rear end and my nose came closer together. Neither one of us seemed to mind.

The enemy stiffened and was giving us all kinds of weapons fire. The commander of our force requested artillery support. Did we get it as time on target followed. Every artillery piece in the division and the supporting artillery guns of the corps laid the barrage down. The earth actually shook! It was very effective. During the middle of the barrage an elderly woman came out of a nearby cellar and ran for the house. I saw her and tried to stop her, but she wouldn't stop until she got to the kitchen where she reached into a closet and grabbed a handful of food and then scampered back to the cellar. At the entrance to the cellar I saw her husband looking out to see if she was going to make it. She did.

Right after the barrage, we were able to get our team together, move out, and take the objective. My platoon continued to assist with the drive, and the tanks started to clank on with our infantry following close behind. I talked to the sergeant and asked if I could be of any help, but he replied, "No, Sir. This is my platoon now and we have them on the run." With that, I congratulated him on his performance in handling his platoon coming across the open field. He nodded his thanks. I wish I knew his name, but it was such a brief encounter and I never worked with him again. There were a lot of examples of great actions by individual soldiers that were never recognized with medals—probably because no one had time to write up the recommendations. When it was over, all we wanted to do was forget those minutes of hell.

While I was still in the house with the stable, waiting for the troops to get on their way, I walked to a large window and stood there looking out. Suddenly the window was shot out. Bullets from a machine gun raked the window. How the rounds missed me, I don't know. Never again did I give the enemy such a good target.

My platoon again followed the infantry, shifting our machine guns to support them. When the objective was reached and all was calm, we were relieved. I took my men back to the company bivouac area where we rested for a day. The time was spent cleaning our weapons and getting ourselves washed and shaved.

About that time Capt. Mattocks was rewarded with a trip to Paris and a three-day pass. He deserved the time off. After he left, the company continued training. When he returned he came in with an empty cognac bottle. With a grin on his face he waved the empty bottle and said a bit sheepishly, "I tried to bring back this bottle to you, but the ride was long and we got thirsty. Guess what? We drank your bottle." We all laughed and were glad to see him back.

The next day I asked Rusty about his trip: what did he see, where did he sleep, and was there anything back there in Paris that was worth the trip? He told us that Paris was so crowded with Army people that a person coming in from the front was lucky to find a bed. He had run into a buddy and the two of them stayed together. He did get loaded. What bothered him most was that all the soldiers there had never seen combat and never would. He saw a lot of officers dressed in pinks and greens. We all agreed that it took a lot of bodies to win a war, but only a few ever saw combat. Even in a division, fewer than half are involved in front-line fighting.

Later I realized that no one in our outfit ever saw any of the USO entertainment perhaps because we were so far forward. Most of the entertainment was provided to the rear echelon people, who probably didn't need much. At the time, though, we were too busy trying to stay alive to even think about such things.

It wasn't long before my platoon got its next assignment—to be under the command of Capt. Johnny M___'s task force. We were to support an action to take over a village near the town of Meijel. After passing through our force's road block, Capt. M___'s task force was to clear the swamp near the town of Weert. All was going well. We ran into some mines but soon got around them. The task force next took the town of Horick. Before we started, I had received two men back who had previously been wounded, Sgt. Totoni and a man whose name I can't remember. I told them to join their previous sections. About that time as we were passing through a small village with buildings along the right side of the road, all hell broke loose. We were blasted by artillery from the left—it was an intense barrage! But the damn stuff was coming from the friendly side. Our force took cover behind the buildings and in a ditch that ran along side of the road. I wound up in the ditch. When the barrage lifted, we reassembled. The private who had just joined my platoon was still in the ditch shaking all over. I tried to get him up with no success. He was mumbling and out of control. I learned then that the reason he had been sent to the rear the first time was for combat fatigue. I had never seen a man act like that before, and I didn't want him with my men in that condition. I sent him back to the command post and told him to check with our medical officer, "Doc" Jell. The task force continued up the road. Suddenly, a fire fight broke out ahead. It was hot and heavy. My platoon was looking for a place to set up to help. We looked ahead and saw our forward infantry troops streaming to the rear. I yelled at my four sergeants, "Stop those men. Have them dig in place." My sergeants had to tackle some of the men to stop them.

Capt. M___ turned to me as he hurriedly walked toward the rear, "Moranda, take over. I am going back to the headquarters and tell them what's going on." Why the man broke I do not know. He had communications with the rear, so he didn't have to leave his command in my lap. His two platoon leaders came back to me and asked what they were supposed to do. I was a new lieutenant. Luckily I knew both of the men. One was a good friend Lt. Corbin. The other young lieutenant had come over with us from England. I said, "I guess we must go on and take the objective." They left, assembled their units again, and we proceeded again toward the objective. Hell!! It wasn't an hour later that the young lieutenant returned to where I was, only this time on a jeep. He was without a leg. He said, "Bob, I'll beat you back to the States." Damn! Damn! Damn! I felt bad. I was the guy who had told him to continue the attack.

The attack went on for a time. The turning point was when Lt. Corbin led his troops across the field into the town. After we had been under fire and pinned down for some time, he got mad about the situation. He stood up and said to his men, "Let's go." With his weapon firing at every step he led his troops to the town. After we reached the town, the two of us sat in a barn, after posting sentries to the outposts, and reviewed the day. Corbin and I enjoyed talking about anything that would take our minds away from the war for a few minutes—mostly about home and family. Later we later found out the first intense barrage had been from the English artillery unit that was supporting us. They had seen us and didn't think that we could be so far toward our objective so fast. They gave us the "sorry old chap" bit, which didn't help much.

It was at this battle I saw something that I have wondered about ever since. A corporal from one of the leading infantry units came back to where I was doing my best to keep things running. He had two German *soldats* as prisoners, marching them back to the rear. Our S2 (intelligence officer), Capt. Fredrickson, always wanted to get information from captured enemy soldiers as soon as possible. The corporal asked how far back the command post was. I gave him the directions, and he left for the rear with the two Germans. It wasn't long before the corporal was back. I knew he could not have taken the prisoners back that quickly. I asked him what had happened and how he could get back so fast. His reply was that they tried to get away so he had to shoot them. I didn't believe him then and I don't believe him now. I felt badly, but there were no witnesses so I couldn't do much about it. I'm sure he knew I didn't believe him.

(I didn't see Capt. M___ again until long after the war was over. I was sent back to the Pentagon for some training when I was a member of the National Guard 40th Infantry Division. I was visiting with Col. Boyer who had been the S3 of the 38th AIB. Capt. M___, then a lieutenant colonel, was stationed at the Pentagon, and Boyer asked if I would go and see him. I said that I never wanted to see the man again. When he asked the second time, I did go down to where M___ was working. I talked to him. He said he was sorry, and with that I left. He had suffered enough years of remembering his mistake. I'm certain a person does not forget his cowardice ever.)

[General Montgomery persisted in his concept of widening the salient in Holland and had given priority of supplies to the British 2d Army. After pressure from Eisenhower to switch emphasis to taking Antwerp, a prime target so the port could be used for the logistics necessary to support the main effort, Montgomery finally promised an all-out effort to do so. On October 16, he altered his supply priorities to the Canadian 2d Army, which proceeded to move to Antwerp, and after heavy fighting took the port city in early November.]

During the month of October it seemed we were in the line fighting most of the time. Our headquarters units were assigned to one command after another, usually small task forces, mostly around the town of Meijel. Our division was protecting the left flank of the First

Army. We had large gaps between our forces. One night that we were in the town of Meijel, it was time to bed down so we placed our security guards around the area and went into an unoccupied house. We never took advantage of the houses other than to sleep in a bed or sit in the chairs. We did not want to hurt any of the Dutch people. This night we had eaten our rations and just gone to bed when we heard a loud bang and something clanged against the front door of the house. We jumped up when we heard the rattle of a machine gun and the whirr of the burp guns. I opened the door and saw a *panzerfaust* shell a few feet away from the door. It had hit the door but must have hit it on a slant and didn't go off. Had it exploded some of us would have been injured badly or killed. We called the engineers, who took the shell away and destroyed it. We learned that a German patrol had come through our lines and tried to wipe out the command post. While fighting in Holland, we had become somewhat lax as we thought everyone in Holland loved us. Not so. Most of the citizens did, but someone had told the Germans where we were sleeping and that it was the command post. We had a Dutchman with us who was one of our guides. Since he was with us at the time, we knew he had not told anyone.

The night after the firefight when I got back to our battalion area, I was going back to my tent. As I passed the medics' tent, our Medical Officer Jell, called out to me, "Lieutenant Moranda, don't you ever tell me that a man is shell shocked. That is the job of the medics."

I retorted, "OK, Doc, it is your decision, but don't send that man to me again. He would only be a continual problem, and it's a bad thing for the rest of us to observe. Furthermore, he shouldn't have been returned to the platoon where he had broken down before."

The doctor grumbled a bit and then to get in the last word said, "And don't call me doc."

I replied, "Why not? It is a term of endearment."

To which he responded, "I don't like the name because a 'dock' is the strap on the harness that goes under the tail of a horse."

"Hmmm," was my response that he didn't hear as I continued to walk around the area.

One of my jobs was to read all the mail that my men wrote. Only one man wrote almost daily, Private First Class Miskowski. He knew the rules of censorship, so I never had any problem with him. As I was reading outgoing letters one day, I came across an envelope that was addressed to a Mr. L. S. Moranda in Chicago. It had been written by Sgt. Totoni. I went over to where he was sitting and asked about the name because it was the same name and initials of my own father. He said he wondered about my name when he first heard it and if I would be related to the Morandas that he knew. I found out that the Morandas he knew were from Albania while our name came from southern Switzerland.

I didn't care for the job of reading mail. The mail from a front-line infantryman was certainly not revealing to the enemy even if it included something about those we were fighting. By the time we got around to writing about any battle, and the mail reached the people at home, the fighting was long past. An infantryman only knows that he survived another round. He wasn't going to tell the rotten story of the life of a GI. Miskowski wrote about the scenery and the churches. He had a good eye so he wrote what he saw and about the people of the area. He was a good writer, and I enjoyed the scenes that he described. But I still hated to read the personal things. This may be difficult to understand, but a lieutenant infantry officer is a lonesome man. He cannot get too close to any of his men because he may have to give the order that would cost a man his life.

We would get the *Stars and Stripes*, "The Armed Forces Newspaper," about a week after an action. The paper wrote about the various skirmishes and battles at the front. In so doing that newspaper told the world about the war but we couldn't. Dumb! I think the reason we were a little mad at the articles in the papers was that they didn't reflect what the hell was going on. I remember reading the *Stars and Stripes* after we had been trying to get to our objective for a couple of days. The paper said how the fighting had been slow. Hell! A hundred yards gained in a firefight was at times a day's or a week's work. Usually more casualties would happen in that kind of action than in those with much greater gains. If we got by with only a few men wounded or dead, we thought we were indeed fortunate.

After I was assigned to the 38th, it took a long time for mail from home to start reaching me. It finally started and was a welcome relief. It seemed everything was going along okay at home. The baby was growing, and Molly kept me posted on the family. The Swains had moved to Lancaster, California. They had entered into a venture with the Eddie Gabberts on a farm where they were also raising chickens and turkeys for a money crop. Mom and the girls still lived in the house on Fourth Street in Oxnard. I am sure they all looked forward to the daily run of the postal carrier, Mr. Pell. They shared the letters received from the members of the family who were away serving in various places.

Overloon and Meijel

During the month of October, we were in some kind of a skirmish with the enemy almost daily. One of the toughest battles that I remember was for Overloon. My platoon was part of the task force headed by Lt. Col. Fuller, new commander of the 38th. During this battle he was near the front most of the time. He was positioned on a small hill where he could observe the front lines. I had my men set up close by so I could watch the actions of the front line troops and had positioned our weapons to protect their flanks. My platoon was held nearby as a reserve for the front line troops. The infantry got pinned down so he called to me, "Moranda, take your men forward to help get out this mess." I got my men and we crawled down to the front on our bellies with our carbines and M1s and helped the riflemen. Finally the battle was over and the leading infantrymen were successful in reaching the objective. I was concerned when given the order, for we had to go down the hill to the front lines dragging our machine guns. When we reached the front lines we were only able to use our rifles. Since the heavy weapon .30 caliber machine gun is fired from the sitting position, my men could not sit behind their machine guns and fire as they would have been exposed to enemy fire. But we helped, and it was enough. I remembered the time during training with the 84th Division when we had to crawl forward with the heavy machine guns and the limitations that I found in such a situation.

When we got back to headquarters, I had a chance to talk to Col. Fuller when he was alone. We had a discussion on the positioning of the machine guns. I was surprised that he listened so intently. After it was over I saluted and left. The next day I had my platoon behind a hedgerow. I had the guns in position standing behind an embankment so they could help the leading infantry get across an open field. Suddenly a mortar shell came right over my head and exploded right behind me. The concussion knocked me to the ground. I felt a sharp hit in the back. All the buttons on my overcoat were knocked off. I got up and called to my runner Conover to come and look me over. I thought I had been hit with shell fragments and wanted him to see how bad the wounds were. He pulled up my coat, shirt, and undershirt. He said there wasn't a mark on my back. A couple of men had been hit, but none seriously.

We had close air support at this battle. Twice our planes came over and strafed the enemy positions. We were being held up by enemy antitank and machine gun fire. The first time our planes made a pass, it didn't do the job, but the second time they knocked out the problem guns, and our troops were able to reach the objective. After the battle, we discovered the reason the enemy resistance was so strong: our objective was defended by elite German paratroopers and former German air force men. For the next few days we were very busy.

One day when I was in the command post, the intelligence officer Capt. Fredrickson told me the story of what happened to him during the battle of Chartres. He was looking for intelligence material. He got out too far in his searching, looked around, and saw that the friendly troops were not with him. He was behind the German lines. He hid in a cellar of a nearby house and decided he would wait, hoping his unit would come back his way and retake the town. For three days he waited. He had to sit through a couple of the barrages from our artillery and mortars, but he was safe in the cellar as long as the Germans didn't find his hiding place. They didn't, and he took a chance to escape back to our lines. He was happy to see the men from the 38th when they came back. He said he had no food or water for the three days and had lost about ten pounds.

While I was in the command post, I was told to work the radio because the radio operator had been wounded. My men were stationed around the battalion headquarters. The CO saw me and said, "Moranda, come in and take over the radio for awhile. We lost our radio man." I had never worked a radio before, but it didn't take long to grasp the knowledge required to operate it. My job was to pass on the reports received from the troops in the front line and from the supporting troops. I would listen and then pass the word on to the CO. I stayed on the radio for twenty-four hours straight. It was at this operation that Conover was worth his weight in gold. Somewhere, somehow, he found a source of potatoes, eggs, and a hunk of bread and brought me a hot meal.

After some heavy fighting, we were to be relieved by the British. We were still on the front lines trying to beat the Germans into submission. The Germans had a different idea, so the battle was almost a draw. We had been on line for some time, and higher headquarters decided it was time to give our outfit a rest and resupply us with arms and men. We were told the relief would be at night. We were in position watching the front, careful not to show any light. The area was quiet. Suddenly we heard a convoy of vehicles approaching from our rear. They had lights on and drew our attention. We knew the Germans were also aware of what was going on. A British officer arrived and told us we would soon be relieved. We discovered how the relief would happen. A lorry drove up a few yards behind our position, and a British non-com came up to us and said in his English accent, "I say there. You chaps can take your guns now. We will take over for you." With that the British troops came up and a contingent took over from my men. The rest of their men sat down and with the lorry lights on started to boil water for their tea. I asked the non-com in charge, "How come you are so careless with the noise and your lights?" His answer was, "We want them to know that we are here, so why should we hide?"

[On October 27, the German Army launched a vigorous attack against the 7th Armored Division in the vicinity of Meijel, Holland, with two Panzer Divisions. The 7th Armored's task at the time was guarding the British 2d Army's right flank. The Germans were obviously attempting to force a diversion from the Allied drive on the Sheldt Peninsula to the west, or to cut the line of communication and supply along the Allied salient toward Arnhem. The Germans made only slight progress, but the fighting was bitter. The 7th Armored contained the drive. After three days, reinforcements arrived to shorten the 7th's front, and British forces combined with them to push the Germans back to their starting positions. More British units arrived; the 7th Armored was relieved and reassigned to the American

Ninth Army. The 38th AIB was part of CCA holding the southern sector near Nederweert during the action.]

Foot soldiers treasure mail from home, a good meal, a good bed, clean socks and underwear, a bath or a shower, and to be no closer than a thousand yards from the action or, better yet, to be in back of their own artillery. Getting away from direct fire was great. Being in a house with the commanding officer was like being at the Ritz-Carlton. For thirty-six hours on the radio, I was almost safe. Finally at the end of the skirmish, I was relieved. I got the men of my platoon into our half-tracks. Cox, the driver, took off. I placed Sgt. Sicari in the observer's seat. I sat between the driver and observer and fell sound asleep in an upright position. I slept in that position for at least two hours. When I woke up, I had a stiff neck, but at least it was rest.

Back in the bivouac rest area we were cleaning ourselves and our weapons when I decided to take a walk around the area. Passing the motor pool, I heard a chicken clucking and scratching around the men who were working on their vehicle. I asked about the hen. They said they had named her Henrietta, and she gave them a fresh egg every day and was a treasure for the motor pool. A few days later I walked past the same group. I didn't see Henrietta so I asked about the hen The answer came back as they pointed to a pot boiling over a burner, "Oh, Henrietta didn't lay an egg for a couple of days, and we found some potatoes so we are having Henrietta chicken soup."

Not long after when I was in my tent, I was awakened from a sound sleep. There was no moon or stars, so the darkness was like being in a closet with the door shut. I wondered what could be so important that they would call me out in the middle of the night. The sergeant who woke me up said he didn't know. He led me to the command track. I ducked my head and entered it. Standing around a map were the brains of the 38th Battalion: the commanding officer, the executive officer, the S1 (personnel officer), S2 (intelligence officer), and S3 (operations officer). Only the S4 (supply officer) was missing. The overhead light was very bright. I reported to the commanding officer. Lt. Col. Fuller said, "Moranda, we have a mission for you. We need your machine guns to support an infantry company." (I think it was company A.) Your guns will support the company in an attack to eliminate a small force of Germans occupying some strategic ground and giving us a problem. The attack is slated to go off early in the morning."

I asked where the rifle company was located. They pointed to the position on the map. I noted aloud that since it is so dark, could they point out an easy way to get there. The CO said, "We have thought of that. The sergeant that brought you to the CP has been to the location before, so he will lead your half-tracks to the assembly area." I saluted and went out into the dark night. And I do mean dark, especially after being in the bright lights of the command half-track. I stumbled around for awhile looking for the area where my tent and my men were bedded down. After trying to get back to my tent for awhile, I knew I was lost. I was completely turned around in our own bivouac area. I stopped, stood still, and listened. I heard the rattle of pans and headed for the noise. It was the kitchen truck cleaning and getting ready for the next day. I asked them where my tent area was and they pointed out the direction. Finally my eyes became adjusted, and I could see the tents and my half-tracks.

Before I left for the CP I had alerted Sgt. Sicari, and he had the men up and ready, so we loaded. The Company A sergeant came by in his jeep and I got in. With the jeep in the lead and the two tracks following close behind, we proceeded to the assembly area. We were very close to the German lines so I wondered how safe we were. Our little convoy was noisy, and it wouldn't take much effort to hit us with antitank weapons. We reached the assembly area at the first light of dawn. I met the infantry leaders, and we looked over the terrain and discussed how best to attack. We decided my guns would set up and fire at the objective with continuous fire. The infantry troops would go along the tree line on the left and along the railroad tracks on the right. I took my men to the area where we were to locate our guns and selected the gun positions and alternate positions. If the Germans came at us with mortars or artillery, we could quickly move to a new position. When we were ready to fire I waved at the platoon leaders, and the attack was on.

The continuous fire kept the heads of the Germans down, and our troops soon reached the objective. The operation was a success. The front-line riflemen captured some Germans. When our troops reached their objective, I moved the machine guns forward so we could set up and help the infantry again. No help was needed as the Germans didn't send relief. The company commander thanked me for the support, and we were dismissed. My men were happy with their work as were the officers in the 38th, especially the S4, Capt. Watson. He was pleased that he had to bring us more rounds of ammunition. He said that he wanted the troops to fire a lot so he could go home to his wife and family. He was a great guy, full of life; I enjoyed our talks together.

Looking back on the war I now realize that for Hitler and the Germans, October was a crucial time. They had lost France, and now for the first time they were defending The Fatherland. When our attack started at Aachen, Hitler ordered his soldiers to hold at all costs. The German command needed time to prepare for a counterattack. He ordered that the ground must be held, and there would be no surrendering no matter what the cost. Aachen was the first large city in Germany to be attacked. I remember the first time our unit crossed over the line into Germany. I had my men get out of their vehicles. We stood in line and pissed on Hitler's fatherland. We relieved ourselves in two ways, both mentally and physically.

It was not long before our outfit moved back to an area near Nederweert and Weert. In that area we did a lot of outposting and patrolling. We would usually be assigned to an infantry company and would help them out when needed, but for the most part it was an easy time for my platoon. I remember one night we were on an overnight patrol. We put out guards around us, and I found a feather bed in one of the houses. I was tired, and for the first time in a long time I had a good night's sleep. I took my boots off, climbed in, and, as they say, "slept so deeply I was on the bottom of the mattress." What a great night!

It was about this time that I heard from Daisy Wood, the mother of our dear friend Wannie Wood. Wannie had grown up with us boys in our family; he was almost another brother. Daisy asked me to join with other men from the Port Hueneme area in establishing a branch of the VFW (Veterans of the Foreign Wars). She was contacting every person from our hometown serving in the war. Naturally she contacted my brothers, and we all joined. The branch was to be called the "Wannie

Woods Post." Wannie, another infantry lieutenant, had been killed in Italy while leading his men in battle. He lasted only a few weeks in combat. (Oh, the great life of an infantry officer!) I wrote to Molly the next day and asked her to give Daisy the money for me to join the post.

Nederweert, the place where Conover and I had taken the rations over the road and liberated the land, had been recaptured by the Germans. So our outfit had to retake the place. It was tough to do, and by the end of October we were in that area doing battle. The Germans came at us, but we were able to hold the ground gained. On October 31, the Jerries hit one more time, but they were repulsed and suffered a large loss of men. On November 1, we were again trying and succeeding, for the most part, in ousting the Germans from Holland. We were to clear the area from Zuid Willems Vaart Canal. For some reason the Jerries didn't want to leave. But slowly and surely the 38th was able to clear the area. My platoon was not used as much during that operation. One reason the attack went so slowly was the mine fields. The Germans must have known that they were out-gunned, so to slow down our attack they had scattered mines around the fields; in most instances the mines were not buried. As we walked gingerly through the mined area, we wondered if more were buried. We used tanks and engineers to do the difficult and delicate work of removing the mines. Finally on November 3, we reached the canal, our objective. The 38th withdrew and when relieved, we went to an area to reorganize and be able to continue the attack.

[The 84th Infantry Division had recently arrived and been assigned to General Simpson's Ninth U.S. Army. Shortly after getting there the Ninth was given the mission of seizing the high ground east of Geilenkirchen, some twenty kilometers north of Aachen. They had the British 21st Army Group on their left flank. British General Horrocks made a surprise visit to the 84th units at the front to see conditions. Stephen Ambrose, in his "Citizen Soldier" told of this visit: "The 84th struck him as 'an impressive product of American training methods which turned out division after division complete, fully equipped…composed of splendid, very brave, tough young men. But he [Horrocks] thought it a bit much to ask of a green division that it penetrate the Siegfried Line, then stand up to counterattacks from two

first-class divisions, the 15th Panzer and the 10th SS. He was disturbed by the failure of the American division and corps commanders and their staffs to   visit the front lines. He was greatly concerned to find that the men were not getting hot meals brought up from the rear, in contrast to the forward units in the British line. He gave the GIs 'my most experienced armoured regiment, the Sherwood Rangers Yeomanry,' told the American battalion and division commanders to get up front, and returned to his headquarters.

"The problem Horrocks saw was becoming endemic in the U.S. Army in ETO. Not even battalion commanders were going to the front. From the Swiss border north to Geilenkirchen, the Americans were attacking. SHAEF put the pressure on Twelfth Army Group; Bradley passed it on to the First, Third, and Ninth Armies; Hodges, Patton, and Simpson told their corps commanders to get results; by the time the pressure reached the battalion COs, it was intense. They raised it even higher as they set objectives for the rifle company COs. The trouble with all this pressure was that the senior officers and their staffs didn't know what they were ordering the rifle companies to do. They had neither seen the terrain nor the enemy. And unlike the company and platoon leaders, who had to be replaced every few weeks at best, and every few days at worst, the staff officers took few casualties, so the same men stayed at the job, doing it badly."]

In Reserve

After being relieved, the battalion left for an area near Zomeren-Maarheeze. For the next few days we spent time retraining the outfit. We had a new battalion S3, Maj. Don Boyer. He was determined to make our 38th a better fighting outfit, so he put the 38th through a few field exercises. These involved the tanks and infantry working together, with more drawbacks than benefits. The damned tanks are noisy, and they draw fire. They can't protect themselves, so the infantry had to guard them at night, which we continually bitched about. However, the armored infantry does not usually stay in the front lines as long as the regular infantry. Like it or not, we had to rehearse.

My troops found an abandoned house that became our base. They made it as comfortable as possible, but being inside has its pitfalls. If one man gets a cold, the whole outfit comes down with it. The weather had changed and we were now in the late fall of the year. We were having cold weather. My men were warm at night, but I soon learned it was healthier when everyone was outside in their tents. Every one of my men came down with a terrible cold. I had a minor cold, but not the kind that they suffered with. After a few days, they recovered enough to function. As for me, I was billeted with Capt. Mattocks in a different house.

While in the rest and training area, Capt. Mattocks, Lt. Kinnebrew, and I left for the rear. The division had located a working coal mine that had a building with showers and a real tub. Not that I needed a bath. Hell, it had only been sixty days since I had taken one. The usual bathing in the field was done out of the helmet. Shave, bathe, and wash your underwear and socks in that order. We would use the water from our canteens to brush our teeth. Not that there was a shortage of water, but when the need for it arrived, the source was often too far away. To prepare for bathing, we drove first to a quartermaster supply point, where we purchased new clothes. I bought everything new with the exception of boots and jackets. Two items that I purchased were life savers later: a wool scarf that was over six feet long and a pair of silk pajamas. The pj's were to take the place of woolen long johns, as I have a problem with wool next to my skin.

From there we drove to the mine. There were hundreds of bicycles parked around the main shaft as everyone in Europe rode bicycles. No one drove automobiles as gasoline was not available for civilians. We went to the area where the baths were located, and the attendant asked whether we wanted a shower or a tub. I chose the tub. A man filled the tub to the brim, handed me some soap and I was soon covered with the warm water. I soaked for a long time relishing the wonderful, relaxing feeling. I hated to leave, but the other two men had taken showers and were ready to get going again, so I reluctantly toweled off and joined them.

The rest of November was the easiest of my experiences in combat, especially compared to the previous month. For the first eight days of November we were called up a few times, and those times were easy for my machine gun platoon. For some of the time we were stationed in the small town of Terlinden, which is located in the Province of Limburg in the panhandle section of Holland. The company troops were spread out in the town. Capt. Rusty Mattocks decided the best place for his command post would be with a Dutch family, the Prickens: Momma, Papa, and the kids Willie, Henrietta Leone, Arthur, Sophie, and Josie. They welcomed us with open arms. The ages of the family ranged from the two older children who were about twenty to the baby in the family. We were given the run of the house. 1st Sgt. Alvie Davis ran the headquarters. Three of us bunked in one room upstairs; the captain and Davis were in the downstairs living room. Alvie also had his clerk and records of the company in that room.

While there I received a letter from Molly, which I kept with me, along with the New Testament, throughout the remainder of my service (and I still have them):

Nov 20, 1944

Dearest Bob,

Well honey, we are up at the ranch, we arrived about 6:00 last evening. Loraine, Tommy, Tomilyn, and I left Oxnard about 2:30, but we had so many drawbacks that we didn't get here until pretty late. First of all the Saticoy bridge was out as per usual in the winter, next I smelled something burning and stopped the car and looked under the hood and a piece of felt lining up under the hood had fallen down across the motor and was blazing away. Boy it scared us silly with two babies in the car, anyway we pulled the felt out and went on our way, then last of all the road up to the folk's house was all full of mud puddles and I had to go about a mile out of the way to get to their place. Well, we were all well received. Tiny [Rozeel] and Mom knew we were coming, but the rest were surprised, especially Daddy because he had never seen little Tommy before and he was sure tickled.

Boy is it cold up here; snow all around on the hills and frost all over the ground this morning. I slept with Daddy's robe on; I'm always cold at nights. Sure wish I could snuggle up to your big, warm body. Oh boy, would I love that, in more ways than one!!! I sure hate this business of not having a husband. We girls here at home all agree that it is sure a dull and lonely life without your husband with you.

Tiny and Eddie are going to take a turkey up to George [her uncle] in Bakersfield, he lives in a boarding house and wants to give the turkey to his landlady.

Nona won't be lonely while we are up here because Jeanette is bringing Marion up to spend a few days with her. And it will be much nicer for them if we aren't there because it is very hard to have three babies in a house at once, especially when they aren't all one family. You can imagine Tomilyn showing Marion around and them all crying at once and trying to bathe and feed them all at nearly the same time. Oh me, I'm afraid that will be the problem too when George [my brother] and Nancy come with little George. They asked Nona to get them a crib so I guess they expect to stay at our house although I'm afraid it will be rather crowded, but we have managed so far so I guess we'll continue to get by. What we need is a few more bedrooms!!

I'm writing this letter in the morning as we will probably go to town pretty soon. I know I won't have a letter from you because Nona wouldn't have had time to forward one until tomorrow at the earliest. Sure hope to get one soon as I haven't heard for about a week, but I know you have been busy.

I'm sending you a poem cut out of the Journal, it did me a lot of good and I know it will you too.

I was browsing thru your last three letters and even if I have read them a dozen times it always makes me feel good to read them again. You're a darling, and I love you so much! Seems like I can almost hear your voice and visualize what you are doing when I read them.

Pumpkin told me to tell you that you are the best Daddy in all the world and to take good care of yourself for your two girls.

Molly & Robin

We love you!

Sgt. Davis was from Mississippi, and spoke with a southern accent. He was the perfect First Soldier. When Rusty was promoted to company commander, there was an opening for an officer to head the Assault Gun Platoon. Rusty tried to get Alvie to take over the platoon and become an officer—a field promotion. Alvie tried hard for about two weeks, but then he came back to Capt. Mattocks and said that he was out of his element and requested to be returned to his previous position. His request was approved, and he again became the first sergeant. That's the time when Lt. Boyd arrived as a replacement to take Rusty's old job, leading the mortar platoon, and Kinnebrew became the assault gun platoon leader. For the short time that Davis was gone we had a sergeant that took Alvie's place. He was a gung ho, tough talking, rough riding first sergeant. He was 180 degrees different from Alvie. Alvie was a kind gentleman who got the men to do their jobs by exerting leadership qualities. The new man was a bastard, determined to "shape up this outfit." His attitude was that he would show them how to be a brave as a great leader of men in combat. The men listened and grumbled and wondered about how tough he would be. It didn't take long. We started to receive German artillery fire on our position one day. That tough talking first soldier ducked into the waiting cellar, and we couldn't get him out to do his duties. It wasn't long before the CO got rid of him, and I know the men in our company were glad to have Alvie back as our First Soldier.

The cast of characters in the company were: Capt. Carl Mattocks, the commander, a tough man (by that I mean at times he talked as if he enjoyed the war, and he was a good leader of men); 1st. Lt. Kenny Kinnebrew, executive officer and mortar platoon leader; 1st Lt. Hugh Boyd, assault gun platoon leader; and I,. running the weapons platoon. Kinnebrew was from Georgia. I asked if any of his relatives were of the Newton name, as that was where Mom's relatives originally were from. He said no. He was a short man with a blonde butch haircut, friendly to me. We had some good talks about home and fireside. Boyd was also from the South. He was very religious and read the Bible at every opportunity. He was a tall man with a gangly frame, spoke when spoken to, but rarely started a conversation. First Sergeant Alvie Davis was a tall southern man. I enjoyed his southern drawl. He loved his men and took an interest in each and every one of them. He was considerate and kind and yet tough—a rugged looking man with a soft heart. The men loved him, and he watched out for them. He and Capt. Mattocks made a good team

The one thing we did at every opportunity was to talk of home and family, though most of the time no one really listened but would grunt at the right time, and the talk would go on and on. Each of us would get that far away look in our eyes and continue with thoughts of home. I put the "we" in here because I know I did the same as the others.

As a replacement officer, I did not know the history of each man. I had to learn by listening to the men as they talked with each other. As I had to censor each man's letter, mostly to their loved ones at home, I learned a bit more about them. Some of the men wrote often and others rarely. As time went on I began to get a grasp of their lives and their homes—where they came from, marital status, and the make-up of their families.

The nights were spent listening to the buzz bombs fly over us. We would hear the motor of the bomb chugging along and knew if the motor would only keep running until it passed over us we were safe. But when the motor quit, the bomb would head straight down. One night one of them did come down about a thousand yards away— quite a bang! It shook the house where we were staying. The next day we went to the crater and saw the results of the bomb. It made a huge hole in the ground. Thankfully it caused no damage other than to the earth.

The Prickens were a clean, well-scrubbed family. Every morning the two older girls would put on their wooden shoes and scrub the courtyard. Mama was in the kitchen most of the time doing her chores, and papa tended to the farm. No one loafed around with nothing to do. All the family could speak English, so we had some good times talking to them. Alvie Davis was able to get some rations from our mess which he gave to the family, and we were rewarded with some fine Dutch cooking. I fell in love with a couple of the youngest children, towheaded and pretty. They could have passed for a sister of my Tomilyn. While we were with the Pricken family one of my men received one of those "Dear John" letters. He was really shook up and got rip-roaring drunk. He had been engaged to the girl and thought everything was going well at home. But the girl had found someone else and was going to get married to her new-found man. Before long he was over the shock, and he said that he was glad to find out the girl didn't love him. I remember wondering how many other "Dear John" letters had been received. What a blow! I had heard about the letters before, but that was the only one I saw first hand.

[By the early autumn, even Hitler knew that the Germans were in serious danger of losing the war after suffering huge and costly defeats on the eastern, western, and Italian fronts. The Allies had crossed into his territory at the Holland, Belgium, and French borders, and his troops were fighting on their own soil. By this time his mind was not reliably clear, and many of his actions were illogical. He had nearly lost his life and suffered injury in a bomb blast in July. However, he seemed to regain some of his

strategic vision, and in mid-September he began to formulate a plan that might avoid defeat by forcing the Allies to agree to a negotiated peace. He recognized that the huge Russian army precluded any offensive on the eastern front as there were no apparent weak spots. The Allies were much more vulnerable. Their logistical support depended on long supply lines that meant water shipments and the capacity of several ports, of which Antwerp was the most important at that time. Hitler's plan was to concentrate forces in the west in order to break through a weak, American-held sector, and retake Antwerp, which would separate the Americans from the British-Canadian 21st Army Group. He wanted to attack the Americans because he believed they were less capable soldiers than the British and unlikely to put up much resistance. That may have been true for the American Army during the North African campaign, but not so two years later.

Hitler planned that even if the British and Canadians escaped encirclement, the Allies would be back where they were in late August, and Germany would have three or four months' grace to deal with the Russians. In the best case, the rout of a major element of the U.S. 12th Army group and the loss of Antwerp might create such a rift between the British and the Americans that the western Alliance would fracture, and Germany would then face only a one-front war by early spring of 1945.

Hitler chose the Ardennes region as the target for the offensive. This was an area of winding river valleys and steep hills, covered with dense conifer forests. The Ardennes was thinly settled with many small villages but few significant towns. It was the region through which the Germans had ruptured the French defenses to win the Battle of Flanders en route to winning the Battle of France in May 1940. He also knew from battlefield reconnaissance and communication intercepts that the area was thinly held by the Americans, and he believed that an immediate breakthrough would be relatively easy. His generals were reluctant to accept all those goals and tried to limit the effort, but to no avail.]

We stayed with the Pricken's from November 10 until the 38th was returned to an American army. We had been with the British Army commanded by the famed Field Marshal Montgomery, doing our bit in freeing the Holland area from the Germans. The division's next job was to receive replacements and be rehabilitated, after which we would be assigned a new mission. For a week we had trained around Terlinden, and then we moved to Schimmert, Holland, and were now quite far away from the front lines and back far enough so that we felt secure and safe.

[By early December, SHAEF had two airborne divisions, the 82d and 101st, as an immediately available strategic reserve and additional divisions in the pipeline in England or en route from the States. Operational reserves were also available to the armies and corps: the Ninth Army had the 30th Infantry and 7th Armored Divisions; the First Army had all or parts of four divisions, the 1st and 9th Infantry, and the 3rd and 5th Armored; and the Third Army also had all or parts of four divisions, the 26th and 80th Infantry, and the 4th and 10th Armored.]

At the end of the month we, the 7th Armored Division, were placed in reserve so that we could support the 84th and 102nd Infantry divisions. The assignment to help the 84th Division was a special few days for me. The 84th was where I started in the Army, and I was with them when they trained in Texas and Louisiana. Now they were in combat, and there was a possibility that my platoon would be assigned to support them with my machine guns. My first assignment was to help the 334th Infantry Regiment of the 84th in one of their first combat missions. The 84th was trying to take the town of Pummeren, Germany. When we arrived, the commander of the 84th decided he didn't need our help. Though I could hear firing of small arms to the front, their commander decided our men could go back to our own area. I didn't understand that decision then and I still don't understand the refusal now, especially after reading of that operation in their history book.

During December, we hoped that the war would be over soon. In the infantry the men always look for clues as to what was going on in the world by using the Army's emphasized special training. When the Army started to hold meetings with the officers and non-coms on how to conduct ourselves with the civilians when we arrived in Germany, it led to much discussion and hope. They told us that above all we were to live by the rules of warfare and the Geneva Convention. The way the Army was talking, the infantry only had to win the next big push and the Germans would give up. Somehow, though, the ground-pounders knew rumors come and go. We knew there was a lot of fighting left to do. For an infantryman, the only way to be away from the front lines was by a wound, being in a bag, being captured, or having the war end. It wasn't all lost time, as the Army conducted specialized training. During one of those meetings, we were introduced to our new commanding general, Brigadier General Robert Hasbrouck. He seemed like a good soldier. I think he was a West Pointer.

By then, the 7th Armored Division moved to Bach, Germany. There we rested and went into another training mode. For the first time in a long period the troops were able to rest and repair and again receive personnel replacements. The tanks and other vehicles needed work. The men also needed a time to write letters and get mail from home. Mail came in bunches, so in the rest area a person could sit back and think of home and write letters and reread ones from wives and families. In November I received a letter from brother Earle announcing that he and Becky (Lorene Becker) were to be married soon. That was good news. Earle had been fortunate in that he had been able so far to stay in Washington D.C. where he was assigned to Army Air Intelligence. It wasn't long after that a letter came from sister Maye telling that the wedding of Becky and Earl had happened.

I wrote to Molly on December 13, and Molly kept the letter:

Hello Darling,

Well honey I'm in the chips as I got four letters from you, two from Mom and one from Maye. Thank you darling they were certainly well received. I've read each one of them three times so far and will reread them a couple more times before burning them.

You asked me a few questions and I'll try to answer them the best way I can. First I'm not a big shot having a C.P. but only a Lt. A C.P. is a command post and every leader has one even in the field. It's a place to meet his non-coms and direct his men. As you go up the ladder, a C.P. is of more importance. A Company Cmdr has one for his officers & non-coms. A Battalion Comdr has one for his staff officers, in other words a command post is where orders are issued and the unit is run from (clear as mud huh!).

You asked too about Overloon and I'll try to answer that by telling you it's close to Venray. We were all over that part of the country, and if you have a map showing the boundaries of the British 2nd you can see where we were. I guess you know by this time where we were though so I'm not telling any news.

Today was spent in the usual way so there is no news from here. We hear now and then some planes flying around and big guns in the distance but other than that we would never know there was a war going on.

Lt. Boyd and I are now in our cellar and he is shaving and dripping water on me. Of course he is cussed out but no one minds that over here. We're not crowded but I doubt if we could get any more in here without a shoe horn.

This is not much of a letter as its hard for me to concentrate with people talking. When I write to you I like to be by myself so I can concentrate, as it's more like talking in person.

So you're still dreaming of me, well honey keep it up and maybe soon I can make them come true. Boy I sure wish I were home and could be holding you in my arms. Sure am in love with you and my love grows every day.

Your Bob

Hi Pumpkin, I sure am glad you like my little letters to you. You're my little sweetheart

Daddy

[Hitler had assembled on the Western Front all that was available as a consequence of his second "total mobilization." A decree of October 18 had raised a "volkssturm," or home guard, for the defense of the Third Reich, conscripting all able-bodied men between the ages of sixteen and sixty years. While the Allies had reached the Rhine in Alsace, the Germans had meanwhile been building their own strength up for a counterstroke. Under the overall command of the reinstated Marshall Rundstedt, this stroke was to be delivered through the wooded hill country of the Ardennes against the U.S. sector of the front, between Monschau (southwest of Aachen) and Echternach (northwest of Trier). The plan called for the Fifth Panzer Army on the left, under General von Manteuffel, with its left flank covered by

the German 7th Army, to wheel north westward after the breakthrough and to cross the Meuse south of Namur in a drive on Brussels. The 6th Panzer Army on the right, under SS General Sepp Dietrich, was to wheel more sharply northward against Antwerp, its own right being protected by a supporting thrust westward from the Roer Valley. Thus it was hoped that the British and Canadian forces at the northern end of the front could be cut off from their supplies and crushed, while the U.S. forces to the south would be held off by the German left.]

Our next mission had been planned by higher headquarters. The 38th was to aid in the attack into the Rhineland over the Roer River, to drive the Germans farther back into their own country. Daily our officers would head to the front line and observe the terrain and plan for our assignment. The 38th was to pass through friendly lines and attack through the lowlands and to seize the high grounds where a dam was located. We were to get control of the dam before the Germans could release the water and flood the lowlands. If we were successful, the war would be shortened and the powers that be thought Hitler would give up. Boy, were they fooled.

I was interested to see in advance what we were going to do. For the first time in my Army experience company grade officers in combat knew what was supposed to happen. Usually it was: take "that hill," "that town," or some other limited objective; then wait for further orders for the next hill or town we were to take. The information was usually that a few disorganized enemy troops were to our front, and that "disorganized" enemy would stubbornly fight for each and every yard of real estate. Infantry company grade officers apparently didn't warrant deep intelligence briefings. Somehow we found out by the rumors that came down to enlisted men from the division and combat commands. Rusty tried his best to keep us posted, but there was a lot he did not know. Typically, when we motored to the front lines in our jeeps, supposedly through safe routes, we had to pass through areas under surveillance by the Germans. When they observed our vehicles approaching, they would lob mortars and fire artillery at us. At one location where we had to make a right turn, it turned out to be particularly dangerous. As we approached the driver said, "Hang on, here we go!" and he revved up and at a high rate of speed rounded the corner and drove to the shelter of some houses nearby. It was like playing Russian roulette. Though we were shot at, we weren't hit. That kind of thing happened to us several times.

We noticed one morning that one of the haystacks in enemy territory seemed to have moved. We called in artillery. We discovered there had been a vehicle under the haystack.

One incident that happened in the rest area was during a poker game. A group of the officers had a game going in the kitchen of one of the houses: Capt. Fredrickson, Capt. Mattocks, Lt. French, and a couple of others. The game had been going on for hours with Fredrickson having nothing but bad luck. A new hand was dealt. The ante was in and the openers had been bet. Fredrickson was about to raise the bet when all hell broke loose. We heard a German plane approaching our area, and it soon came over and dropped a bomb. Then the pilot maneuvered his plane around and came back down the road strafing the area where we were all billeted. The poker players were under the table, in a closet, in the pantry, or on the floor. I dove toward the outside and watched the plane from behind the open front door. No one was hurt so I went back in. The players were gathering themselves together, picking up the cards and chips, and placing the chairs around the table. Fredrickson was on his hands and knees, still had his cards, and was crying, "Come on let's go. I've still got my hand." The others didn't so the hand was called off. "Damn! Damn! Damn!" he moaned, "I have four aces." Somehow none of the other players displayed any sympathy.

On one of those days, Lt. Corbin and I were driving to see what we were soon going to be doing when I saw the sign on the road announcing that my old outfit, Company M of the 84th Division, was billeted nearby. I wanted to see my old friends, so Corbin and I took a detour to where they were training. As we came into the area, I saw my enlisted friends from the 84th. They were in formation standing at ease. I asked permission from my old company commander, Capt. Burns, to visit my former bunk mates. He gave me the permission gladly, so I had a few minutes with Sallee, Marshall, Emeterio, Ashford, Klein, Bird, and others. One of my old friends had just received a battle field promotion; Sgt. Esteridge was now a second lieutenant. So for a few minutes we were enjoying each others' stories. They asked about

Hugh West. I told them I had come overseas on the same boat with him, but we parted in England and I hadn't heard from him since. The most asked question was, "How is combat?" What do you tell them? You don't want to frighten them, but you want to be honest. All I could do was to tell them to be aware of everything—to keep their eyes and ears open. But they knew what I was trying to tell them. The sad part is I never saw them again and wonder how many of my friends made it through the war. At times I have wished that I had remained as a sergeant with the 84th. With those men I belonged. As a replacement officer you have to, time and again, gain the respect of your men—men whose capabilities, strengths, and weaknesses were unknown to you and with whom you had no experiences. Even over fifty years after the war, in many respects, it is still the same. The men who served throughout the war with the same unit have more to talk about. For example, when they ask if you remember the training in the desert, and you come back with, "I wasn't there," the conversation stops.

Battle of the Bulge Begins

[At 1730 on December 16, Brigadier General Robert W. Hasbrouck, commanding general of the 7th Armored Division, was ordered to get ready to move south to an assembly area near Vielsam, where he would be assigned to VIII Corps of the First U.S. Army. The 7th Armored Division had been located near Heerlen, Holland, and in Scherpenseel, Germany, northwest of Aachen, and was then an element of the III Corps reserve as part of the Ninth U.S. Army. The First U.S. Army commander, General Hodges, had planned an attack and was not about to "...let the Germans dictate the timing of my attack..." and said he did not need the 7th. Knowing that General Hodges had not wanted the 7th, his staff did not give them road clearance immediately. General Hasbrouck was told to move out as soon as he received information about his route of march. At 2000 he called Brigadier General Bruce C. Clarke, commander of his CCB, and told him to go to Bastogne and report to Major General Troy Middleton the VIII Corps commander for instructions and information.

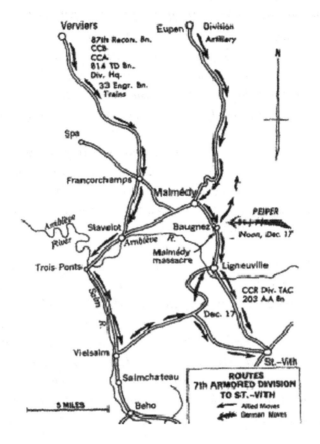

Routes 7th Armored Division

Shortly before midnight, General Hasbrouck was told to take two parallel roads behind two corps of the First Army. The western route went through Heer, Verviers, Stavelot, and Trois Pont to Vielsam; the eastern route went through Aachen, Eupen, Malmedy, Recht, and Poteau to Vielsam. He then issued orders to elements of the division: the western road was to be used by the 87th Cavalry Reconnaissance Squadron, CCB, CCA, the 814th Tank Destroyer Battalion, Main Division Headquarters, the 33rd Armored Engineer Battalion, and the division trains; the eastern route was to be used by CCR, Division Tactical Headquarters (TAC), Division Artillery, the 203rd Antiaircraft Battalion, and smaller units. The units using the eastern route were to commence at 0800, December 17. Hasbrouck had not been told that VIII Corps had told General Jones, Commanding General of the 106th Infantry Division, that the 7th Armored Division *would reach St. Vith and the 106th Division by 0700 on December 17. However, the information given to the elements of CCR did not indicate that it was anything more than an administrative move, and the unit commanders could not understand why the move was being made as the VIII Corps had the 9th Armored Division already assigned to it as the corps reserve. Some surmised that either General Patton's Third Army had made a breakthrough and was screaming for more armor to exploit the penetration, or that Patton had borrowed the 9th AD and the 7th AD was to replace the 9th as corps reserve. It wasn't until they saw the heavy stream of traffic of American forces going west that the realization came that it was more than an administrative march and that there was a serious emergency facing the American Army in this area.*

After three false starts, because the Ninth Army's Military Police had trouble clearing the roads, the 7th Division's western column started moving at 0430 and covered the sixty-five miles quickly. They reached the Vielsam assembly area without difficulty at 1100, where orders were waiting for them from General Clarke. On the eastern road the column had trouble. Col. Peiper's spearhead elements for the 1st Panzer Division hit the column south of Malmedy. The Germans captured Battery B of the 258th Field Artillery Observation Battalion, which had inserted itself into the column between TAC and Division Artillery unbeknownst to the 7th Division— which led to the Malmedy Massacre. The last few vehicles of TAC were also hit, and Col. Church M. Matthews, the division chief of staff, was killed.]

On December 16, rumors started that our division was going back to General Patton's Third Army or back to the British we had fought with at Overloon, Holland. We knew our present mission, which was to support the divisions trying to capture the dam on the Roer River, had been changed. Now we waited for our next orders.

The Combat Command Reserve (CCR) commander called a conference that night. I saw our company commander Rusty Mattocks go to battalion headquarters about 0300 on December 17. There was an anxious feeling, but we company grade officers didn't know why. Lt. Boyd read his Bible even more. I thought of home. For some reason, I had a down-deep fear of some pending action.

Sgt. Sicari asked me, "What's up, Lieutenant? The men want to know."

"I don't know, but something's up. Get your men to bed and get rested. But have your half-tracks ready to move out soon."

It wasn't long before a runner came and said, "Lieutenant Moranda, we are moving out. Report to the company command post." When I did, Capt. Mattocks gave me the word. The 38th Battalion was to be attached to CCR and proceed to St Vith, Belgium. I remember asking, "Where is St. Vith?" But I never got an answer.

[Hitler planned the "Wacht am Rhine" (the term used for the cover plan. The actual operation was called "Herbstnebel" or Autumn Smoke) to use the Sixth Panzer Army to deliver the decisive blow in his Ardennes offensive. Commanded by General Sepp Dietrich, the Sixth Army contained four SS Panzer divisions, a Parachute division, and four Volksgrenadier (Infantry) divisions. The infantry formations were to tear holes in the American lines between the Losheim Gap and Monschau for two Panzer divisions to advance over five pre-selected routes to seize the bridges over the Meuse River from Huy northeast to Liege. A powerful task force under veteran tank commander Lt. Col. Jochen Peiper, containing more than half of the armor of the 1st Panzer division along with supporting panzer-grenadier, engineer, and artillery troops, was to lead the exploitation. The plan called for the breach to be made within twenty-four hours and for the lead units to reach the Meuse that same day. Then the panzers were to push on rapidly toward Brussels and Antwerp, leaving the volksgrenadier divisions to hold the northern flank. Once Antwerp had been taken, the Army was to hold a line from that port city eastward to the Meuse around Maastricht.

The Fifth Panzer Army on the Sixth's southern flank, commanded by General Hasso von Manteuffel, was assigned the task of isolating and destroying the American 106th Infantry division in the Schnee Eifel massif and seizing the critical crossroads of St. Vith immediately west of the Eifel. Farther south other divisions of his force were to break through the American 28th division, isolate and bypass Bastogne if defended, and then advance through Houffalize toward the Meuse crossings around Namur. Once the initial breakthrough had been achieved and the immediate geographic objectives had been seized, the Fifth Panzer Army was to shield the southern

143

and eastern flanks of the Sixth Panzer Army along a line roughly from Antwerp to Givet. But the key to the operation was St. Vith. Without the communications center there, the focal point for highways, and the rail lines, the armored, infantry, and supply columns would be immobilized because the rugged, hilly terrain was heavily forested and permitted limited cross-country movement. St. Vith was to be captured on the first day of the offensive, for it was to be used as an advance rail depot for both the Fifth Panzer and the Sixth Panzer Armies.

The southern positioned Seventh Army under General Erich Brandenberger was to protect the southern flank of the Fifth Panzer Army and hold a line between Givet and Echternach.

The breakthrough was to be aided by "Operation Greif," led by Col. Skorzeny, in which German officers and solders dressed in U.S. uniforms (worn over their own German uniforms, so they could discard the outer garments after the breakthrough) would seize the bridges across the Meuse and, as a secondary mission, spread confusion and panic.

On December 16, at 0530, the attack began with a massive artillery barrage in the 6th Panzer Army zone. The volksgrenadier divisions were repulsed initially by the American 2nd and 99th Infantry divisions, but on the 17th, Peiper's Task Force found a hole and advanced, in three and one half hours, nearly ten kilometers into the American lines near Bullingen. His column then pushed westward to Moderscheid, on to Schoppen, Ondneval, and Thirimont, but had to backtrack when he found an impassable quagmire and turned northwest toward Malmedy. There, at about 1300, his men ran into an American convoy moving south, and the Germans shot up the vehicles.

To the south, the Fifth Panzer Army did not use an artillery preparation, as General Manteuffel preferred to infiltrate his units without giving any warning. This penetration was made through the American 28th and 106th Infantry divisions. The106th, with a squadron of the 14th Cavalry Group (Reinforced) was positioned across the Losheim Gap at the western foot of the Schnee Eifel and on 16 December had been there less than a week. The Our River meanders through the Gap, which is cluttered with abrupt hills, some bare, some covered with fir trees and thick undergrowth.

Two main roads were macadam and ran through the American positions directly to St. Vith. The division's front was about eighteen air-line miles, but when traced on the ground it was actually more than twenty-one miles. The 106th's northern neighbor was the 99th Infantry Division while the 28th Infantry Division was on its southern flank.

The 106th division's units and the troops of the14th Cavalry were so sparsely situated that when the attack came before dawn, the German forces moved through gaps, many of which were undetected by American units until after daylight. By nightfall on the 16th, the German attack had gone according to schedule and had penetrated through the Losheim Gap, had overrun American artillery units and the troops of the14th Cavalry to reach Auw, and were preparing to send through heavy armor units the next morning on its drive to St. Vith. Two regiments of the 106th Division and an artillery battalion were surrounded, while its 424th Infantry Regiment and its neighboring unit, CCB of the 9th Armored Division, halted the German advance along the line from Neidingen-Maspelt-Hiereberg.

The American High Command, meanwhile, was reacting to the German offensive. Among other changes made in the dispositions of the 12th Army Group, General Bradley ordered the Ninth Army to send the 7th Armored Division from its position about fifteen miles north of Aachen to Bastogne, some seventy miles to the south. The division was preceded by Brigadier General Bruce C. Clarke of CCB, who reported before the dawn of December 17 to the Corps Commander in Bastogne for further orders. General Troy Middleton, VIII Corps commander, was told that the 7th Armored Division, already on the move, would report to St. Vith to help the 106th Division, which had two regiments marooned on the Schnee Eifel. General Clarke proceeded to St. Vith, arriving at 1000 and reported to Major General Alan W. Jones, Commanding General of the 106th. General Jones told Clarke that he wanted an immediate counter-attack towards Schonberg to relieve the two regiments of the 106th Division.

The 7th Armored Division, which had been expected around 0700, was at that time fighting its way across muddy roads clogged with vehicles fleeing westward. Lead elements of the division did not arrive in St. Vith until late afternoon. About 1530, General Jones turned over the defense of the St. Vith sector to General Clarke who, at that time, still did not have elements of his command. Included in the scattered units given to General Clarke was the 275th Armored Field Artillery Battalion (Separate), a Corps Artillery battalion that had remained in place despite the panic and the fact that there were no friendly units between it and the enemy. He also assumed command of two engineer headquarters companies and a platoon of infantry. At that time, the Germans were only three or four thousand yards from the town. East of the town, several critical roadblocks were being manned by the engineer troops across the road near Prumerberg.]

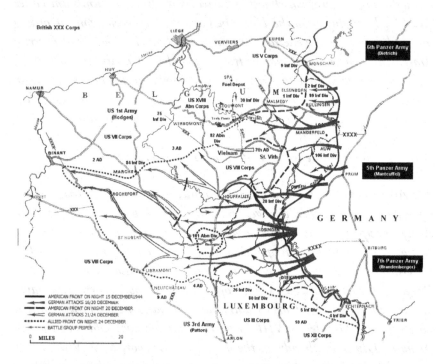

The route for our march went through the following towns: Aachen, Eupen, and Malmedy, to Vielsalm. All I saw that night were the dark roads, black night, and shadowy people along the roadside. Cox and I were in the front seats of the half-track. I stood up as the observer to help him drive. It was snowing, blustery, cold, dark, and difficult to see anything but the small red lights of the jeep in front of us. The weather was cold and damp and there wasn't any moon. It took a lot of stamina to stand. My nose was cold, my eyes continually watered. Because it was so dark and the lights could not be on, it was necessary I continue to help guide the half-track. As we drove along, a ghost of a vehicle or a man would suddenly appear beside the road. No words were spoken, only a wave of a covered flashlight and the convoy continued.

My men seemed exceptionally quiet. They seemed to know we were marching toward doom. The questions were, "What's going on, Lieutenant?" I couldn't answer, but I too had a very bad feeling in my gut. Infantrymen seem to know when a battle is pending and what the odds were going to be before they ever get to the line. There is something in the air that spells out in advance how tough the battle is going to be. From the actions and quiet of the men, I sensed they were worried. Infantrymen know they are the expendable parts of the war, and one of their jobs is to stop the enemy and plug the hole in a line if there has been a breakthrough. From the attitude of our command, we knew something serious had happened.

The farther we went, the more traffic we saw—but not going forward. They were going fast westward to the rear. This caused more concern among my men. The one person I saw the most during the march was our S3, Maj. Boyer. He seemed to be everywhere, picking up stragglers, keeping the march going, and doing a great job. He commented to me during a rest break, "For the life of me I cannot understand why some persons of higher rank can't see what's going on and stop a few of these fleeing officers and make them form some kind of defense. No, those guys all seem to want to run and get out of the way. They don't think about stopping and defending. I can't help from being proud and thrilled at the spirit of you guys and the rest of my men for what you've done—loading vehicles, spinning tracks, gunning motors, and taking off for a fight which others are running away from, when all we know is that somewhere down there are krauts and that there is going to be a fight. And here we run into all these guys bugging out. I'm proud of belonging to the 7th Armored, a fighting outfit."

[Near Stavelot, CCR ran into more of Peiper's German units, who apparently were as surprised as the Americans by the meeting. CCR brushed them aside and arrived at Vielsam with no serious damage late in the afternoon. German air was more active than usual, and the column was attacked several times.]

Somewhere along the road we were alerted to man our machine guns, that it was thought German paratroopers had been dropped into the area, were disrupting the march, changing road signs, and that snipers were shooting at the troops. So now my men were really awake. We placed another head above the side armor to have more eyes observing. I went back to the following half-track and advised Sgt. Sicari to do the same.

My God, but it was dark. I was without my glasses, so I had trouble seeing details but by squinting I could get by. It was snowing. It was cold. It was scary. One of my men, I think it was Conover (who was my eyes) said he saw a parachute hanging in the trees. Now we believed the rumor. Now it was a fact. The men became even more questioning. We were passing a forest and feared a burst from a machine gun or bazooka. We were easy targets—they could see us and we couldn't see but a few feet at any time.

We continually met vehicles coming from the opposite direction. What was their hurry? My men were very quiet. Funny, we never saw any civilians. The farther we went, the colder it got. We saw Military Police on occasion and they seemed nervous. I couldn't grasp what was happening. All I knew was that we were in convoy. We saw many vehicles going in the opposite direction, and my men and I wished to know what in the hell was going on.

Finally, on a break I found out more news. Germans were in the area dressed in U.S. Army uniforms. They were disrupting traffic, changing road signs, killing people, and generally stirring up trouble. Their mission was to do anything to stop or slow down the functioning of our Army.

Capt. Mattocks told me all he knew: "There has been a breakthrough by the Germans and the vehicles we are seeing rushing to the rear are Americans in flight. No one is in charge, and they are trying to save their asses."

[The heavy stream of westward moving traffic, which was a disorganized rout, caused Lt. Col. Fuller, commander of the 38th AIB, to divert Company A and Headquarters Company from the route and ordered them into an assembly area at Rodt. B Company was also diverted, but Company C and Service Company got separated from the battalion column and was snarled in the traffic jam. This concentrated the battalion, minus C Company and Service Company, about three miles west of St. Vith. Meanwhile CCB,

with the 31st Tank Battalion and the 23rd Armored Infantry Battalion attached, had been all but immobilized by the traffic maelstrom which jammed the Vielsam-St. Vith road. Lt. Col. Fuller and Major Boyer of the 38th AIB helped Lt. Col. R. C. Erlenbusch, commander of the 31st Tank Battalion, clear a path for one medium tank company and one armored infantry company before the western bound traffic double-banked each other and again closed the road.]

We convoyed for most of the day and finally pulled off the road near the small village of Rodt. There was a schoolhouse where we all got out and relieved ourselves. Rusty came by to see us and offered me a drink of cognac. I saw an old upright piano, so naturally I had to sit and play a couple of tunes. It must have been quite a scene: men listening to me while waiting, concerned about what they were seeing—trucks, jeeps, tanks, and command cars fleeing from the direction we were going. In those vehicles were all ranks. And there I was playing the piano. The song I was playing was "My Blue Heaven." The words went, "A turn to the right, A little bright light will lead you to My Blue Heaven. Just Molly and me and baby make three the reason for My Blue Heaven." When I look back at my piano playing then, it was dumb of me. The piano is one of the easiest things to booby trap. Lucky for me it wasn't, or I might have gone immediately to "My Blue Heaven."

I remember on December 17, as I was waiting with my platoon in the schoolhouse, I looked out on the main road full of our troops fleeing the battle, completely out of control. Their vehicles were packed with men who were yelling at whoever they saw, "Run! The krauts are coming!" They were throwing away their weapons, but what surprised me most were the many officers among them who could have exerted some control but made no effort to do so. One man jumped off one of the trucks when he saw our unit and yelled that he came to fight and wasn't going to bug out. I don't know what outfit he hooked up with, but he didn't join our unit. It was a sight that I never dreamed I would ever see: a U.S. Army unit completely out of control.

St. Vith

[As the first units of CCR of the 7th Armored Division crept towards St. Vith, two hours had passed since General Clarke assumed command. The final traffic jam at a crossroads several hundred yards to the west of the town was cleared by General Clarke himself. When the first column of Sherman tanks arrived, Clarke directed them towards Schonberg, until they met the engineers. Thus began the defense of St. Vith. The initial plan for a counterattack by CCB had long since been scrapped because of the delay caused by the congested roads.

The Corps of Engineers trained its engineer combat battalions not only in the primary role of facilitating the movement of troops and supplies by keeping the road nets open for rapid advance and creating obstacles to the enemy forces, but also to fight as infantry when necessary. That training and experience proved itself many times but especially in the Battle of St. Vith. On the morning of December 16, Lt. Col. Thomas Riggs, commander of the 81st Engineer Combat Battalion of the 106th Infantry Division, whose headquarters was in Heuem, learned from a messenger from his Company A, which was supporting the 422nd Infantry Regiment, of the German attack. Col. Riggs checked in at the Division headquarters at St. Vith and learned that it was a concerted German attack; he was given orders to assemble his unit and serve as infantry. Riggs' B and C companies were already committed within their respective combat teams, and one platoon of A Company was also involved with its assigned infantry troops. Those elements of his command were fighting a delaying action and were slowing the enemy in the various places where they had been assigned. He rushed to Schonberg and evacuated most of the bulldozers and other heavy equipment.

Then back at division headquarters, Riggs learned that the 7th Armored Division and CCB and the 9th Armored Division were en route and scheduled to arrive at 0700 on December 17 and that he should withdraw from Heuem to immediately west of St. Vith. Three hours later he was told to assemble all available men from his battalion and the 168th Engineer Combat Battalion, a VII Corps unit commanded by Lt. Col. W. L. Nungesser that had been operating saw mills and maintaining the rear road network. He was able to put together slightly more than two companies, comprising his Headquarters and Service Company and about one third of A Company and elements from the168th Engineers, commanded by Lt. Col. W. L. Nungesser. With these troops, Lt. Col. Riggs established a defensive position along a wooded ridge about one mile east of St. Vith, near Prumerberg. Mines were laid to their front and the troops dug in. Several German tank and infantry attacks were repulsed during the day. During the night German patrols were stopped, but the lines were anything but clear as both American and German troops became commingled. Maj. Boyer checked in with Col. Riggs that night. At a meeting with officers of both engineer battalions, Troop B, the 87th Reconnaissance Battalion, and an attached platoon of medium tanks of the 7th Armored Division, it was decided that Company B, 38th Armored Infantry Battalion, would relieve the 168th Engineers troops.

Col. Riggs had his platoon leaders tell his troops about the incoming infantry of the 7th Armored Division and instructed them to lead the new arrivals into position and to avoid firing on them as his engineer and the German troops were intermingled on the ground.]

Finally, the superior leadership of Maj. Boyer and Capt. Mattocks got the convoy rolling. My platoon was again loaded and on the alert. I don't know whether Boyer and Mattocks were ever decorated for the job they did on the convoy, but they should have been. I remember one incident: I had walked from the school to the road and was watching and helping where I could. We were trying to get our troops back on the road. A command car came down loaded with some of the high-ranking officers of the fleeing troops. They apparently wanted to continue to get away from their responsibility. We needed their space to get our vehicles back on the road. They would not move, so Maj. Boyer told them to get off the road or he would get one of his tanks to push them off. I am sure they didn't like the order from a major, but they got their vehicle out of our way.

My men wondered what kind of hell we were getting into. I could read their minds easily because I was thinking the same thing: Why are we going forward when all those troops and officers are leaving? It didn't take long for me to come to an answer. We were going up to the front. We were the infantry, and it was up to us to do the messy jobs. We didn't know what we were getting into, but we knew it was going to be a dirty mess of some kind. Some one had goofed up again and it was up to our troops to stop the enemy somehow, some way.

[It took CCR six hours to get to get from Vielsam to St. Vith—a twelve-mile run—because of the disgraceful traffic jam caused by the fleeing Americans, a delay of combat units that might have saved elements of the 106th Infantry Division if they could have reached St. Vith earlier. During the night Gen. Clarke supervised the extension and thickening of the thin line of engineers that ran roughly from Hunningen, north of St. Vith, through Prumersberg to Weisenbach, where it loosely joined the left flank of CCB of the 9th Armored Division. To the south he knew that the 422nd and 423rd Regimental Combat Teams (RCT) of the 106th Division had been cut off and completely surrounded; that to the southeast, CCB of the 9th Armored Division was attacking to retake Winterspelt; and that the 424th RCT of the 106th south of the 9th AD was retiring to take up new positions. By 1630, Clarke was in his command post in a schoolhouse in St. Vith, which was also the CP of the 106th Division. Only three units of the 7th AD had been able to enter the town: one cavalry Reconnaissance Troop, one medium tank company, and one armored infantry company. When Lt. Col. Fuller and Maj. Boyer reported to him, Clarke told Boyer to, "Go in town and get B Company of the 23rd, which you will find in the main street. Have them take positions here," (pointing to the southeastern approaches to St. Vith). Boyer asked who would be on his right and left. Clarke answered the only way he could: "We don't know about the right; CCB of the 9th is there somewhere. On the left, some engineers from a Corps Battalion, farther to the left, a reconnaissance troop from the 87th." Gen. Clarke then told Fuller to coordinate the defenses of St. Vith with the commanders of the engineer units then in position about 2400 yards east of the town and in the woods to the right of the Schonberg road. At the same

time he attached the reconnaissance troop, the armored infantry company, and the tank company to the 38th AIB.]

By early evening, we arrived at St.Vith. It was dusk. My men unloaded and went into a vacant building to wait for orders. I wandered about the town for a short time trying to find out what the hell was going on. There were a few civilians. They didn't seem to relish the idea that Americans were in their town. A young lady at the last rest stop had been crying, "Le boche. Le boche." We tried to understand her, but no one in our group understood German or whatever she was speaking. We saw that the town was in a confused mess.

When Maj. Boyer first got into town, he was fired at by a sniper from one of the windows overlooking the street. The sniper missed. One of our armored vehicles was passing at the time and had a .50 caliber machine gun mounted on it. The gunner adjusted, aimed, and fired. The sniper was killed with one burst and was left hanging out of the window.

Soon after our arrival in St. Vith, a Military Police motorcyclist raced into town from the direction of Malmedy. He skidded to a stop against a building on the other side of the street from where Maj. Boyer was directing traffic. The MP's uniform was ripped and torn, and he was bleeding from surface cuts apparently sustained from a spill. He was highly excited and out of breath, but he was able to gasp out the news that our Division Chief of Staff, Col. Matthews, had been ambushed by a German tank about two miles north of St. Vith. Col. Matthews in his jeep, escorted by two MP's, had left town about 1730 en route to Recht with orders for CCR. As they rounded a turn in the road, they came almost face-to-face with an approaching German tank. In an attempt to get away, the vehicles got stuck. The driver and Col. Matthews bailed out and tried to escape on foot. The MP said he stayed in the area of the incident for more than an hour but had not seen his buddy, the other MP, Col. Matthews, or the driver. Maj. Boyer directed the MP to the schoolhouse to report to Gen. Clarke what had happened to the Chief of Staff.

That report about a German tank being two miles or less from town meant the road to the north was cut, and that the krauts would probably try to force the town from the north sometime during the evening. It sure wasn't a comfortable feeling, for I knew that Capt. Anstey of Company A was not yet in position. The only troops that were in line were a few engineers of the 106th Infantry Division.

I ran into First Sgt. Alvie Davis, who was trying to organize the command post. Davis said that no officer was around and that Capt. Mattocks was trying to find out what the new mission was and how long we would be able to rest—and would we have time to feed the troops? We hadn't had a good meal for a couple of days. He found out that we didn't have time, and the mess truck was not with the forward elements of our group. In fact, he didn't know where the truck was.

I went back to my men. They, too, were waiting and wondering. I had been back for only a few minutes when a runner came and said, "Lieutenant, you are wanted at the CP." I found the command post. My orders from Capt. Mattocks were, "Moranda, take your platoon up this road about a mile or so. You will come to a small house on the left. Report to either Lt. Col. Fuller or an Eng. Lt. Col. Riggs. One of them will give you the mission. Good luck!"

"Strange," I thought, "What's the 'good luck' bit? He had never said that before."

Back where I left my men, I called Sgts. Sicari, Simeneaux, Totoni, and Curtin and gave them the word, "Let's move out." We loaded the half-tracks and drove to the house. When we arrived, I looked at the men sitting around the command post. They seemed to be in a daze. Not many smiles on their faces. They were milling around, waiting. They didn't seem to be eager to continue what they had been doing, whatever that was. By now it was dark. I went inside and found Lt. Col Fuller, Lt. Col. Riggs, and a Lt. Holland conversing. As I approached I saluted and said, "Lieutenant Moranda reporting."

Col. Fuller introduced me to Riggs and Holland. Col. Riggs gave me a brief history of the previous action. They were from the Engineer Battalion of the 106th Infantry Division. Their division had been broken through, and the division was in a full retreat. Col. Riggs and Lt. Holland were ordered by Gen. Jones of the 106th Infantry Division to make a stand on the outskirts of St. Vith—an important hub on the route the Germans had to take for their operation. When the 38th Armored Infantry arrived in St Vith, Col. Fuller was ordered to join

Col. Riggs' men. As Col. Fuller was the senior Infantry officer, he was to be in command. The 38th Battalion was to join with the engineers and stop the attack of the Germans. My mission was to go with Lt. Holland and support his men. Col. Fuller had no more information except to say the enemy was only a few hundred yards away.

(I discovered later that Lt. Holland and a few of his men had been in a series of skirmishes before our troops arrived. When the 106th Infantry Division had been overrun by Germans, some of the American soldiers broke and ran. Holland came across some of those men that were trying to save their skins. He watched some of them throw away their weapons, so he stopped them and made them members of his unit. Soon after, on December 16, he and his men stopped the Germans by first knocking out an enemy tank and the infantry following it. Holland's men had used some of the discarded American weapons—a .50 caliber machine gun and a bazooka.)

While walking to the forward troops, we held our conversation to whispers, for the enemy was near, and we didn't want to draw fire before we even got to the front lines.

December 18

[The defensive cordon around St. Vith was established piecemeal with units placed in line as they arrived. Some such as Troop B, 87th Reconnaissance Squadron had to fight its way into its assigned position. Another example as related by Lt. Col. Erlinbusch, who commanded the 31st Tank Battalion: "Company A, 31st Tank Battalion, was ordered to take up a defensive position on the high ground about 2000 yards east of St. Vith. Lt. Dunn, the leading platoon leader, preceded his lead tank in a quarter ton to reconnoiter for positions. About 1500 yards from St. Vith, upon rounding a bend in the road, Lt. Dunn spotted, about 800 yards to his front, three German tanks and about one company of infantry moving in the direction of St. Vith. He turned his vehicle around, issued instructions to his platoon by radio, climbed into his tank, and led his platoon to the point where he saw the enemy approaching. The German force and his first platoon met head on at the bend of the road. The fight was short and at point blank range. We destroyed the enemy tanks and killed or wounded about fifty of the enemy with no loss to our own forces. Company A secured the high

ground, blocked the road, and extended its position north from the road along the ridge."

Traffic jams on the St. Vith-Vielsam road were still increasing as those American forces who had been in the area before the German breakthrough were trying to get as far west as they could as fast as possible. It took Capt. W. H. Anstey with his Company A, 38th AIB, two and one-half hours to cover three miles. By 0700 on December 18, troops were dug in along a U-shaped arc from the Prumerberg road on the south to the Malmedy road on the north—the sector assigned to the 38th AIB by General Clarke. On the left of the 38th was, at first, the 87th Cavalry Reconnaissance Squadron and later the 31st Tank Battalion. On the right was CCB of the 9th Armored Division. During the night of December 17 there was some probing by the Germans and some small arms fire, but no major attacks. The weather, which had been bitterly cold all day with gray, overcast skies, turned into a cold, drizzly rain late that night. The ground was muddy and soggy, making vehicular movement almost impossible. Even so three German tanks and two of their 75 mm assault guns were destroyed in front of the 38th's arc.]

After about 500 yards, we came to the front edge of the forest. Lt. Holland and I trooped the line. His men were dug in and were glad to see some help arriving. After walking around the area, Holland and I decided we would split our forces. He would take Sgts. Sicari, Curtin, and Totoni and a section of machine guns with him and bolster his defense on the left side of the road. Sgt. Simeneaux and his section, along with a few of Lt. Holland's engineers, would come with me and establish a defense on the right side of the road. It was very dark that night and difficult to establish fields of fire. While we were moving forward, we could hear the rattle of machine gun fire to our left. Lt. Holland remarked, "Sounds like the Jerries are still trying to break through the line."

Capt. Carl K. "Rusty" Mattocks   Sgt. James Totoni

Pfc. Maurice Conover   Cpl. Glenn Fackler

I walked back to the CP with Conover, who had accompanied us. As we were walking through the trees we heard the clop of footsteps coming toward us. Conover went to the side of the road so he could cover me as I challenged the man. It was an elderly civilian who kept repeating "Le boche, le boche," while pointing toward the east. My interpretation was that the enemy was close. We continued to the command post and placed the half-tracks nearby. With the platoon in tow, we all went forward. No words were spoken. The men sensed the situation was serious.

We placed our .30 caliber machine guns on either side of the road so their fields of fire could cover our entire front. The rest of the squad and the engineer troops were dispersed so they could also fire their weapons through gaps in the trees. We placed the other men back into the woods for cover and protection from the enemy in front. They still could have fields of fire.

I told each soldier, "Dig in. We will be hit early in the morning." They understood and began. Few of them had entrenching tools. Those that didn't dug with their helmets or whatever they had, and soon all had foxholes. I didn't dig one as I usually jumped into the nearest one when the need arose.

[At 0800, December 18, medium small arms fire broke out along the front of Company B, 38th AIB, along with close direct fire from two German tanks and one assault gun. This firing decapitated trees, causing limbs and chunks of wood to fall into and behind the foxholes. One light machine gun was destroyed, its crew and one rifle squad annihilated by panzerfaust fire. This heavy fire overwhelmed the center platoon of Company B, and the platoon withdrew about 300 yards. Tech Sgt. J.P. Revels, the platoon sergeant, quickly rallied his men and launched a counter-attack. There were no reserves available. The attack shifted about forty-five minutes later to the right platoon of Company B, commanded by 1st Lt. J. H. Higgins and the engineer troops under the command of 1st Lt. W. E. Holland. The German troops were very aggressive in trying to widen the breach. This showed that seasoned troops were involved. By 0920, contact was broken and the Germans withdrew, leaving one tank and one assault gun burning.]

Early in the morning we heard troops moving in to our left. It was Company B, 23rd Armored Infantry Battalion moving in. This made the line almost continuous for a few hundred yards. All of the American troops were on the edge of the forest.

I met with Lt. Holland to discuss our plan, and then went back to the right side of the road. For a few minutes, I had a short rest. But it wasn't long before I was awakened by an enemy patrol probing our lines.

A few rounds came in. A tank was seen near a small house to our front. It was rumbling but not advancing toward our position. I discovered that being back in the forest had its benefits but also its drawbacks. The artillery coming in hit the tree tops and we suffered casualties from tree bursts. The incoming shells exploded and the fragments of steel did their best to kill or wound you. Someone said the damned fragments seemed to have eyes. We soon learned that the safest thing to do during a barrage of incoming artillery that hit the trees above us was to hug a tree. We soon placed our foxholes near one, but even then we had to don our helmets—even while trying to sleep in the hole. We found the best way to build an emplacement was to establish a field of fire, then build yourself some overhead cover, and have it near a tree.

I was hit on the nose and above the eye by a shell fragment, and another piece hit me on the right leg, none very serious. Then it dawned on me, we didn't have a medic with our bastard outfit of half 106th Engineers and half of our 38th Headquarters Company machine gun platoon. When we first got there, we used a medic from one of the other nearby units.

The first real attack occurred at about 0800. The Germans hit first along the entire front of Company B/23 and our team of engineers and machine gun platoon. Attacking were two tanks with accompanying infantry. One of the light machine guns of B/23 was destroyed along with its crew, and the enemy fire had annihilated the men of the adjoining infantry squad. Their front line withdrew about 300 yards, but the officers and non-coms soon reorganized the men and retook their positions on the defensive line. In the Infantry School at Fort Benning they had called the line the FPL—Final Protective Line.

The second attack came at about 1100. The Germans had not given up trying to come through us and again hit the front of our position, this time with two platoons of infantry supported by a tank. As I was going toward the rear to get to my other men and not expose myself too much, I came close to our battalion CP. I saw Lt. Col. Fuller and Lt. Col. Riggs talking to a captain with a tank destroyer crew. This was what I hoped for. I asked the officer in charge of the TD if he would take on the tank in front of our position. He said he would. With that the tank destroyer rumbled up the road; he got the weapon into position and with a couple of shots knocked out the enemy tank. The tank destroyer departed right after the firing. It was a short-term relief because we soon heard more tanks to our front and to the right of our position.

[About two hours later the Germans tried again and hit the right platoon of Company B and the engineer troops, this time using two platoons of infantry supported by a tank. The tank section of Company A, 31st Tank Battalion, took care of the German tank with a ricochet shot that left it burning about twenty-five yards in front of the defense line. The attacking infantry were unable to stand up against the withering hail of rifle and machine gun fire which was poured into their ranks and they soon broke and fled.

Meanwhile Company A, 38th AIB, and Troop B of the 87th Recon were having a quiet time, except for an incident in B Troop of the 87th, according to Capt. Anstey, who described one action: "One of his armored car crews was in a concealed position near the boundary of Company A and the 87th Recon when a Tiger tank approached at right angles and ran along a trail in front of the Main Line of Resistance; the armored car slipped out of position and started up the trail behind the Tiger, accelerating to get closer; the German tank commander saw the armored car, and started traversing his gun to bear on it; it was a race between the Americans in their vehicle with a puny 37 mm gun trying to get close enough to be effective in the Tiger's vulnerable rear armor, and the Germans, who were desperately trying to get its main gun to bear in order to blast the "fools" who dared to fight a sixty-ton tank with their little pop gun. Suddenly, the armored car got to within twenty-five yards and quickly pumped in three rounds; the lumbering Tiger stopped, shuddered, and a muffled explosion was heard followed by flames which billowed out of the turret and engine ports."

At 1300, Company A, 23rd AIB, under Capt. J. R. Foster arrived and was put in line between Companies A and B of the 38th AIB to relieve B Troop of the 87th. From 1445 to 1730 the Germans attacked again. This time they meant business for they slashed into Lt. Higgin's platoon and Lt. Holland's engineers with an estimated battalion of infantry on a two-company front, with direct support from four tanks and eight assault guns. Two of the tanks and two assault guns attacked with the infantry, while the rest of the armor placed direct fire on the Americans from the vicinity of Wallerode. Initial penetrations were made. It was only the heavy enfilade fire poured into the assault ranks by the Machine Gun Platoon of the 38th AIB, commanded by 2nd Lt. R. E. Moranda, and the direct fire placed on the attacking tanks and assault guns by Companies A and C of the 31st Tank Battalion that broke up the attack. After almost three hours of vicious fighting, much of it hand-to-hand, the Germans were forced to withdraw. The American lines still held, although several gaps had been opened and some German patrols filtered through. B Troop of the 87th was pushed into line to plug a gap between Company B of the 38th and the engineer troops.]

About mid-afternoon we were hit again by infantry and tanks. It was during this fray that one of my gunners on a machine gun broke and ran away from his gun. Conover and I stopped him. He was a young blond kid, twenty years old and scared to death. I talked to him and told him the seriousness of his running away. Then I talked to Sgt. Simeneaux, and we decided to put him back as the gunner.

During one of the attacks, a squad in Lt. Higgins' platoon reported one machine gun section was seen taking off. Higgins asked them to check, but they never found them. No one knew whether they had been captured or killed.

Usually, when the infantry is under fire from artillery, mortars, Nebelwerfer rockets, and tanks—as well as in range of small arms fire—the best way to overcome the fear of the enemy is to attack. We couldn't do that. We had orders to hold at all costs, so stay we did. And we always had to fight the urge to withdraw.

At 1745 we were kept on the alert, with the enemy was still probing our lines looking for a weak spot. Their mission was to push through our position and capture St. Vith.

[The night was reasonably quiet except for the ever-present probing attempts by the Germans patrols, but the Americans heard vehicular movement, including tanks, to their north in the vicinity of Wallerode. German 88s and artillery concentrations were placing continuous harassing fire on St. Vith and all roads. The weather was bitter cold, overcast, with snow flurries

during the day. The rain had stopped, but the roads were slick and covered with a thin coating of mud.

The actual count of German losses included five tanks, two assault guns destroyed, one assault gun damaged, and 249 killed.]

During many of the lulls I had all my men take their shoes off and massage their feet. There was some grousing, but the men followed the order. The weather was very cold and we didn't need to have any frostbite cases. The hardest thing was keeping warm as we only had our regular outfits, inadequate for the weather. I was fortunate in having bought some silk pajamas to wear underneath and that long muffler I could wrap around my head and body to keep old Jack Frost away. The men were not so lucky. Most of them had only one pair of socks and no long johns, so it was very difficult for them to keep warm. During breaks in the action, they would usually pair up, two men to a foxhole, and position themselves back to back so their body heat helped some. Sleep? I don't think I had more than an hour's sleep at a time for five days, and that seemed to be with one eye open for a foot step or any unusual sound would cause me to be wide awake. I think all of us were in the same state of alert.

December 19

The next day there were more probes. We heard German tanks to our front. One of our left flank units broke and withdrew farther into the forest. Their leaders were soon able to control the men and get them back into position.

About that time, Capt. Mattocks told me about the U.S. Army Searchlight Company. As we were making our way to St. Vith, their commander had asked the commander of our convoy as we were leaving Uback, if they could follow our convoy. Our CO agreed. When we were coming into Rodt, the searchlight convoy took the wrong turn and wound up in Malmedy. The unit was captured and massacred. Word got around about that slaughter, and I think it was one of the reasons our outfit and others fought so well at the Battle of the Bulge. It did not take long for the news to spread about the killing of Americans who had surrendered. It was understandable that my men were concerned.

For two days they had observed American troops fleeing from the front; they had probably not heard of the Malmedy massacre. Even so, it is questionable whether it would have made a difference in their attitude or whether their fears could have been overcome, enabling them to stand and fight. Yet here we were, doing our job and doing it well.

One of our problems was that we didn't know anything about the enemy, or where we were, or who or what kind of units we were fighting against, or who was retreating. There was supposed to be a friendly unit on our right flank. In all the time we were in the line, the right flank unit never materialized. At one time we did hear some tanks clanking around on our right, but we never saw them. For one brief period, we heard some tanks firing their weapons, but they never came near us. We knew we had no help from the right and were exposed. It worried me—knowing we had no friendly troops there to protect our flank. I wondered if another of our own outfits had bugged out on us.

Lt. Holland was my main source of information. To me, he was one of the heroes of the Battle of St. Vith. There were many heroes; most were lieutenants and sergeants. I saw only one field grade officer in the front lines after we were in position: Maj. Boyer, who was there during all the battle. He was with B Company on my left most of the time. The right side of the horseshoe was still under the Holland-Moranda group.

The third attack that day came about 1700 hours. The enemy meant business this time. They came down the road with tanks and infantry—it seemed like an army of tanks to us. The decision to have our positions back into the forest trees protected us somewhat from the tanks. Our machine guns and infantry with bazookas were finally able to stop the Germans. Even so, it seemed as if the battle would never end.

When Company A's line had been broken, I saw that Sgts. Curtin and Totoni and their sections were withdrawing deeper into the forest. Curtin had his men under control. To get to him I had to go back about fifty yards and then cross an open area to the other side of the road. Curtin had his men standing behind trees and firing into the oncoming enemy. Curtin was in his glory. He must have thought he was playing cowboys and Indians. With the tanks knocked out, it wasn't long before this German attack was over. I remembered what Sgt. Sicari had told me earlier about Curtin: that when the chips were down he would be the platoon's best leader during combat.

On the right side of the road, my gunners were firing into the advancing Germans. The young lad who had fled the first fire fight, and who we had turned around, was firing his weapon even after being wounded with a shot through the arm.

[In Maj. Boyer's After Action Report he wrote: "The devastating effect of the enfilade machine gun fire was aptly demonstrated along one fire break in B Company's area. Yesterday the Germans broke through the line and immediately pushed a platoon of paratroopers through to exploit the gap. They quickly dodged down the reverse slope, but as they broke through the trees one of the machine gun sections of 2nd Lt. Moranda's platoon on the right flank quickly traversed the guns and laid down fire at the break. When the Germans crossed the open break about one hundred yards away, they were perfect targets. There they lay, nineteen men laid out in parade ground intervals five yards apart, dead with slugs in their chests. We had stopped them!"]

I saw Lt. Higgins right after he was told to take command of B Company and asked him what had happened to Capt. Green. He told me that when they had their first "visitors"—apparently a probe, nothing very serious—Capt. Green was going down the line checking his men. As he got close to the last of them, he heard some machine gun fire in the nearby woods. He thought it was his troops firing, so he ran to see what the problem was and ran into a platoon of Germans. He was taken prisoner.

As I was coming back from Sgt. Curtin's side, I stopped by the CP to pick up some machine gun ammunition from the half-track parked near the command post. I saw Lt. Col. Fuller; he was ashen. He asked, "What the hell is going on up there?" I told him, "We are now OK. The troops have stopped the krauts, and we have re-established our front lines." That was the last time I saw him. Soon after he went to division headquarters and told Gen. Clarke he was too sick to continue in command. His command was taken over by Maj. Boyer and Lt. Col. Riggs, the engineer commander.

I will not take credit for the "kills." My section sergeants were the heroes. They were the ones who kept the machine gunners firing. They encouraged the men. I was kept busy going from one side to the other. The sergeants and their men were on the front all the time.

[Field Marshall Model, Commander of Army Group B, which had the responsibility for the offensive and breakthrough, reminded Gen. Manteuffel that St. Vith was the exception to the orders to bypass all heavily defended towns. Even though St. Vith had been outflanked from the north and south, the town had to be taken in order for the roads and the rail lines to be used in support of the Fifth and Sixth Armies. Therefore, the Fuhrer Escort Brigade, the Fifth Panzer Army reserve, was diverted from an exploiting mission and turned against St. Vith. By the morning of December 18, two Volksgrenadier Divisions and a combat command from the 1st SS Panzer Division began the first of a series of attacks which were to extend for six days.

At 0200, elements of the 1st SS Panzer Division struck north of St. Vith; at 0800, CCB of the 7th Armored Division (U.S.) was hit by infantry supported by tanks; at 1000, service elements west of St. Vith were engaged by elements of 1st Panzer Division which had flanked St. Vith from the north. By late afternoon, however, CCB and CCA, 7th Armored, by aggressive counterattacks, had recaptured the vital crossroads lost in the morning.

During the nights of December 18 and 19, two attacks against CCB were repulsed. By the end of December 18, the German probing attacks had found St. Vith ringed on three sides by the 7th Armored Division on the north and center and by CCB of the 9th Armored Division (U.S.) to the south. The defensive perimeter, almost twenty-five miles long, was completely isolated from friendly forces. The gap to the south now stretched eighteen miles to Bastogne; to the north, the fifteen-mile gap to Malmedy was filled with the Sixth Panzer Army troops.

All day on December 19, probing attacks for soft spots were made. Attacks in turn were made against 7th Armored Division/CCB's left flank, then at the center of CCB, and then against CCB's right flank. All attacks were beaten off by combined fires and numerous individual acts of heroism.

By noon Model was again pressuring Manteuffel to seize St. Vith. The traffic jam to the east of St. Vith had tied up German supply convoys and trains, not to mention the 1st Panzer Division. This time it was Gen. Manteuffel's turn to unsnarl traffic as Gen. Clarke had done two days before by personally directing traffic.]

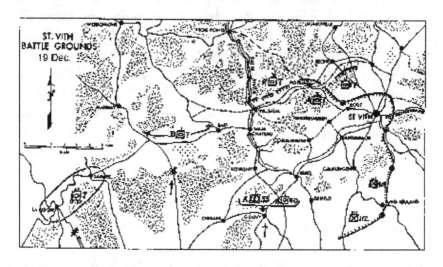

Sketch showing situation 19 December 1944

December 20

The morning came, finally! I trooped the line with Maj. Boyer, Lts. Higgins and Holland, and Capt. Mattocks. We saw where the furious action had occurred the day before. We saw many dead Jerries. Our rifles and machine guns had saved the day.

[During the check of the positions, Maj. Boyer found that Lt. Holland was completing the reorganization of his company, but on his left, Company B was licking its wounds after the savage fighting of the day before. There was a gap between the 1st platoon under 2nd Lt. W.A. Jamiel on the left and the 2nd platoon under 2nd Lt. W.C. Fradenburg in the center of the line. The 2nd platoon had suffered too many losses, so Maj. Boyer combined it with Lt. Higgins' 3rd platoon, and told Higgins to take command of Company B since Capt. Green, the commander, had been missing since the previous day's early attack. Maj. Boyer had been told to take command as Col. Fuller had gone to the rear. Lt. Holland told Maj. Boyer that he

considered his engineer troops as being under Boyer's command, and this gave Boyer a task force of four companies with about 450 men, including a reserve of 70 soldiers.

While the lines were being adjusted, Maj. Boyer and party surveyed the scene of the last attack. The only Germans they found were dead ones, most of them killed as they apparently tried to dig themselves in behind trees, logs, or any cover they could find. Those who did not have shovels had tried to scoop shallow holes with their helmets, bayonets, or even their finger nails. The accuracy of the defenders rifles and machine gun fire had been too much for them. They counted more than 200 dead Germans within the defensive positions and did not count those in front of the lines. They also identified from their insignia two Volksgrenadier divisions, a panzer division, and a regiment of the Gross-Deutschland—a unit that provided the guard for Hitler's headquarters when in the field.]

At that time the Germans who had been attacking us were identified. They were a Volksgrenadier Division along with a Panzer group. When I told my men who the group fighting us was, Sgt. Curtin said, "Hell, if you have seen one, you've seen them all." I agreed. When someone is trying to kill you, it doesn't make much difference what kind of identifying uniform patch he is wearing.

The next attack came at mid-afternoon. An estimated enemy company supported by a heavy Panther tank was knocked out by a bazooka. The enemy was picked off by our rifles and machine guns. In my mind I can still hear the German non-coms directing their troops from the rear. What heavy voices they had—and how well they controlled their advancing soldiers.

Snow came again. I tried to give the men individual attention as we were all uneasy. At least we didn't see our own troops fleeing the front. All day long we were under artillery fire. Most of the shells went over us, but we were plagued by those damned "screaming meemies." What a scary sound! When we heard them coming, we automatically looked for the nearest hole. I would dive into the nearest foxhole, usually on top of one of my men. When I piled in on Conover, he would invariably say, "Welcome aboard, Lieutenant."

[By the morning of December 20, the situation at St. Vith was becoming increasingly difficult for the defenders. Although bolstered by the arrival of division artillery and the addition of the 112th Infantry Regiment from the 28th Infantry Division (which had been thrust aside by the initial German penetration and out of contact with friendly forces until December 19), the defense was greatly hampered by the lack of supply, aerial support, and aerial observation for artillery fires. Ammunition was especially scarce as it had to be obtained by locating abandoned dumps and then running the gauntlet of the German-infested rear area with truck convoys.

However, the Germans were also having difficulties. By this time their timetable was three days behind schedule. The St. Vith salient stuck deep into the road net to the west, impeding support of the exploiting panzers racing toward the Meuse. Traffic was jammed bumper-to-bumper for miles from the original line of departure at the Westwall. The effect of the jam was indicated by the fact that it took the Fuhrer Escort Brigade three days—until December 20— to plow through the jammed roads to get into position to attack.

During the day of December 20, Maj. Boyer was ordered to the town of St. Vith to meet with Gen. Clarke, who wanted an update. Boyer gave Clarke his assessment and said that there had been a penetration of the Allied lines in the engineer troop area that Boyer wanted to attend to. Gen. Clarke stated he wanted to think about it and check other data. Boyer told him to "Go to hell" and took off for the breakthrough area. Years later, when Col. Boyer was serving under Gen. Clarke again at Fort Hood, Texas, Clarke often commented, "Col. Boyer is the only one who has told me to 'Go to hell' and survived."]

Our troops finally got support from our own artillery and from the 38th's Headquarters Company. Lt. Kinnebrew opened his forward observer position for his mortars. Lt. Boyd was still looking for a good observation spot for his platoon of assault guns. The 275th Artillery opened up a forward observer post. It seemed as if we were getting stronger all the time. Our main trouble was having no replacements for the infantry losses. Our front lines were beginning to have too many blank spaces.

We were continually probed. The Germans would open with burp guns and mortars. We could hear their NCOs ("Feldwebels") yelling at their men. We were using ammunition sparingly. Many times we didn't answer their fire because I was sure the Germans were logging every one of our positions for later artillery and mortar barrages. A fifteen-man German patrol came into the draw in front of the unit next to us. Our machine guns opened up on them as the patrol came nearer. We continued to fire at them until they withdrew. Early the next morning our troops sent out a patrol to see what the results were. When they came back, they reported seeing blood on the ground along with bandages, but no enemy. Apparently, they had taken back their wounded.

As I recall my action, I was continually on the move, going from one side of the road to the other. One day when I was going from my squads on the right flank to my squads on the left side of the road, I heard a fire fight up ahead. As I went toward the firing, I heard someone coming through the trees toward me. I dropped and covered the noise with my weapon. From the front lines came Capt. Rusty Mattocks. He had been trooping the line and had participated in a small fire fight. That was the last time I saw Rusty until 1987, when I attended the 38th Armored Infantry Battalion, 7th Armored Division reunion in Pennsylvania.

I was uneasy and couldn't seem to grasp the situation. Sleep didn't come easy. I couldn't show my uneasiness as the men would have picked up on it, but sitting and waiting was hard. Why couldn't we get more troops, more support, so we could attack? Defense is no way to win any battle, but with what we had, we couldn't attack.

[During the day and the night of December 20, the defenders consolidated their positions, while the Germans moved their units around for a final attack against the salient from the north, east, and south. Considerable pressure was put on CCA to the north, but the critical road leading from Becht to Poteau was held. On December 21, two German infantry divisions and the Fuhrer Escort Brigade launched unceasing attacks along the entire front. Infantry, tank, artillery, engineer, reconnaissance, and service troops stood their ground inflicting huge losses on the attacking formations. Five major corps attacks were hurled against CCB in the center until by 2000

the CCB line was penetrated in three places. CCB then withdrew to the high ground west of St. Vith and tied in with CCA to the north and CCB of the 9th Armored Division on the south. On that day, eleven distinct and separate attacks had been made on the entire front, in addition to the constant probing and patrolling.

The schoolhouse in St. Vith had been the command post for the 106th Division and later for Gen. Clarke. On December 18, Clarke moved his command post to Krombach. When the command building received a direct hit by artillery fire on December 20, the 38th AIB moved its CP into the schoolhouse.

Also on December 20, 2nd Lt. Bundy of the 434th Armored Field Artillery Battalion reported to Maj. Boyer as forward observer. That battalion was from VIII Corps Artillery, originally in support of the 106th Infantry Division, and had remained in position and offered their services to the 7th Armored Division. Prior to that the 275th Artillery had the job of supporting the entire 7th AD as there were not enough forward observers for every battalion. On December 19, a liaison officer and two more forward observers arrived and were placed in positions where observation was the best. However, the 38th AIB had to rig up a communication system where messages could be relayed by telephone and radio to the firing batteries. Meanwhile the assault gun platoon under Lt. Boyd and the mortar platoon under Lt. Kinnebrew performed miracles in making up for the shortage of artillery. Boyd's three guns were augmented by a 105 mm howitzer from a tank company and Kinnebrew's platoon manned six 81 mm mortars. Their reactions to targets were almost automatic, and they were issuing fire orders even before a rifle company could call in its mission.

At mid-morning German tanks and armored vehicles (including a captured American one), followed by infantrymen fanned out behind, attacked the 38th AIB area and were met by heavy artillery and mortar fire for over ten minutes which slaughtered the infantry, destroyed four tanks, and forced the attacking armor to turn and flee through Wallerode in the direction of Born.

At mid-afternoon, another attack came. When the Germans had closed to within twenty-five yards of the American lines, bazookas and artillery knocked out the armored vehicles. By placing withering machine gun fire on the burning vehicles, all the German personnel were killed except two SS troopers who were seriously wounded, taken prisoners, and identified as members of the 1st SS Panzer Division.

Then a company-sized unit was seen moving through the woods to the south of the Schonburg road. Some mortar rounds came into the American positions and some automatic rifle fire, but the Germans did not close. They were apparently trying to get the American defenders to disclose their positions, but the fire discipline of the defenders must have been disappointing to the attackers, and they withdrew.

All during that night there was heavy tank and motor movement to the north, northwest, the immediate front, and the south. From map data only, some American artillery was called for, which had some success, for the defenders heard a muffled explosion, followed by a larger one and shortly thereafter a red glow was seen above the trees, which probably meant a hit on an ammunition or gas supply truck.

German losses in the 38th's sector were tallied for December 20 as five half-tracks destroyed, four tanks damaged, and forty-three killed.

All night the 38th could hear the build-up of tanks and other vehicles along its entire perimeter, with an especially heavy concentration of armor in the northwest, which indicated a full-scale attack was imminent. By 1100, a fifteen-minute barrage hit the defenders, and by noon the entire front was locked in combat as the Germans attacked along the Schonburg road. At 1400, the 31st Tank Battalion received a one-hour barrage of heavy artillery fire and an infantry attack by a full regiment.]

December 21

On the fifth day when dawn broke—it had snowed during the night—we knew something was going on. All night we had heard the build-up of tanks and other noises. We knew we were going to be in a fierce fight. Years later when I read the After Action reports I found out where we were, who was with us, and who was against us. But a platoon leader in an on-going operation doesn't know much. His world is what he can see a few yards in front of him.

The German attack started at 1100, not in my area but on our left. Company B of the 38th commanded by Lt. Higgins was getting the brunt of the attack. They had tried Holland's and my area before. This time they really laid it on. I was kept busy checking both areas. There were no casualties. The artillery and "screaming meemies" were away from us.

It wasn't long before we were under the most intense artillery fire imaginable. I was in a foxhole and every time enemy rounds hit the ground I would bounce. Right in the middle of the barrage the radio operator yelled at me, "Lieutenant, the headquarters wants you." I jumped out of the foxhole and ran about twenty-five yards through the barrage to the radio. It was Sgt. Davis at headquarters, "What's going on?" My reply was, "We are receiving a heavy barrage. Enemy is attacking center and on my left." I then ran back to my foxhole with Conover. The savior of the battle was the artillery support and the guts of the riflemen and the machine gunners. The Germans had us plotted but our men had the fortitude to hang in. They were great!

The attack became fiercer all the time. There was no let up— continuous artillery and direct fire from their tanks. About noon the Germans again started their advance on us. First, a barrage of artillery and soon the whole front was attacked by their infantry. This had to be the one attack that must be repulsed. We could see that the enemy had built up their forces and were going to make an all out effort. I was so damned busy I didn't know what was going on anywhere else but in the immediate front of my positions. I knew the other American troops were as fully engaged, but there was no way I could help them, or they us. Our artillery was going out and the German stuff was coming in. We had been in combat almost constantly for five days, with practically no sleep, and no food except for K rations.

The Germans kept coming all day long. Every time they got close, they were stopped by our rifles and machines guns and by bringing our own artillery fire to within fifty yards of our positions. The artillery forward observer, if I remember correctly, was Lt. Shanahan, who did a masterful job saving our lines time after time. He would yell to our troops, "Duck, here it comes just over your heads." The Germans had positioned their machine guns where they could fire at our lines, and we were saved by our artillery knocking them out.

In the late afternoon we had another intense barrage from the Germans. Though the regular artillery does more damage when their shells land, the "screaming meemies" did the most damage to our nerves. The sound of their shells coming was nerve-racking. Everyone would jump into foxholes and then, at times, we would hear the screams of the wounded. So it was screams coming in and screams going out.

The Germans had tried to break through the center of our Task Force position for most of the day. Now it seemed they were going to try the lines directly in front of us on the right. We were again successful in stopping them. Right in the middle of one of the barrages two of my men, Totoni and Marowski, were wondering about mail call. That broke us up for the moment. It reminded me of the last letter I had received from Molly which was still in my pocket—that along with my small New Testament. I don't remember how many times I said the 23rd Psalm. It was my steadying thought.

As the day was coming into darkness, their attack continued. I had trooped the line at every lull. When I saw Lts. Holland and Higgins, they were very much like everyone else—beat! The continual pounding, the loss of people killed and wounded, and the need for fresh troops made us all anxious. But we were still alive. I thought of home, Molly, and the baby during that day and wondered how they were doing. But I couldn't dwell on them too much.

I was proud of my little troop of men. They had guts. I recall the first encounter we had at St. Vith when one of my gunners broke and ran. I had decided at that time to leave him in his job as gunner on one of the machine guns. His name was Ryan. As I walked around the area to see how the men were doing, I came to Ryan. He had been wounded in the arm. I said to him, "Get on back to the medics and take care of the wound." He refused saying, "I'm going to stay and do my job." I then ordered him to go back to the medics. He went but only on the condition the job would be his when he got back. I thought to myself when he departed, that's the last that I'll see of him as the medics will probably send him to the rear. I was fooled. He was back at his gun within a couple of hours, smiling and saying, "Told you, Lieutenant, that I would be back!"

During the lulls, I didn't hear many complaints. For some reason, the men were quiet. No laughter, only serious looks. We constantly had our ears open and our eyes to the front. I know each man was deep in the thoughts of home or some were worrying what was going to happen next. That's where my mind was, and still wondering where in the hell was the support that was supposed to be coming and how much longer did they expect us to hold out?

We had a couple of hours without incoming artillery and mortar rounds. The men were taking stock of themselves, resting in their foxholes, eating anything that was available. Some of the rations were awful. In fact, because of the cold weather, most of the rations were frozen. We didn't want to build any kind of fire because that would bring more artillery in on us—God knows that we had enough of that without asking for more. I remember the cheese in the K rations. It seemed the longer a person chewed it, the larger the wad would get in his mouth. I always kept the cigarettes, chocolate bars, and the crackers out of the K rations. Those I kept in the lining of my overcoat.

The calm didn't last long. The Germans had close support from tanks with assault guns, "screaming meemies," and the yells of the German's NCOs making a bad combination of loud noises. Our troops picked them off as they came in. What saved us was the artillery fire coming from Mike Shanahan's artillery battalion. The Germans retreated again after leaving many dead and wounded.

The next attack was away from my troops. According to reports from Lt. Higgins and Maj. Boyer, the Germans hit hard on our left. The Germans did break through our lines; they kept coming until by mass of numbers they caused our line to yield, but we fought them back. I could hear the explosions of the artillery and the rattle of the small arms fire. We knew they would soon be coming our way if they were successful where they were attacking. But the valorous effort by Higgins, Boyer, and my machine gun sections supporting B Company stopped the Germans again. Soon after that our line was restored.

The line had been held by the actions of some very brave men. Later, one report from B Company was from Glenn Fackler of Company B: "On December 21, I had dug in with my .30 caliber machine gun next to a tree. I had a good field of fire in front of me. As I surveyed the area ahead

I spotted a dug-in German tank in front of my position. It was about 500 yards ahead of me. I crawled back to a friendly tank that was near me and asked for help. The tanker commander said that he didn't want to give away his position. His excuse was: 'Before I could get a round off the German tank could wipe me out.' So I started back to my position. As I was going back, all hell broke loose. An intense combination of German shells started to come in. I didn't get all the way back because our outfit was ordered to withdraw to a new position about a hundred yards back from the front line positions. After the barrage, which caused numerous tree bursts and much havoc, our unit was ordered to return to our first positions. I arrived and saw that the tree that I had been under had taken a direct hit. The top half of it was gone. It had been hit about six feet above the ground and was destroyed. I knew then that the German tank I had seen must have had me in his sights."

That night the Germans attacked again. Fackler and his unit held the line. It was dark, and the men couldn't see the approaching enemy, but they heard them coming. When Fackler started firing his weapons, our machine guns and rifles along the front joined in sweeping the area in front of their positions. We fired at noises and the faint images that we could see. Many Germans were killed. All during the night we heard the moans of the wounded coming from the enemy side. The attack was finally over. The rest of the night everyone was keenly alert.

We were in need of more support of any kind—air, infantry, tank destroyers, or tanks: anything would help. I knew with the enemy's continual build-up and our strength going downhill, we would soon be unable to hold them back. We were in a small area vulnerable on our right, as the support that was supposed to be there didn't exist, and our strength was not enough to keep the enemy from breaking through.

It was dark and dreary and cold. After the Germans to our front had pulled back, I trooped the line again. One of the men from the unit on our left was a runner for the company. He had been sent back to the battalion command post to learn what was going on there. When he arrived, a tank was standing with its motor idling outside the old building. As the runner did not see the battalion commander or any one else, he rapped on the side of the tank. The voice that came back was not speaking in English. What he heard was, "Vas is los?" He left as fast as he could and came back to advise us that there were Germans in the battalion command post.

When I came looking for Sgt. Sicari, I was told he had been back at the company command post. Capt. Mattocks had called him back for a rest from the front lines. What happened to him after that I do not know. He never returned to my platoon. Apparently he departed for the rear with the headquarters unit when they pulled out ahead of Capt. Mattocks and Sgt. Davis.

My troops on the left were OK. Sgt. Curtin's men had taken a beating but were still in good spirits. They were running low on ammunition and food, but that wasn't anything new. I went back to the right side of the road. I was about ready to get some rest when Maj. Boyer and Lt. Higgins came by with Lt. Holland. They had received word of a command decision that had come over the radio: "Break up into small groups and try to get back." It was then that I finally realized the truth: we had been sacrificed. Our small group had held back the Germans long enough to let our forces regroup and build up enough to meet the Germans on more even terms. That hit me in the gut!

Donald P. Boyer, Jr.

This picture was taken in the spring of 1964 when Col. Boyer commanded the 11ᵗʰ Armored Cavalry Regiment.

Many years later, I received Major Boyer's "Personal Report, Narrative Account of Action of 38th Armored Infantry Battalion, 7th Armored Division, Battle of ST. VITH, 17-22 December 1944." The report tells of that day and perhaps gives a larger picture of what went on than what I knew and experienced. It reads:

After 1300 [21 December] I was so heavily embroiled in the fighting within my own sector that I had no further knowledge of the general picture. Despite our standing there and tossing back attack after attack, by 2200 German tanks had blasted their way through the center of the line and were entering St. Vith. Although I didn't know it at the time, the same thing had happened in the North and on the South, and tanks were also entering the town along the Malmedy and Prum roads This cut off those elements of the 38th then East of St. Vith, and those few men who were still alive—dazed from almost 12 hours of continuous pounding by the artillery; rocked by 12 hours of ceaseless attacks by overwhelming forces of infantry, supported by heavy concentrations of *Panther* and *Tiger* tanks; and almost unnerved by 5 days of constant combat with no sleep, little food, and suffering from frost bite—were forced to break up into small groups of 5-10 men each in an attempt to regain friendly lines by infiltration. I use the phrase 'still alive,' for of an estimated 670 men who had manned the line to the right of the Schonburg road in the morning (my force plus B/23), there were only approximately 185 men alive at 2300. The rest were dead or severely wounded.

> 1150: Patrol returned with information that an estimated battalion of infantry was advancing against our positions, 2 companies abreast, astride the Schonburg road.
>
> 1200: Heavy automatic and semiautomatic weapons fire broke out to my left along the front of Foster's and Higgins' companies (A/23 and B/38).
>
> 1200-1315: 'Jerry' kept up an unceasing series of infantry assaults against Foster and Higgins' left platoon, making strong use of *panzerfausts*, but their efforts to break through were unsuccessful. B/87 and Higgins' right platoon were only lightly engaged.

1300: The expected attacks against B/87 and the entire B/38 were launched in force. I estimated the assault troops to consist of 2 battalions of infantry, each battalion attacking on a narrow front with 2 companies abreast.

1345-1510: The 'Krauts' kept boring in; no matter how fast we decimated their assault squads. As fast as we could kick back one assault wave, another would return. It certainly looked as if the Germans were determined that they were coming through, but their spirit alone was not enough to sustain them against the merciless hail of small arms fire which we were hurling at them.

All machine guns were employing swinging traverse and taking a deadly toll. But again and again there was a flare of flame and smoke (the explosion could not be heard because of the general din) as some 'Kraut' got in close enough to heave a grenade into a machine gun crew or to launch a dread *panzerfaust*. (One caliber.50 squad which hitherto had been dishing out a deadly hail of fire all along the front, was hit by a panzerfaust which struck the barrel halfway between the breech and muzzle. The gunner fell forward on the gun with half his face torn off; the loader had his left arm torn off at the shoulder and was practically decapitated; while the gun commander was tossed about 15 feet away from the gun to lie there quite still.)

The men were magnificent, and as long as there were targets, their fire never ceased. Whenever a machine gun was silenced by having its crew killed off, other men leaped from their holes to take over the gun so that its devastating fire could be continued. Artillery: we were using it like mortars, and never before have I seen artillery do so much damage with almost no friendly casualties because of 'shorts.' As fast as Higgins, Holland, or Rogers (new CO of "B" Troop, after Stewart was wounded Tuesday night) called for fire, I relayed the request to Shanahan (FO from 275th, who had reported to me as the noon attack started). In a few, minutes we could hear the shells whistling over our heads.

Frankly, I didn't see how our men could stand up to this pounding without any cessation and no replacements. And always there were more Germans, and more Germans, and then more Germans. Where they were all coming from, I did not know but it looked as if battalion after battalion must have been massed up behind the original assault waves. That's the only way they would be able to keep on attacking, attacking, and re-attacking for better than 1 1/2 hours.

Again and again the 'Jerries' were able to emplace machine gun teams where they could rake our lines, and where it was difficult for us to get at them. Again and again I called on Mike Shanahan for fire to wipe out these guns. Whatever the fire commands, he always relayed them although he knew he was bringing fire down within 50 yards of our men. It was taking a terrific chance but never once did the gunners of the 275th AFA make an incorrect laying! How they did it so accurately while receiving missions from more than 20 different F[forward] O[observers]'s scattered throughout the St. Vith horseshoe was beyond me.

1515: Contact had been broken all along the front, and the Germans had withdrawn. Quickly I dispatched orders to Higgins, Rogers, and Holland to readjust their lines, to redistribute ammunition, and to get their wounded out. How much time we would have I did not know, but I felt that this was only the 'lull before the storm.' Von Rundstedt apparently was making his supreme effort this day to reestablish the counter-offensive's timetable, the timetable which we had done so much to disrupt.

1520: Higgins arrived at my foxhole, and quickly we sketched what had taken place. When he asked for men from the Platoon of F/423 which had been our reserve, I had to tell him that they previously had been used to plug gaps which were torn in A/23's line during the noon attacks. *We had no reserves!*

1545: I heard the 'screaming meemie' batteries go off to our front, and for some reason I 'knew' they were coming in on us. I remember yelling 'Down,' and as we slid into our holes in came the worst hail of steel and screaming metal that I have ever seen or heard. Back and forth, right and left, then back and forth and again right and left across our positions came the crushing, thumping, tearing scream of steel followed by steel. Huge gashes were cut in the logs over our holes, and all around us we could hear the crash and ripping of tree tops and even of trees as the merciless hail of steel swept and lashed through the forest.

Again and again we heard the anguished scream of some man somewhere who had been hit, and yet all we could do was cower in our holes with our backs against the forward walls, hoping that we would not receive a direct hit. It seemed as if our very nerves were being torn out by the roots as the screaming steel crashed around us, coming in with increasing and ever-increasing waves of hideous sounds.

1550-1620: Artillery added its din to the heavy 'screaming meemie' preparation that was being placed upon us, switching back and forth along the front and converging on the center of the line in the vicinity of the SCHONBURG road. After 1600, the preparation definitely concentrated against the areas of B/38 and B/87. This time the main effort was to be through us—they had failed through the center; now they would try the left (Jerry's left, our right).

1619: I could see the German infantry starting to come through the woods, running a few paces, hitting the ground, then getting up to run again. This is what I expected—that they would try to charge into our positions as the barrage was lifted at the last minute and before we could recover from the stunning shock of all the steel they had poured down on us. As I called out 'Heads Up!' and the men poked their heads out of their holes with rifles and machine guns at the ready, almost simultaneously the awful hail of steel was lifted from us and into the woods to our rear.

1620-1700: This attack followed the same pattern as the two earlier ones, except that there was close support from tanks and A[assault] G[guns]. Although we slaughtered the attacking echelons and very few 'Krauts' ever managed to cross the logging road in front of our positions, 'Jerry' kept boring in no matter how much we piled up the dead. Still he could not force a breakthrough. One AG which got within 10 yards of our lines was left a burning hulk with a beautiful deflection 'bazooka' shot through its side armor, and in front of B/38; a *Panther* was destroyed on the logging road when one soldier with a 'bazooka' climbed out of his hole, ran forward and pressing his tube against the fender-line, pulled the trigger, and as he fired, he slumped to the ground dead.

Our stubborn stand, however, was beginning to show signs of weakening; gaps were appearing which we did not have the men to fill. Had it not been for the deadly support of the 275th AFA, I feel certain that the 'Krauts' would have forced a gap somewhere. The deadly massed fire that Shanahan was bringing down was a little bit more than 'Jerry' could stand, and we could hear the screams and cries of the wounded in ever-increasing numbers. By 1705, the impetus of the German drive had been lost, and practically all small arms firing had ceased except for a few rifle shots when some 'Kraut' exposed himself while trying to withdraw.

1715: Mortar fire started clumping into woods around us, and once more we could hear the 'burp-burp-burp' of the 'Jerry' guns as they opened up with assault fire about 150-175 yards in front of us. As they moved in we could hear the guttural voices of their *Feldwebels* as they 'talked it up' among their squads. This assault apparently was to be aimed at Jamiel's Platoon (left platoon, B/38) in an attempt to open up one side of the Schonburg road.

1735: Heavy tank fire could be heard above the small arms fire fight to our left. At about this time Higgins called over the radio with tears in his voice asking where were the T[tank] D[destroyers]? I tried to relay this situation to the Battalion CP, but both the radio and phone hook-ups with the Forward CP were out. I did reach Lt. Col. Riggs through Holland's phone, however, and emphasized that if we did not get TD support to break up this tank attack, I was afraid that some of the *Tigers* would get through.

1805: Jamiel reported that the Tank Section from A/31 which had been covering the Schonburg road had either been knocked out or had withdrawn; that 2 *Panther* tanks were shelling his foxholes systematically, 1 hole after the other, with direct fire.

1850: I called Lt. Col. Fuller through Holland's phone and reported: 'Our lines are still holding. A few Krauts got through, but we'll take care of them. I believe that we can hold through the night, but we must have relief in the morning.'

1905: Higgins and I were preparing to sweat out the night, and I was about to leave him at his CP hole while I checked the line, when 'Jerry' artillery and screaming meemies started coming in again. Once more they started a systematic raking of our entire area, and I knew that before long we would have tanks and infantry on us again. Far to the South (B/23) and to the Northwest (31st Tks and A/38) we could hear the scream of steel, as those positions also were subject to the barrage.

This looked like it, as I told Higgins, and then I directed him to go to the Fwd CP and acquaint them with the desperateness of our situation; that I didn't believe we could hold back a new assault such as this one promised to be; that we needed tank and artillery support; that we needed reinforcements and that we needed them in a hurry!

1935: Jamiel called over the SCR-300 [radio] in a voice so choked with emotion that I could hardly understand him: 'G--D--I--, they've 2 heavy tanks here on the crest, and they're blasting my men out of their holes one at a time! They're all gone, and the same thing has happened on the other side of the road. D--I--, can't you do something to stem 'em?'

Even over the radio I could hear the barking of the '88s, and Jamiel reported that one of the tanks was on the other side of the house in which he was in. Our position was desperate for we had no tanks to counter this slaughter. All we could do was use artillery, and I had little hope of this proving to be more than a nuisance value to *Panthers* or *Tigers*.

1945-1955: The initial concentration was fired by Shanahan, was corrected by an FO with A/23, and then followed by several additional concentrations but they had no affect on the tanks. (During one of the corrected concentrations, the FO with A/23 was killed when he brought the fire in on his own position in an effort to destroy the tanks.)

During one of the earlier attacks, Foster who commanded the tank company, and the other Foster who commanded A/23, were both hit by German artillery or tank fire. The tank captain was killed, and the infantry captain was badly wounded.

> 2000: I could hear heavy tanks clanking and creaking down the Schonburg road, behind the MLR (Main Line of Resistance) and toward the Fwd CP. We shifted machine gun and mortar fire to the road in an attempt to stop the infantry whom we knew would be following the tanks. By now it was quite dark, but I still hoped that if we stopped the infantry, someone would deal with the tanks in the town, and that we might be able to hold through the night. At the same time Shanahan placed all available artillery fires on the Schonburg road from the MLR East.

> 2015-2115: For an hour we kept the Schonburg road under heavy machine gun and bazooka fire. Although 1 Mk VI was destroyed, and 'Jerry' dead lined the ditches on both sides of the road, the 'Krauts' still kept pressing forward to follow their tanks. We were unable to stop all of them, and for the ones that we killed we were paying a terrific price! No machine guns nor bazooka team lasted more than 10-15 minutes, and each gun already had been manned by several or more teams. As soon as one team was destroyed, it was replaced by other men who crawled into position only to be killed in turn a few minutes later. Finally I refused to pay the price any longer and directed 'B' Co to hold up on replacing teams along the road.

> 2200-2300: Higgins and Lt. Col. Riggs came up with essentially the same information: that the Fwd CP had been wiped out; that at least 8 *Panther* or *Tiger* tanks were in town, and that infantry were pouring into St. Vith. Higgins had tried to send a patrol across the road to learn the situation in A/23 and A/38, but the patrol could not make it. He also reported that Jamiel's entire platoon had been wiped out.

Lt. Col. Riggs and I then reported to Brig. Gen. Clarke, using Shanahan's FA FDC net, and asking them to relay: 'Road cut. At least eight heavy tanks and infantry were in town. What are our orders?'

About 45 minutes later, we received the following answer: 'To Riggs or Senior Officer present: Reform; save what vehicles you can; attack to the West through St. Vith; we are forming a new line West of town.'

> 2355: When Gen. Clarke's orders were announced to the assembled Co Commanders (Higgins, Rogers, and Holland), they insisted that their men were not in shape to launch the attack envisaged by Gen. Clarke. I agreed with them, especially when Rogers confirmed through his Maintenance Officer (then in St. Vith) that at least 8-10 heavy tanks were in the town.

The decision was made to 'peel off' to the right, carrying all personal and crew-served weapons. A messenger was dispatched to the Mortar Platoon to destroy their vehicles, but to salvage their mortars and bipods. Holland reported that the Tk Sec originally in support of his company had taken off earlier in the evening, and it was believed that they had regained the town ahead of the German tanks. Boyd's AG Plat we hoped would have been warned by Kennebrew whom we understood had escaped from the Fwd CP before it was overrun, and had gone to the schoolhouse to warn Maj. McDaniel (Battalion Executive Officer). Higgins was to try once more to get word across the road to A/23, so as to tell them what we were doing and to direct them to 'peel off' to the left through A/38, joining the 31st Tk Bn on their Northern flank across the Malmedy road.

Rogers had 5 men severely wounded who could not be moved. These were to be left with an aid man who volunteered to stay with them, and in the morning he would try to surrender himself and them to a German medic. (Personally I was dubious of this arrangement, but there was nothing else we could do.)

Rogers was to order his Maintenance Officer who had 'B' Troop's vehicles in the RR yards in St. Vith to destroy such vehicles as he could not man with a crew, and to attack through the town and regain the lines being formed West of St. Vith.

Higgins and I were to move out immediately, working our way down to the right, informing each Platoon Leader along the way of what we were doing. When we reached Britton's Co, we learned that their right flank had vanished and that the Prum road was cut. According to 1st Lt. G. A. Taylor, who was the senior officer still with the company, the 'Jerries' had been pouring tanks and infantry up the road into St. Vith and Westward towards Krombach for more than 2 hours.

This was the "blackest" news of all, especially since snow had been falling for more than an hour and gave every indication of being almost knee deep by morning. When the column came down the hill, we swung out through the trees on an azimuth of 270. The progress was slow for the forests were thick, the snow was piling deeper and deeper, and the men were experiencing difficulty in keeping up. Of the estimated 150 men with me, over half were wounded in varying degrees, and all of us were suffering from the pounding we had taken all day. Twice we avoided 'Jerry' combat patrols by only a few feet, and as the gray light of dawn began to come up we still were not across the PRUM road. It was then that I issued orders to destroy all but personal weapons, to break up into small groups of 5-10 with a non-com or officer in charge of each group, and to attempt to infiltrate our way to our forces fighting somewhere in the West.

> 22 Dec 44 - Fri: By morning the full extent of the price which the 38th AIB had paid for its stand began to be realized. There were no Assault Gun, nor Mortar, nor Machine Gun Platoons— neither men, nor vehicles, nor weapons. Company's 'A' and 'B' consisted each of the Antitank Platoon plus the company's half-tracks with their drivers. Of the attached troops, the picture was even 'blacker' if such were possible. There was no A/23, and only 1 Platoon from B/23. 'B' Troop had ceased to exist, as had the 2 Provisional Engineer Companies. The only 'bright spot' was at 1200, when A/31 was discovered to be fighting with CCB of the 9th Armored, with whom they had joined forces after fighting their way out of St. Vith.

Throughout the morning various men worked their way back through the lines, but their numbers were pitifully few, and most of them came from A/38 and A/23. By mid-morning a composite armored infantry rifle company had been formed, consisting of approximately 110 men, and had been placed in position on the high ground Northeast of KROMBACH, where they became part of a force under the command of Lt. Col. Erlenbusch of the 31st Tk Bn.

About 90 other men filtered back through the lines, but they had to be evacuated because of wounds and almost complete exhaustion from their struggles to regain the lines. The 38th had done its job, and done it well, but it had paid a price. Those who were left had only the satisfaction that they had exacted a price far more terrific from the troops who had assaulted their positions in vain for 4 days, and who had broken through on the fifth day only after one of the most vicious attacks the 7th Armored Division had ever seen. Dead Germans actually counted totaled 604, and it was to be a rather accurate estimate if we said that they had lost in the neighborhood of 4-5 times as many killed but not counted, and 5-6 times as many wounded.

[One can imagine the physical and mental condition of the troops at this point. Five days of constantly fighting a determined enemy; fatigued men with little sleep or rest and most with wounds; the weather cold, with sleet and snow and rain; bearded men with blank stares, mouths open, drooping eyelids partly covering staring eyes, hungry, concerned with rumors, smelling the odors from the dead, the gunpowder, fuel, and burned trees and vegetation. Then, after all they had done, to get orders to quit and get back as best they could!]

Maj. Boyer gave me the order to destroy our heavy machine guns. So I gave the men the word. He thought we could salvage my platoon along with Higgins' men. My platoon was to follow Higgins' troops. Higgins and I were to go with Major Boyer and to join him on the point to see if we could find our way back to our lines. That is when I found out we were many kilometers ahead of our lines. All of our support troops had pulled out and left us to hold for them while they moved to the rear.

I called Sgts Curtin, Simeneaux, and Totoni and told them the plan. Destroy machine guns and follow us. We leaders on the point started going to our right. Maybe we could find the support that was supposed to be there. Where we were going, I didn't know, but I supposed that Boyer knew. The snow was coming down. We kept walking through the woods. It was so dark we almost had to hold hands. We continued through the forest. At a halt, I asked Conover to go back along the line of troops we were leading and see how the platoon was doing. When he didn't return I went back and searched. I couldn't yell as the

Germans were nearby. After a while I gave up and returned. As I look back on the whole operation, the decision which caused me to leave my platoon gave me the worst feeling ever. But I was following orders. I should have asked permission to stay with my men, but I thought the platoon would and could keep up with the leading officers. Apparently, they lost sight of the leading troops, were worn out, and were too tired to keep up.

[At 0200 on December 22, the line between CCA and CCB was severed. The line was pulled back and by dusk, contact with CCBs of the 7th and 9th Armored Divisions had been reestablished. Contact with CCA to the north was not regained, however. On December 22, the 9th Panzer Division from Dietrich's II Panzer Corps was hurled into the battle, and pressure continued to increase along the entire front. By this time the position of the defenders had become untenable. General Hasbrouck sent a message to the corps commander, General Ridgeway, that unless reinforcements were forthcoming immediately, "there will be no more 7th Armored Division." Later that day the following message was sent by Field Marshall Montgomery: "You have accomplished your mission—a mission well done. It is time to withdraw." The withdrawal involved breaking contact and using a secondary road west from Vielsam. On December 23, after continuous fighting for six days, the 7th Armored Division and its attached units broke contact and withdrew behind the 82d Airborne Division and took up positions in the defense of Manhay, which was astride the only primary road leading due north from the north flank of the German salient.]

We walked until dawn and then rested in the forest. We could hear and see the enemy fifty yards below us. The road was filled with a German artillery unit. Now, what to do? After a short conference, we decided to wait and see what the German action was going to be. Could we get around them? Should we try to wait until dark and see what we could do then? So we hid from the Germans to our front.

It wasn't long before a squad of Germans came into view from the rear. I was in plain view of them. I had positioned myself behind a tree that was hiding me from the Germans to our front. As I tried to move around to the other side of the tree, a rock came loose. The Germans heard the noise. There, twenty yards away was a squad of Germans aiming their guns at us. Lt. Higgins, who was thirty yards away from me, took off but Maj. Boyer and I were dead ducks. The Germans had yelled to troops on the road who set up their machine guns, aiming at us from below. So with great reluctance we stood.

Maj. Boyer and I were lucky. Our group was so far ahead of our own lines that we were captured by a German artillery unit. They were getting their guns ready to go down the road to get into position closer to their front lines. I remembered the stories that we heard of our troops being lined up and killed after being captured. Artillery units weren't out in front like the infantry soldiers who were fighting and watching their buddies being slaughtered, so they usually didn't develop the hatred that front line troops do for the opposing forces. Emotions run pretty high when you see your buddies go down. There were many prisoners on both sides that were killed after surrendering under such circumstances. So we were probably very fortunate to be caught by that artillery unit.

We were frisked and steered to the road. I was very down in spirits. Never had a group of men fought so hard and lost. Not because of their efforts, but failed because of unlucky circumstances.

If I could speak to the men in my platoon today—Sgts Secari, Curtin, Simeneaux, Totoni, and Corporals and Pvts Bartz, Thompson, Marowski, Dotson, and Ryan, and, of course, Conover, Cox, our driver, and others whose names I have forgotten—I would say to them, "You were the bravest group of men I have ever known or read about." I would say the same thing to Lt. Holland and his engineers. What I learned about the American soldier (except for a few) is that he will fight, and he will stand. At St. Vith, and I am sure throughout the Battle of Europe, the infantry soldier was usually thrown into battle not knowing where he was or knowing anything about the enemy. With leadership and a given purpose, he fought and fought well. And I think I know the one big reason he fights so well in combat is that he will not allow himself to let his buddies down. The bond between the men is difficult to describe, but it is there.

In our case at St. Vith, I still wonder what happened to the men who had the responsibility for the area before we got there. Where did they go? How could a few stand so well, and a whole division could not handle the same forces that we encountered? The American soldiers who held fast in the Battle of the Bulge, whether at Bastogne, St Vith, or any of the other great stands, were heroes. And I believe if it had not been for the great effort of the men at St. Vith, there would not have been a stand at Bastogne.

I wonder, too, about the men and officers who broke and ran, so full of fear they could not even try. What do they do with their minds and consciences when they keep bringing back scenes of where they broke and ran? They must be ashamed. Are they able to forgive themselves?

A letter from Capt. Carl K. "Rusty" Mattocks I received long after the war ended told what had happened to him at the time we were captured:

> My first indication of a real problem was when Lt. Hugh Boyd, our forward observer of the Assault Guns, called on his radio and whispered he thought there were Germans in the house that he was in. My instructions to him were, "Do what you have to do."
>
> Shortly thereafter a Panther tank crested the hill, firing high velocity shells flares destroying the four Sherman Tanks that were located in the valley below. They did not bother any of the small houses on the right of St. Vith in which our battalion headquarters had been located. Soon thereafter they fired directly into our 81 mm Mortar position and also my old CP on the east side of the town. Thankfully I had moved my people out of there when the action started and no one was injured.
>
> The Germans were swarming over the area and I could hear the German non-coms barking out orders. Those were the busiest times of my life. I tried to call you. And it was then that I got the orders from Major McDaniels to get on the "Chattanooga Choo Choo" and head west out of St. Vith. I sent runners out to all the Platoons instructing them to head west following the railroad but I believe that all the runners were either captured or killed.
>
> Following the orders of Major McDaniels, I took my small group south of the town to a hill where the assault guns were emplaced. They had been positioned incorrectly so that we

could not get them out of their present position. They had no "Route of Withdrawal." So I gave the order to "spike them."

I then took the men from the guns and my headquarters group down the reverse slope to the railroad leading to Cromback where General Clarke had installed Battle Police to pick up stragglers. Cromback is about four kilometers southwest of St. Vith. There we were directed to set up a road block utilizing twelve stragglers of Americans and an abandoned 57 mm antitank weapon. We did and a short time later a German tank came around the bend and in one shot wiped out the gun and all the men. One of the men killed was a man you knew, Shorty Masterson.

Next they came at us with tanks and infantry. Major McDaniels wanted to surrender, but First Sergeant Davis and I said, "No thanks." With us all during the night was a woman with a baby girl. She would be safe in either way as long as she could avoid the shells. We soon had to leave her and I have wondered about her ever since. There was no way we could have helped her. As she was a native we were sure that she would be okay. We soon left that building.

About 1 p.m., two Germans came into what was left of our CP. They were looking to loot our dead soldiers. One flashed a light on Sgt. Vaughn. Vaughn killed him with his carbine. The other one ran out yelling "Americans." I shot him with a burst of my sub-machine gun. He fell on the snow covered road and for the next three hours he called on us to surrender or to get him a "Doktor."

I kept on trying to contact anyone who could give me any information and/or directions. But it was a hopeless task. Finally I was able to make contact with some one from the 31st Tank Battalion. The CO recognized me by my nickname "Rusty." He knew that I was one of "Fuller's Boys." He suggested that I go on to the north and west. Sgt. Davis and I decided to start out at the crack of dawn.

The temperature dropped and we were bitterly cold. The engineers had left some mines outside of one of the buildings and we felt we might place then in the snow near the man who we had felled. He was still alive but it wouldn't be long as he was getting cold and was still asking for the "Docktor." We smashed his weapon and threw the ammo into the snow. "We had one more little fracas when Tomko, the mail clerk, ran into a German. The German missed and Tomko hit him so that was the end of the German.

The next morning I gathered my few men together and we traveled west using the railroad as a guide. As we were about to turn north to Hinderhausen, I saw a dim figure running along a nearby fence. I drew down on him but at the last minute I saw that it was your driver Cox. Somehow he had made it back.

We finally made it back to Hinderhausen but not until I had a real Donnybrook with our own 87th Recon. Bn. They wondered if we were Americans. When I cut loose with some good old American swear words they finally believed that we could come toward them.

Well, that is the story about what was happening to us while you were trying to get back. We were lucky and you were not. There was so much going on and so much confusion that I know that you people on the front lines wondered why you didn't hear from the troops at the headquarters.

Rusty

In September 1997, I received a copy of some of the Morning Reports for Headquarters Company, 38th Armored Infantry Battalion, for the period December 18 to 28, 1944, while stationed at St. Vith. Morning Reports were the means the Army used to keep track of each man and the company-sized unit to which he was assigned. On December 18 the strength data showed one captain, two first lieutenants, two second lieutenants, 127 enlisted men present and two absent. On that day two privates (Girtie A. Fountain and Frank B. Murawski) were reported as going from duty to hospital as battle casualties. On December 20, Pvt. Paul H. Ryan was reported wounded. On December 21, 2nd Lt. John P. Marion and Sgt. Ralph B. Roush went from duty to 56th General Hospital with battle wounds. Entries for December 28 showed a strength of one captain, one first lieutenant, and 67 enlisted men. The following names were entered as "From Duty to Missing in Action as of 22 Dec 44:"

Hugh K. Boyd1st Lt.
Robert E. P. Moranda2d Lt.
Richard K. BatesT/Sgt
Howard L. HeacockT/Sgt
Jay P. MoserT/Sgt
Andrew F. FergusonS/Sgt
Rosco PiganellS/Sgt
Joseph W. RussellS/Sgt
Lionel A. SimoneauxS/Sgt
George A. VincentS/Sgt
Herbert E. BrownSgt
Joseph M. BrzezowskiSgt
Herbert G. BurtonSgt
Thomas H. Cooke, Jr.Sgt
Edward J. CurtinSgt
Maurice D. GalatasSgt
Robert KarnesSgt
Paul G. MashburnSgt
Howard W. McCordSgt
Eugene A. SkillernSgt
James TotoniSgt
Eugene AdamsTec 4
Richard J. BasnerCpl
Woodrow I. HudspethCpl
Donald C. LambethCpl
Cletus H. PhillipsCpl
Vergil A. RobbinsCpl
Edward C. WehlingCpl
William W. KempTec 5
J. B. WhiteTec 5
Joe D. AldrichPfc
Earl E. BarbamPfc
Frank BartzPfc
Maurice W. ConoverPfc
Alfred FalterPfc

William FischerPfc
David B. GardnerPfc
Paul P. HallmanPfc
Thomas E. Jenkins, Jr.Pfc
Orval D. LunsfordPfc
John E. MastersonPfc
Robert F. SpringerPfc
Ozie C. AlexanderPvt
Ralph D. AllenPvt
Anthony BavusoPvt
Robert E. BiddlePvt
Florentino CarrilloPvt
Lonnis C. CatoePvt
Clair D. CookPvt
Thomas B. CooperPvt
Isaac H. DotsonPvt
John W. GilesPvt
Samuel A. Gromis Pvt
Lewis T. MashishneckPvt
Watson PettyPvt
Doyle J. RossPvt
Paul H. RyanPvt
Leo T. SizemorePvt
Richard A. WaltersPvt
Clinton G. WalkerPvt
Wayne W. WolfePvt

When I read about or see the pictures of the Battle of the Bulge, it always seems that the main reason for the losses was very poor leadership displayed by the field grade officers from the colonels down through the major ranks. They were the ones who broke and ran. They were the ones who surrendered whole large units without as much as a shot fired at the enemy. They were the ones I saw fleeing down the road four and five to a command car. Where were their troops? Did they leave them? Or was it fear that broke them? I cannot say that about my immediate commanders. They were with us all the way. One got so sick that he had to leave, but he left a great operations officer to take his place.

Another reason for the losses was that the high command didn't believe what they heard from the front: that there was a big build-up in front of our lines. The Intelligence people ignored the reports. They thought the Germans were finished, and all they had to do was to make points with each other through their Public Relations Departments. I am sure that if they were honest, they would say that they had made some mistakes. I have always been amazed at the generals and their public relations. When pictures are taken showing the general in action, the action is in a safe place.

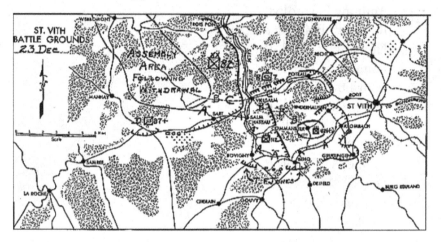

Sketch showing situation 23 December 1944

When I hear about the great work of General Patton, I smile a bit. Sure, he got to the general scene in a hurry, but it took him more than four days to get up the road ten miles from Bastogne. During that time, thousands of GI's were slogging their way back to where our troops had been. My hat is off to the men at Bastogne, for in that battle there were also heroes, especially among the engineer troops, who held long enough so that paratroopers could get to the town.

Finally, we who were there wondered all through our ordeal where in the hell were our planes? It seemed to us there surely were a few hours of daylight or breaks in the cloud cover where our planes could at least drop some bombs on the enemy supply lines, which must have been long and full of vehicles and personnel. But, no. Not one of our planes flew over. But the Germans did.

After the war ended and I was separated from the Army, I wrote to Capt. Frederickson, our battalion intelligence officer, and he responded telling me what had happened after my capture. His letter follows:

Dessau, Germany

2 June '45

Dear Bob, you ol' piano hammering bugger,

Was I glad to hear from you and more pleased you wrote to me. First, congrats in escaping from St. Vith and the rest of it. Sorry to hear of Boyer's illness, but further sorry that we have never heard since from him. You're right in Higgins, a swell unappreciated officer. Glad for Boyd's escape also.

Fuller became exhausted on the twenty-first, was evacuated by ambulance and taken to a hospital. He returned on the 24th after we had withdrawn back to Harze. On the 24th we were ordered back to stop the Jerries at Grandmenile and Manhey. We did and were relieved by the 75th Inf and Third Arm'd who came up the other way. Fuller and Gen. Clarke did not hit it off too well and Fuller was transferred on Jan 2nd to Army Hdqs. We pulled back to Verviers for refitting and reinforcements. "On the 18th of January we started our comeback around Born, and then took Hunningen. On the 21-22 of January retook St. Vith, on the 24th took Wallerode, where Mattocks was shot in the stomach. He was evacuated to England and the last I heard he was O.K. In February we started on the Siegfried line taking Strauch, Steckenborn and helping the 78th Inf on the Schmidt dam deal.

After, we pushed to the Rhine hitting it at Bad Godesburg. In March, about the 23rd or 24th we started our drive across the Rhine, spearheading the First Army's drive to Marlborough, Limburg and the Erft dams. Then we doubled back and cleaned out the Ruhr pocket. On the 16 of April four generals and 21,000 men surrendered to the 7th Arm'd Div; in fact on the morning of the 16th our column began its push and attack. At 0645 a German car bearing a white flag met Lt. Col. Griffin our Bn Commander, and offered terms. Five hours later the surrender became effective. After that we [were] sent to the

British Second Army for the push north of the Elbe with the 82nd Airborne. On May 3rd they began to surrender en mass. For two days they filled the roads, thousands of them. We are now temporarily stationed at Dessau, Halle and close to Leipzieg.

Carmen, you old son of a gun (see how excited I am). I also heard from Capt. Emmons who is recovering in the States. Kinnebrew is Hdq Co Commander, Corbin A Co., Meades C Co. Lots of luck.

"Curly" Freddy

Another letter from him dated August 17, 1945 from Liebenstadt, Germany, gave me additional information about some of my associates and troops:

Hello Bob,

Glad to hear from you.

First—Nick is OK, he's with us. All of your M G Platoon are accounted for except Conover. All others have been heard from. First Sgt Davis got hit on April 14th and was evac to England.

Second, all vehicles of Hq. Co. were lost but two jeeps.

Third—you said Capt Ansley, you meant Capt Anstey didn't you. He got most of his men out, in fact all but a couple. He was wounded in the leg on the retake of St. Vith two days before Carl [Mattocks] got it. I took Carl back to the medics. He was nearly frozen and it was a long way.

Yep, I remember Overloon. Some fun eh kid. But I remember one year ago today more. It was then those kind little fellows had me for 3 days behind their lines training on me in the use of M. Gun grazing, point blank and tracking fire. Gosh how I ever got out I'll never be able to say. At night the rascals threw up flares and tried to find me. Gosh I wasn't a chow-hound then for I didn't eat for 2 1/2 days (prices too high, Germans asking too much).

By the way, I recommended you for the Belglum Award for the action at St. Vith. In the course of several months you should receive it. I didn't know of any person more worthy. I spoke to Major McDaniel and he concurred.

We have but 450 men left and 14 officers. We don't know when we shall be sent back."

Lub & Tisse

Olga and Freddie

Lt. Higgins received a letter from Don Boyer dated October 3, 1945, which he shared with me. It brought us up to date about what happened to some of the troops:

Dear Higgins,

This is a far cry from the last time we were together in that glass factory near Limburg, isn't it. Certainly we are much happier and more comfortable than we were then. When I learned through a letter of Boyd's to my Mother, that you, he, Moranda, Shanahan, and the others had come through OK — well, I cannot describe how relieved I felt.

As for myself, I seem to have spent the better part of the summer in Walter Reed General Hospital in Washington, getting over a severe attack of yellow jaundice. This time I believe the cure has taken, and since I came home on Friday I have felt better than at any time since we were captured. True I am listed for temporary limited service until February, but I am looking forward to receiving orders to a new assignment starting about the 23rd of this month. While it may not be troop duty until after a final check-up in February, I am looking forward to getting back to work—even if it will be a desk job for a few months.

Capt. Anstey was a patient at Walter Reed this summer, but has been up and around most of the time. He was wounded in the leg when the battalion went back into St. Vith in January. You wouldn't know it to see him, however, for only occasionally does he limp. He does have several mortar fragments in his chest, and he probably will be retired for physical disability.

Anstey tells me that Rusty Mattocks was made CO of "B" Company after St. Vith, and that he rebuilt and reorganized it into the fighting outfit it was before it got hurt so badly. Higgins, I don't exactly know how to say it — but you and your men did a super-human job there at St. Vith, and I couldn't have asked to fight alongside finer men and better soldiers. And one of the reasons that the men did the epic job that they did was the example that you set for them. I would be proud to have you with me anytime, anywhere!

I have had some correspondence with the battalion trying to learn if certain men had received awards or not. Sgt. Revels, I feel is deserving of the Silver Star. Two other men whom I feel are deserving of awards are T/Sgt. George and S/Sgt. Hogan. These men are recorded as K[illed] I[n] A[ction] on Monday, 18 December 1944, and no posthumous awards. They were killed in the attack that morning when the center platoon gave way, and I seem to remember your telling me they were killed in an attempt to close the gap in the line.

Aerial photograph of St. Vith taken after its capture by the German 5ᵗʰ Panzer Army and aerial bombing by Allied air forces in late December 1944

By the way, can you shed any light on the identification of "Frenchy?" I think he was your runner whom I took over, although he may have been Capt. Greene's. Along this line, do you remember the name of a radio operator from either yours or Van's platoon who took over and operated my SCR-300?… He was of medium height, wore steel framed glasses, and could not have been more than 20 or 21-years old, and was either a pvt or pfc. He was with me when my group of 5 was captured, and I would like to get in touch with him.

Rusty was wounded in January and has since been evacuated to the States. Junie East was evacuated for combat exhaustion in January, and then later was with a reinforcement depot near Marseilles. Kinnebrew is a captain, commanding HQ Co, while Newman has been transferred to the 1st Armored Division, 14th AIB, as part of the Army of Occupation.

You may be interested to know that Freddie [Capt Frederickson] also writes that Jamiel was with the battalion until about a week before he wrote me. I imagine he went down the hill to report the situation when those tanks started shelling his platoon's position that night, and that is how we didn't find him when we planned to pull out. I am glad that he was able to make it.

Here is one you may not know. When I reached Oflag XIII-B at Hammelburg, Germany, late in February, who should be the first one to greet me but Capt. Greene. When the first firing started that Monday morning, 18 December, he heard a machine gun firing in the woods on the other side of the trail behind which the company was dug in. He thought it was one of "B" Company's guns and ran across the trail to stop them from firing so as not to give away the position. The rest you can guess, he ran smack into a German squad and became a prisoner. He was taken to the rear, and he says that Von Rundstedt had his stuff parked almost bumper to bumper back along the road to Schonburg — that the Germans were expecting to move on that day, and that they were certainly surprised when they didn't get through. Seems that they took a little of the exasperation out on him when he wouldn't tell them what was holding them up. He is OK, though, and happened to go home on the same train that Colonel Fuller did this past June.

That about exhausts the news.

With best wishes for you and your family, I am

Very sincerely,

Don Boyer

St. Vith as it looked when Bob made his return visit many years after the war

In 1975, I returned to St. Vith. I was on a trip through Europe with my sister Maye, my brother Bill, and his wife Jeannette. One stop that we made was at St Vith. As we passed through the small towns before arriving at St. Vith, I became very nervous and upset. I remembered the hassle we had trying to get to the front. I was still upset that everyone was running away and we had to go forward to save them from themselves. To this day I do not understand why the return bothered me so much, but it did. The town was repaired and all the stores and homes were occupied. We got out and I wandered about for a short time. I went into a building that was serving drinks and looked around. For some reason I was not comfortable, so we left. We left by the road that took us past the small building where I met with the commanders in charge and where I met with Lt. Holland. I noted the road through the woods to the front lines, but I didn't take the walk. Maybe I should have, but I was too emotional.

[What did the heroic defense of St. Vith accomplish? Why is it considered the turning point in the Battle of the Bulge? First, the six- day delay it caused in the German timetable was fatal to the entire German plan, for it gave the Allies, initially completely surprised, time to rally, regroup, and attack. Second, the defense caused the immobilization of truck and rail

201

columns east of St. Vith, which disrupted the supply to the Fifth and Sixth Panzer Armies and slowed their movements because of the lack of gasoline and ammunition. Third, German reserves of both the Fifth and Sixth Panzer Armies were committed to the final assaults on St. Vith and thus could not proceed with the advancing troops. Fourth, the weather cleared immediately after St. Vith was taken and the supply routes were cleared, so Allied Air could decimate the supply columns by air strikes and St. Vith itself was made impassable by massive bombardments. And lastly, it prevented General Manteuffel from going to the aid of General Dietrich's surrounded 1st Panzer Division and reopening the northern penetration, thus preventing the quick encirclement of the 2nd and 99th American Divisions holding the northern shoulder at Monshau. Dietrich had to detour his second wave around the horseshoe at St. Vith to exploit the gap created by the Fifth Panzer Army, one division of which was used at St. Vith and another bogged down in the traffic jam to the west.

After the war, General Manteuffel stated: "I wanted to have St. Vith on December 17. Although I had expected Bastogne to be defended, I did not think that the Americans would be able to defend St. Vith. This unexpected defense was one of the outstanding achievements of the (Allied) campaign... The devotion of the American soldiers and their courageous defense of St. Vith introduced the final phase of the defeat of the German Army in Western Europe; the subsequent counter American offensive brought about the ultimate defeat of these German forces in the west...Morale factors are all-decisive, for battles are won in the hearts of men. Therefore, the dramatic weeks of December 1944 occupy an important role when the history of the U.S. Army is being written. The courage of the men and the command of the troops--especially of Combat Command B of the 7th Armored Division in action around St. Vith was, from the German viewpoint, of the highest order."

And Prime Minister Winston Churchill wrote to President Franklin Roosevelt that the 7th Armored and the 1st and 99th Divisions had performed "the highest acts of soldierly devotion at heavy personal sacrifice."]

Prisoner of War

Taken Prisoner

I sat on a rock wall and waited to see what they were going to do with Maj. Boyer and me. Soon they took us to a nearby house where we stayed until we were joined by thirty U.S. solders. We were marched through St. Vith, the town we had been defending. As I walked down the road, I saw my half-track being driven by a German *soldat*. I knew our command post had been overrun. I wondered what had happened to Col. Riggs and others at the forward command post. I did not have to wait long to find out, for Col Riggs and several others soon joined us.

I remember thinking to myself, "I have to get back. No one is going to stop me from seeing my family again. Molly and the rest of the family will be sending prayers to God to watch over me. What would happen to them if I didn't survive or return? Look for opportunities to escape. I can't let my family down. Could I ever face my brothers again if I didn't at least try? So first to live, and next to escape, but play it cool and see what next happens and don't be foolish. I don't know where we are or the direction to go. Cool it for now.

They marched us on to Mannheim where we spent the night. That night I had the first cooked food I had had for six days: three small cold, cooked potatoes. And those came at midnight.

The first day on our POW march, our bombers came over and seeing us they dropped bombs. We dove for ditches and any cover. But many of us asked the question, "Where in the hell have you been?" For days we requested, pleaded, begged for air support. Not one of ours came over. And yet the Germans used their aircraft. We were not very happy about the lack of air support. In fact, if you ask anyone who was at the defense of St. Vith what they thought about it, they always came back, "We were sacrificed!" A few saved many. Perhaps that was worth it all to win the war—but it is tough on the men that were sent up and left to be sacrificed. No one came to our support.

On December 24, we were marched to Prum. But the aircraft, ours, had destroyed the town so on we went to another town, Gerolstein. We made about forty-five kilometers during the day. We had to drag some of our men who could barely walk. They were exhausted, but by encouragement and assistance all kept going. Maj. Boyer was becoming weaker all the time with dysentery, but he carried on. The Germans placed us in an old building that night. We were exhausted, tired, and hungry, but we didn't receive any food. The civilians snarled at us and apparently wanted to attack us, but our guards kept them away.

December 25. We stumbled along for another day and ducked bombs from our planes again several times. The planes weren't after us but mainly roads and buildings, and we happened to be on roads. Surprising as it may seem we, the POWs, knew the war was soon coming to an end. The Germans had exposed most of their reserves of equipment and men on the push through the Ardennes. Now they were in the open and extended. We knew if we could survive for a time we probably would soon be freed.

That night was the first time that we were interrogated. I was called into the anteroom of a schoolhouse where they had placed us. A captain (*Hauptman*), a lieutenant, plus a guard or two were the interrogators.

I reported, "Lieutenant Robert Moranda. Serial number 01326108." They asked, looking at the patch on my shoulder, which unit I was with. I again gave the speech, "My name is Lieutenant Robert Moranda, 01326108. According to the Geneva Convention that is all I can report to you." When the *Hauptman* saw the crossed rifles of the 2nd Lieutenant Infantry on my collar, he knew that we in the infantry never knew anything of the big picture, that we only knew our assigned mission. The German *Hauptman* laughed, said to the interrogator, "A second lieutenant infantry, Ha! He could only see a few yards in any direction." He laughed and dismissed me. When I got back our men wished to know what they asked. I told them. From then on the interrogation went rapidly. Their replies were all the same, that they were in the infantry.

That night a few Psalms were recited and a few Christmas carols were mumbled, mostly as a prayer, not a celebration. "Silent Night" was sung softly and with great feeling. I heard the German guards singing along with us, vocalizing their words in German.

At dusk one of the German *soldats* came around to each one of us. He had an open can of molasses. We put out a filthy hand and he dipped a spoonful of molasses into our palm. That was our Christmas meal.

On this Christmas night one of the officers in our group told me of his capture. He was the payroll officer for his outfit. When he saw he would be soon captured, he got out of his vehicle and buried the money. He didn't have much time so he didn't get the money buried very deep. Now he wondered whether the Germans would find the money, or what would happen to the money and how long would it be there. He said when he got released he would try to find the spot again. He was quite worried about his problem. When he was released would the U.S. officers believe his story, especially if he could not find the place again? The only cheer I could give him was, "First you must survive. After that then worry. But I'm sure the Army would believe you. They certainly know of the confusion going on then."

December 26. Maj. Boyer was in bad shape. He had dysentery so bad he could barely walk. But with a lot of guts and help from others he made it to the next stop. There we were joined by another large group of American men and officers from other U.S. divisions, even two Air Corps pilots who had been shot down. We marched to a small town where we were again placed in a school building. We had covered another twenty-five kilometers. Again no food.

December 27. This was one of our worst days. It was bitter cold. We had to continually move to keep warm. We were going cross-country, plowing through snow. We had to stand for about two hours while our guards ate, rested, and asked for directions. Finally we moved along slowly for another ten kilometers to a large warehouse in Mayer, Germany. At midnight the guards woke us and handed each POW eight small boiled potatoes. It was the first food for a couple of days, so we ate them slowly.

December 28. Maj. Boyer was taken away by the Germans. He was very sick. That was the last we saw of him, and as he left I said a silent prayer for him and all the rest of us. The troops were in bad shape with frostbite, pneumonia, coughing. No treatment was available, so all we could do was help each other along. We were exhausted, mainly because of lack of food, not much water, and no rest. Tempers became shorter all the time. We went about twenty kilometers where they placed us in another old building with no heat. But body heat from the group helped. At night we would sleep in the "spoons" position. My group was Lts. Boyd, Justad, Higgins, and Tate.

Boyd was very religious, and read his Bible at every opportunity. He was from Louisiana. Justad was from South Dakota, a farm boy and a great kid, who had never been out of his state before the war. Higgins, a brave and quiet man, had assumed command of our B Company at St. Vith. He was forced to when, during the first battle, his commanding officer disappeared. Tate was a youngster from Texas. That night we received a Red Cross parcel to split ten ways, and it was well-received. Boyd gave me his cigarettes, which made Tate unhappy. When people are worn out, hungry, and tired, sharing becomes a problem. At times a cigarette can start an argument, so I shared with Tate, too. I had made it a practice to stuff the cigarettes and chocolate into the lining of my overcoat. Those cigarettes and chocolate bars came in handy for a short time. I don't know how much weight we had lost by then, but my pants were much looser.

December 29. We were out early and crossed the Rhine north of Koblenz near Neuwied before noon. We were all surprised at the width of the river—it was quite a barrier to cross.

On this day I was spit on as we were walking through the streets. The sight of so many POWs was news to the German population. The civilians were on the sides of the streets as we proceeded. One man spat at me. It didn't hit me, but the hate in his eyes and his clenched fist showed me he had little love in his heart for us.

Only a few blocks after that a pretty lady forged out into the street and pressed a coin into my hand, a silver coin. I don't remember the amount, but as she pressed the coin in my hand she said, "God bless you." I wish I could have known her name or how to contact her after the war. So in one minute I was hated and the next minute blessed.

That day we had our first hot food—potato soup. The warmth of the soup and the amount, a whole cup full, made a lot of men sick. I was sick for only a few minutes. Fortunately, the hall where we were placed had a toilet—with toilet paper. So after squirting out the soup I was able to clean myself. I was lucky to be sick at a place where I could relieve myself. All night we could hear the men up-chucking or rushing to the toilet. We stayed that night in that large hall. It looked like a Nazi headquarters with all the German Swastika flags draped around. I wondered if Hitler had ever been in this hall.

December 30. A light day. We were marched about twelve kilometers to a glass factory, where we had to wait for a train. The building had a high ceiling. The roof either leaked or the bodies of the many POWs caused enough warmth to melt the ice on the ceiling glass. It was very cold outside. At this place I met the first men from other countries being used as slave labor. Two Poles were assigned to keep the slit trenches (outside latrines) in order. I tried to communicate with them but was not successful. They acted like zombies. The light in their eyes was gone. They mumbled and sort of dragged themselves along.

On New Year's Day we had a feast. All we needed was table cloths and candles. We each got one-sixth of a loaf of bread, one small slice of cheese, and a patty of butter. We should have dressed for dinner. We were happy to get that much food.

Our daily routine was simple. We did anything to keep warm. Many men were still ill with dysentery and respiratory forms of sickness. It was so cold, the lion's share of the time we spent huddled together to keep warm. I did some exercising mainly to keep warm, but for most of the time we rested, waited, and saved our energy.

January 3 to 6. We were loaded into a boxcar, forty men in each car. There was no sanitary facility. We received a Red Cross package, six men to a package. Again Boyd gave me his cigarettes. We didn't move for the first day but sat in the railroad yards. I remember the fear I had: would the Allied aircraft bomb and strafe our cars? All the newsreels I saw before coming overseas to the war zone showed our planes bombing and putting the railroads out of action.

After pounding on the door and getting the Germans to understand, we got them to bring us a small barrel into our car where we could relieve ourselves. Did you ever take a crap with thirty-nine men watching and complaining? I was lucky as my position was near the door. The cars had many cracks especially near the doors so we who were near the openings had some relief from the odors. On the third day, we were fed a soup of potatoes and oatmeal. We needed the food as the men were getting weaker by the hour. We would feel the train move for a time and then sit on the side tracks. We were not a high priority. We could hear trains passing us going in both directions.

Not much talking went on in the boxcar. Talking took energy. We had some very sick people. I heard one of our men saying to another, "If so- and-so dies, we won't say anything to the guards. We can then share his food." That was soon stopped as the rest of the men in the boxcar came down on the two. I'm pleased to say the sick man survived.

Molly wrote a letter at this time which was returned to her marked "Missing, verified by J.M. Burford." I read it when I returned:

Jan 5, 1945

My Darling,

Gee I sure hope I get a letter tomorrow because I didn't get one today and I sure miss your chats with me.

Today we took George to the bus. He left at 11:00 and I felt so sorry for Nancy because I know how she felt. This darn war is always making someone feel bad.

In the afternoon we drove around the beaches and Nancy enjoyed seeing the ocean. We then went to Port Hueneme and had coffee with the gang. Clara [Barr], Bill Woodard (who has a new granddaughter), Glen Dewar, Clyde [Welch], Marie [my aunt], Nancy, Nona, Tomilyn and me. While we were there Billy Van Delinder came driving up in a huge, big, black, shining Buick convertible. He is a pilot in the Air Corps of B24's—a 2nd Lt. and he looked very nice. He sure is a big fellow. He is married now and has a two weeks old baby daughter.

Nona said to tell you that John Fitzgerald [I grew up with John during my teenage years] was commander of a submarine that went down, may still be alive as some of the men off his sub have been picked up. I don't know the fellow but Nona said you did.

You know what? We have a mouse in our pantry of all things! He runs around at nights and has a merry old time. And you know how scared I am of mice, well if I even hear a little noise I run back out the pantry door. The other night he strolled up the hall and looked at us when we were all in the living room. What a character. Today we bought three traps, we'll get him good!

Nancy is sort of expecting George to call her either tonight or tomorrow sometime. He is great on phone calls, she says.

Tomilyn was sure sleeping tonight, she runs around and plays so much when we are down at the office [my Mother's, who was Clerk for the Justice of the Peace, a job she continued after Dad died]. They all give her so much attention and does she love it.

George went out to see the Howell's [whose son-in-law was Wannie Woods, killed in Italy] last night and stayed until about 10:00 and we had a houseful here waiting to see him. Anyway he blew out the 27 candles on his birthday cake and got to talk with them all a little bit. Ted [my uncle] & Dorothy [Newton] had to leave early as she is a policewoman at the base and works nights. And Johnny [Bott] had to drive the 11:00 bus to the beach.

I ran across some bananas today for Tomilyn and then Loraine saw them and bought some too so we have an abundant supply for a while anyway.

Marie, Nona, Nancy & Tomilyn and I are going to Ventura tomorrow. Nancy has some distant relation over there she wants to see and Nona wants to get some things that Ted needs. Scarfs, gloves, etc. Must be cold where he is too.

Bob darling, please take care of yourself for us. We love you so.

You're our precious Daddy!

We love you,

Molly and Robin

The fourth day was more of the same. We were hungry from one ration to the next. The men were weak and dehydrated from lack of water. I wondered how much more some of them could endure. But the human body, we discovered, can be abused for a long time. The mind is the key. Men who were mentally strong seemed to have more endurance than the ones who allowed themselves to lose their basic values.

We arrived at Stalag 4B. After a long wait the doors were opened and the guards told us to get down from the railroad cars. At first we had a difficult time standing as we had been confined without exercise for so long. We were marched to a nearby building. Each of us walked through the outside building that stood adjacent to the fences of the compound and was sprayed with a delousing material.

From there we were marched into a large building within the prison compound. We were greeted by a large number of POWs. The place was overcrowded. The men were standing around, gathered in groups. Most of them looked up as we passed some with a smile, some with a stare, and some would not look at us.

We were briefed by an English officer who was in charge of our barracks. We were told we should fill out a registration card the first thing, which would be sent to our homes. It didn't take any time at all for me to fill out the card. I wrote telling Molly and Mother that I was OK. I was glad to be able to do that because I knew they were worried about me and I hoped it would get there. I knew if or when they got the news they would pass the information to the rest of the family.

The camp was run by English soldiers. Some had been there since the African Campaign, and that was a couple of years before. They had things well organized. The first thing they did was to give us a cup of tea. Then each of us was given a shave.

As we entered the compound I heard a voice calling out, "Hey, Lieutenant Moranda, over here." I looked in the direction of the voice and there was Conover, my runner. It was like finding a brother, that man who had watched over me all the time since I had joined the 38th AIB. In civilian life, he was a wheat farmer in Montana, farming hundreds of acres. Wherever our outfit went during my time in the war, he was my eyes and my provider. He watched out for me—in combat he was a Godsend to me. We had a good visit, but they soon hurried us along to our new assigned spot.

Later, sitting with my group talking to fellow POWs, I overheard a young major talking to his little group telling them he was from Lancaster, California. I walked over and started to talk to him, telling him my name and that I had family in Lancaster. His name was Maj. Jim Burns, who had been with the 28th Infantry Division. He, too, was captured during the Battle of the Bulge. He had been the S3 (operations officer) of a battalion in the 28th Infantry Division. With him were Lts. Duffy, Ed Kazarin, and Vince DeGort. We all became good friends, but it was Jim Burns who became close to me. He lived near my in-laws, the Swains, in Lancaster. After the war we saw see each other often.

We began to recover from all the exposure. Our rations were steady. Daily we got two inches of a loaf of black bread, a small hunk of cheese or sausage, and a mug of soup. A mug was issued that took the place of a mess kit. I still have the cup sitting on my dresser to remind me of the time spent as a POW.

Our daily routine was to sit around and talk as there was not enough room to exercise and we were not allowed to go outside. It was still cold and we'd had enough walking for a time.

On January 12th, eighty officers and six enlisted men were called out, lined up, and marched to the railroad yards where we were loaded into boxcars again. The cars were the same; the count per car was the same, forty men. This time they remembered to give us a bucket to be used as a toilet.

A new leader was appointed for our group. His name was Col. Hurley Fuller from the 28th Division. His assistant was Lt. Craig Campbell. Craig had been an aide to General Eisenhower in Africa and had been captured there. Also assigned to help Col. Fuller was Maj. Jim Burns.

[Col. Hurley E. Fuller commanded the 110th Infantry Regiment, 28th Division, which had been assigned a wide sector of about 9.4 miles from Kalborn south to Stolzembourg. He positioned his main elements in a string of villages and covered the gaps with patrols—there wasn't enough manpower to do anything more--an average of about sixty infantrymen to cover each kilometer of front. After the German forces broke through, surrounded the strongpoint held by the 110th, Col. Fuller was captured with a group trying to escape to the west. Fuller was a Texan who had enlisted in the Army in 1916. He went to Officers Training School, served in France during World War I, and had fought in the bitter campaign in the Ardennes Forest. He was embittered by that experience, but stayed in the Army and established a reputation as a tough, irascible curmudgeon. He had been assigned to command a regiment in the 2nd Infantry Division and brought the unit to Normandy on D-day plus one. He lasted in combat only ten days, when he was relieved by the division commander, apparently because he had maneuvered his regiment into an untenable position. Fuller went to his old friend General Middleton, commander of the VIII Corps, who obtained another chance for him by assigning him to the 28th Infantry Division when a vacancy occurred in the 110th Infantry Regiment in late November. One of the first things he did was to move the regimental headquarters from a farm village to the more comfortable tourist city of Clervaux and into Hotel Claravallis.]

Poland POW Camp

We arrived at *Offlag* 692 in Poland around the 18th of January. The *Offlag* was occupied by fifty French and other foreign officers. When we arrived, the count went up another eighty plus.

The ride from Stalag 4B near Berlin to the *Offlag* took us six or seven days—in a box car with only the cracks in the sides and a two-foot square opening at each end for visibility. Our food was a small one-inch hunk of black bread and a small slice of sausage. We were given a small amount of water daily. Our toilet was a large bucket that was emptied only once in the whole trip.

With forty men in a boxcar, all weak, some with dysentery—the stench was unimaginable. One officer had been constipated for a couple of weeks and was worried. After three more days he decided that it was time to really try. He got on that stinking bucket and kept trying and trying. Finally after almost an hour of grunting he was able to get some relief. The men in the box car stood around and were rooting for him. It was the first and last time I ever rooted for a man trying to crap!

The weather was cold. To keep warm we crowded together. We had no blankets and felt that we were lucky to have all our clothes. When we first became prisoners I was with Col. Riggs, and a couple of the German *soldats* were looking at our paratrooper boots. They had decided that they were going to make us take off our boots and keep them for themselves. Col.Riggs stood up and fought for our rights; he called to an officer and registered a loud complaint. That is the last we ever heard about them taking our boots.

In this boxcar I saw the deterioration of some of the men, but others were able to control those who started to break down. Being together made time pass more easily, but there was very little talking. Most of the time our minds were far off. Toward the end of the six days things were getting bad. Men were getting weaker. There was more bickering; more heroics by the sane, more tenderness shown, more selfishness by some. Some were waiting for death, and some waiting for the rations of those who were very sick. A few kept things going and encouraged the rest to "buck up," by promising that it would soon get better. On January 18, it did get better. We were received at the *Offlag*. The address was Camp No. M-Stammlager 4B, Deutschland, located near Poznan, Poland.

[On the Eastern Front, by the end of 1944, the line had stabilized on its northern and central sectors along the East Prussia border extending southward along the Narew-Vistula line to the Carpathians, but was threatened on the south by the Red Army's flanking movement through the Balkans into Hungary. Hitler had placed General Guderian, a brilliant armored force commander, as Chief of General Staff, but left him with only twelve armored divisions and fifty infantry divisions to face what intelligence sources estimated to be 225 Russian infantry divisions and twenty-two armored corps. Hitler shifted two Panzer divisions from Poland to Hungary without consulting Guderian. Despite Guderian's pleas for reinforcements, Hitler was committed to the Ardennes Campaign in the west and was unable to help him out.

In mid-January 1945 the Red Army started its major offensive and breached the German defenses on a 200 mile front toward East Prussia's southern border. Warsaw was captured on January 17, Lodz on January 19. The Russians had advanced a hundred miles in a week. By then it was obvious to Hitler that the campaign in the west had failed, and he shifted the Sixth Panzer Army, against Guderian's advice, to Hungary rather than to Poland. Thus, the Red Army could continue its advance for two more weeks; their spearheads crossed the Oder near Breslau and cut Silesia's mineral resources off from Germany, and drove forward from Warsaw to the frontiers of Brandenburg and Pomerania. Another Red force isolated East Prussia by driving to the Gulf of Danzig. They reached within eighty miles of Berlin on February 13.

On the Western Front, Allied Forces had, by the end of January, eliminated the Battle of the Bulge and were moving eastward on a broad front.]

A person never realizes what it's like to be confined within a box car until he has to stay in one for a prolonged period. Debarking was done quickly as we needed to stretch our bodies. It was good to be able to walk, to have some space, to breathe fresh air, to have a cup of cabbage soup even if it had a couple of crickets or other animal in it. We didn't complain. One of the men said, "Goody, fresh meat." And finally, we had a hunk of bread. That eased the hunger pains. It doesn't sound like much but was an improvement over the past weeks. It was so much better than what we had while in the box car.

The prisoners were kept in one large room, equipped with double bunks with straw mattresses—I can't remember a blanket the first few nights. As the weather was below zero, some of us slept in the spoons position to keep warm. My bunkmate was Lt. Boyd.

On the third day we all received a Red Cross package. What a great gift. The box contained little tins of food, chocolate bars, cigarettes, raisins, powdered milk. Some men wolfed things down, others hoarded the things. I hoarded. What I enjoyed most were raisins in a mixture of dried milk and water. I let the raisins soak until plump and then ate them slowly. And with a cigarette—not bad!

There was a courtyard where we could exercise at any time. I stayed out there as much as possible. Being outside relieved me from thinking about being in prison.

I remember some of the personal habits and character traits of the men. Some kept busy; some slept almost day and night. There was not much talking. Some found ways to keep busy by making things out of the tins that were in the Red Cross packages. Some read the Bible. A few were like zombies, having a difficult time in adjusting to imprisonment.

Col. Fuller from the 28th Division was our CO. Before the war he was a professor at a college in Pennsylvania. He was older, and the trip had taken its toll. He seldom joined the rest of us. He had separate quarters; Craig Campbell and Jim Burns stayed in the room with him and they stayed to themselves.

In late January, Mother wrote to Molly:

Dear Amelia,

Your letter arrived this morning, thank you for it. The enclosed also arrived this morning & I opened it thinking if it was any further good news, I'd phone you this morning. But it's a regulation letter & not urgent so I'm sending it on by mail & not phoning.

Yesterday I had a telegram from Earle [a lieutenant in Army Air Corps Intelligence in the Pentagon] which said "Shocked at news of Bob. Can't give up hope. Most likely prisoner. Won't get word for about 60 days. Casualty branch to advise me, in addition to telegram to Molly if any news. Will phone you when hear. Molly to receive letter confirming telegram. Writing Hugh West." The letter Earle mentioned is this one I'm enclosing. I can't remember whether Hugh West is still with Bob or not but Earle is going to write him. If you know the names of any of the men with Bob you might write them. I still believe that Bob is alright & that we'll hear good news of him.

George & Nancy came over to the house with me & yesterday they & Marie scrubbed down the walls of the kitchen. I felt awful about it but they said they wanted to do it. Yes Jeannette will be up Sat. so will have a little time with Nancy. I don't know whether Bill & Marie will feel like going to Lancaster Sunday or not. It looks & feels like rain—but may not—but I'll get word to you later.

Sure hate to see George leave again, but who knows he may be around for awhile yet.

Mary Moore had a baby son yesterday. I was surprised as I didn't think her baby was expected so soon.

Hope you are feeling alright now. You must keep up & be as cheerful as possible both for Bob & Tomilyn.

Lovingly,

Nona

The enclosed letter from Major General J.A. Ulio, the Adjutant General, was addressed to Mrs. Amelia Moranda, dated January 20, 1945, and said in part:

> This letter is to confirm my recent telegram in which you were regretfully informed that your husband, Second Lieutenant Robert E. P. Moranda, 001326108, has been reported missing in action in Belgium since 21 December 1944.
>
> I know that added distress is caused by failure to receive more information or details. Therefore, I wish to assure you that any time additional information is received it will be transmitted to you without delay, and, if in the meantime no additional information is received, I will again communicate with you at the expiration of three months.
>
> Experience has shown that many persons reported missing in action are subsequently reported as prisoners of war, but as this information is furnished by countries with which we are at war, the War Department is helpless to expedite such reports.
>
> The personal effects of an individual missing overseas are held by his unit for a period of time and are then sent to the Effects Quartermaster, Kansas City, Missouri, for disposition as designated by the soldier.
>
> Permit me to extend to you my heartfelt sympathy during this period of uncertainty.

The letter had an enclosure that explained the entitlements of missing persons and their dependants.

The Russians Are Coming

We had been at the POW camp for a short time when we noted a change in attitude of the Germans. We heard them include the names of Russkie or Bolshevik in their conversation. They seemed excited and moved at a faster pace. And they were packing things. The ones who could speak English were saying, "The Russians are coming."

It was even implied and sometimes asked of us, "Would we fight with the Germans against the Russians?" We listened and by our actions, they got the message we wouldn't.

On January 21, we were told to gather the warm items needed to protect us from the cold. They even allowed us to take things that belonged to the Germans. Apparently, they were going to save us from the Russians.

For all the time we had been at the Offlag, I had exercised and walked in the courtyard with Col. Riggs, the engineer officer who was with us at St. Vith. We would walk the compound for at least an hour at a time, doing it twice or three times a day. We would talk about escape. The problem was where would we go, which direction, and how would we survive? The two of us got ourselves in pretty good shape.

On January 21, we were lined up and counted at least twice. With the *Hauptman* leading in a horse and cart, we took off. My costume was a coat, a scarf that was at least six feet long and eight inches wide, and a blanket. I gathered the food I had saved, what was left of my Red Cross package, anything we had hoarded, and anything we had stolen from the Germans. The scarf and my large cup for the daily soup ration were things that I made sure I had.

The convoy was the *Hauptman's* wagon plus six horse-drawn wagons carrying the Germans' supplies, followed by eighty-six Americans (eighty officers and six enlisted men), plus a few French and other foreign officers walking. The foreign officers had been at the Offlag when we arrived.

By the *Hauptman's* attitude, we could see that he hated us all—how I disliked his arrogant manner. He continually drove up and down the convoy, urging the guards to hurry us. When we saw there was a possibility to slow the convoy down and let the Russians catch up with us, we did. We did whatever we could to delay the march. The *Hauptman* always had his pipe in his mouth. He was a short, stocky man with glasses and a permanent frown on his face. *"Roush Mit!"* he would yell at us, which meant for us to hurry up!

According to the German guards, our destination was Berlin and that was a long, long way to go. "Why Berlin?" we asked, but we got no reply because the guards did not know either.

Our interpreter, spy, and interrogator was a German lieutenant, Paul Hegel. He had been at the Offlag and was always trying to get more information from prisoners by being nice to them. He was allegedly pro-American, having been educated in America, where he had studied banking. He said he wanted to be a friend, but I did not trust him. He stayed with Col. Fuller most of the time, doing what he could for the colonel, what is known in the Army as "brown nosing." In retrospect I realize that he was only trying to save his life.

"Krieges" [POWs] was what the Germans called us. On the first day, we walked fifteen miles. Not many miles considering how long we were on the road, but we were not the only ones traveling. Most of the German population in and around that part of the country was also trying to escape the Russians. Wagons pulled by horses, wheel barrows being pushed, and even one dog cart passed by us. The Germans had the right of way, so we would have to wait on the side of the road and allow wagons and all to pass. Any wait was followed by the usual line up and the count. The people were loaded down with their possessions. What hate was on their faces as they passed us! They would look, snarl a word at us, and then face the road ahead. They were trying to hurry, and there was a fearful look about them.

At dusk of the first day, they placed us in an old barn. As always in barns there was hay and manure and that combination creates heat, so we were comfortable. The German guards were able to scrounge a half-way decent ration for us. All night long we could hear artillery in the distance. Now we could understand the nervousness of the Germans. The Russians were coming, and they were getting closer.

On January 22, my mother's birthday, we were lined up early in the morning. The usual counting the lines of men, the usual shifting of the men so we could disrupt the *ein, swei, drei* and so on. The Germans would have to count us at least twice. Our delaying tactics were working. Our breath was white in the bitter cold. Men kept stomping their feet and wrapping their arms around themselves.

We walked only about fifteen miles. The pace was slow. Trying to keep men in line was difficult. Many men had bad feet. Even though they had a few days in Stalag 4B to try to cure the frostbite, the pain was still there. The guards were continually trying to keep us moving. The *Hauptman* would walk up and down the lines trying to get the guards to move us out. We finally reached a German youth camp where we were fed and bedded—tired but otherwise okay.

Most of the time no words were uttered, a grunt or two as most of the men were within themselves. Some were talking about escaping. Four men from the 28th Division—Maj. Burns, Lts. Duffy, Kazarian, and one other young officer were planning to give it a go when the opportunity was there. The question always came up, escape to where? The Russians? We didn't know where we were. Col. Riggs and I discussed plans and the possible problems; we wanted to succeed and not have to go through this again. We agreed it took a lot of luck, but we were willing to try.

January 23 was really tough. We were up early and did the usual stomping to get our blood circulating. It was below zero the whole day. It was so cold that our skin would feel like it was burning. As they do in cold countries, we mushed it—only without the dogs and sleds. We walked or trudged on and covered about twenty miles. That night we were put in a large barn with cows, and we didn't complain. The cows' body temperatures, their willingness to give us milk, and the abundance of hay made us comfortable. We took off our boots and massaged our feet back to life. Damn, it was so cold walking that day—no thought of escaping. We were only trying to survive.

January 24 was a short day; we covered about twelve miles. We had to fight the snow all day. That night we were rested in a German *bier* hall.

On January 25, we made about twenty-five miles. We crossed the border into Germany, the border town of Filchens. That night we were placed in a cold barn, still bitterly cold. By then the German civilians and others were moving out in large numbers. It was very hard on the women and children, and I sympathized with them.

After we rested, the guards would form our lines again and count us. *Ein, swei, drei,* and so on. As often as we could we would jump ranks so the count would be wrong. Delay was the order of the day. The Germans were having a hard time getting the count correct.

I learned that sometime before the day's march Col. Riggs had escaped. I had walked the courtyard with him the day before, and we were still working on plans to get away. Now he was gone. I was glad for him but wondered how he had gotten away without any of us seeing him. (Years after the war, I talked to him by phone after learning where he lived and asked him how he had escaped. He said on the morning they were lining us up, he was in the toilet. No one was looking for him, so he waited a short time and saw that he could go over the fence easily, and he did. He had quite an experience before the Russians came along and took care of him.)

Our men were rapidly going downhill. We were spending a lot of effort helping the weak to continue. I saw one man reach down and pick up a frozen sugar beet and try to eat it. After a trial bite he threw it away.

This reminds me of a poem written by a Lt. Phelan. Every night, we had been given some soup—one cup full and sometimes a slab of bread, so he dreamed of the good food at home. Phelan dedicated this poem to his wife. He knew that she would understand.

> I dream as only a captive can dream
>
> of life as lived as in days before.
>
> Of scrambled eggs and shortcake thick with cream.

And onion soup and lobster thermador.

Of roasted beef and chops and T-bone steak.

Of turkey breast and a golden leg or wing.

Of sausage, maple syrup, buckwheat cake.

And chicken broiled or fried, a la king.

I dwell on rolls or buns for days and days.

Hot corn bread biscuits, Philadelphia scrapple.

Asparagus in cream or Hollandaise.

And deep dish pies, mince, huckleberry, apple.

I long for buttered cream oyster stew.

And now and then I long for you.

On that day, we were walking along with thousands of German civilians, their wagons piled high with possessions. The weather was so cold that many had their heads covered with burlap sacks with holes cut out for their eyes. They would stare at us and we would stare back. No words were spoken. It would take too much energy to talk.

A bag dropped from a wagon as it passed us. As the bag was paper, it split when it hit the road. I reached and scooped a handful and tasted it. It was sugar. I slowly ate the sugar and told the men about it—and many scooped up some of it and did the same. It seemed to give us a small spark of energy.

One thing I could not understand was why so many of the slaves from Poland, Denmark, and France helped the Germans to escape from the Russians? Were they happy as slaves of the Germans? Did they know something about the coming Russians? I assumed that they would rather help as slaves than face the Red Tide that was coming.

One Sunday morning we had stopped to rest close to a few houses. One of the officers in our group was a French priest. Though he was ordained, it made no difference to the French, for when the men were drafted everyone in an age group was drawn into the French army. There were no exemptions. He had been with us for some time, but none of us had known he was a priest; however, we did notice he had been carrying a small case. When we halted to rest that day, a wagon was parked on the side of the road. The priest went to the wagon, opened his case, laid out the necessary items, put his vestments on, and started to say Mass. From houses, from wagons, from *soldats*, from men in our group people came to participate in the Mass. For a few minutes they were with God, alongside a road in a cold, cold place. Enemy soldiers, civilians, and prisoners were worshiping with heads bared. I remember thinking that it does not matter what governments do, they cannot stamp out man's belief in God. The soldiers from Germany, the Americans, the French, the slaves from Poland, the women all ask God to love us and protect us. For a moment there was peace.

We stayed in another barn that night. It was somewhat warm, and we survived the night.

The next day, January 26 was still bitter cold. The guards were getting jumpy. One of our group said, "The guards were as nervous as a whore in church." Our antics did not help their attitude. Some of the men had toes that were frozen, which made it difficult to walk in the snow. The wind was blowing hard, and the cold cut right through our clothes.

We finally reached a *bier* hall and, as the guards had had enough, we went in. The meal that night was soup and bread. Most of us ate the soup and saved the bread for morning.

We started January 27 in the usual manner though it took longer to count that morning as it seemed someone had taken off. When the guards counted, we were one man short, so they went up and down counting and recounting. The *Hauptman* even got down and counted. The interpreter walked along the lines with the *Hauptman*. They would ask, "Who is missing?" To that question he got blank looks on our faces. At the first line up, I didn't know who was missing, and I don't remember the name of the man who had left. That made it two men who had departed from our group as Col. Riggs had been the first to get away. (After the war my brother George met Col. Riggs when he attended the Army War College at Carlisle Barracks in Pennsylvania. When Riggs heard the name Moranda, he asked him, "Are you related to Bob?" It was then that I found out that he, too, was picked up by the Russians and was repatriated. He offered no apology for leaving without me. As it turned out maybe it was for the best.)

The weather was still bad, but we made about twenty miles. It was one of those days that a person puts his head down and walks on. It brought back memories of the comment of Lt. Babb, my first platoon leader, who said at one of our first formations, "A man can walk one hell of a lot farther, even when he is dead tired, than he thinks he can."

That night we were again placed in a barn with cows. We didn't complain about the smell. The warmth was great, and we all had warm milk to drink. I was pretty good at getting next to a friendly cow and using the Swiss style of milking (that I had learned from my Uncle Walter when I had visited him on his farm near Goshen in the San Joaquin Valley) to fill my cup.

The men were going further downhill physically, deteriorating more each day. They all needed help—medical help. Their feet were frostbitten. We who were in the best shape would go among the men in the worst shape and get them to rub their feet. We all needed encouragement. My feet were almost okay, with only a tinge of frostbite, so I was able to walk easily.

On the next day, January 28, the weather had not improved. After a good night's sleep in relative warmth and plenty of milk to drink, we were rested. Even so it wasn't long until the weather had beaten us down again. No longer did we share the road with the people who were fleeing. It seemed that we were the only ones left. We could make much better time. But then what the hell was the hurry?

Wugarten

We passed through the town of Waltenburg in mid-afternoon. We continued for about five miles, and in an hour or so we arrived at the small town of Wugarten. No matter where we were, there was an air of fear. The German soldiers obviously feared the Russians. The civilians feared the Russians, their soldiers, and us. The guards were uneasy about everything. They wanted us to speed up, and we wouldn't, and some couldn't. I am sure the soldiers of the Third Reich had heard of the pillaging of Russian towns, raping the women, and killing the men. That news must have been passed on to the civilians, so they became even more fearful as the sound of artillery came closer.

Some Germans still expected the Americans to fight against the Russians. I recalled that in the POW camp the Germans had put out a feeler asking the British and Americans if we would help them stop the Russians. Needless to say, the offer was flatly refused.

One thing that continually slowed our column down was dysentery. Many men had the problem. When the urge hit them, they would head for a snow bank, drop their pants, and relieve themselves. Some had brought paper to wipe with, but that was soon gone. Wiping was done with anything available: cloth, weeds, or even snow. And as there was no way to be hygienic, the dysentery got worse. The only paper I had with me was the last letter from Molly and I wasn't about to use that. I read it daily. It seemed to me I could hear her voice as I read it.

We halted on the road. I noticed the guards and the *Hauptman* were together in a bunch and talking several yards away from us. Lt. Paul Hegl was with them, and the discussion seemed feverish. Some of us wandered off. All at once I realized I was alone. I waited for a few minutes making certain that the guards were not coming for me. They were not. I was following at a distance. The group was coming into the town of Wugarten. Then I saw the column was going into a school, and the guards were leaving!! I soon discovered what was happening.

The Germans had decided to try to save their own necks and took off. Only one German stayed with the group, the interpreter, Lt. Hegl. That apparently was what the heated discussion had been about with the Germans. Col. Fuller had told Hegl that if he stayed with the Americans, he would save his neck. He would dress Hegl in an American uniform, give him an insignia, and make him a lieutenant of infantry, U.S. Army. So when the Germans left, Hegl became Lt. George Mulbauer, named after an escaped American POW.

I watched from a distance. I was alone in the town, going over all my options. Could I find my way to the American line? I couldn't speak German. Would it be better to get back with the group? Good sense told me to get back with the troops. I started up the road. Suddenly there loomed a tank. I knew it was a Russian tank. Now, what do I do? Do I run, hide, or bluff it out? I kept walking right up the middle of the road, straight at the tank. I could see the man in the turret watching my every move. I yelled at the driver. The guns were aimed at me. I kept yelling at the tank crew, "Americanski! Americanski! Americanski!" The commander finally understood. He climbed down from the tank. He looked me over, looked at the bar on my shirt collar, the shoes on my feet, and walked around me. Then he embraced me and there followed much hugging and pounding on the back. Out came the vodka. A drink was poured and I downed it. Being emaciated, I left the group and went to the side of the road and upchucked it. Back again. Another drink poured and this time it stayed down. They called the drink "Spiritous"—a cheap vodka. I learned the Russians are given a daily ration of the stuff. I think the Russian soldiers fought half drunk—it helped their nerves and bravery. I climbed aboard the tank, and we motored up the road.

Our conversation was mostly by sign language and the few words of English they knew. Stalin, Roosevelt, Studebaker trucks, Churchill, Hitler, the German *Kaputt* and *Alles Kaputt*. All of this time there were smiles and gestures. They let me out, and I joined my group in the schoolhouse.

So there we were, about one hundred Americans, Italians, and French. One of the French officers who had been a prisoner for some time was Alex Bertin, a tall, young, intelligent man. He was great in languages and could speak seven of them, so he became our interpreter. We became good friends and later great partners at bridge. Earlier I had become well acquainted with the French chaplain, so I had acquired two fine friends from France.

Soon we were visited by the German local Burgermeister. He requested that three or four of the Americans stay at his house, which was located across the street from the school. Lt. Higgins, Tate, and I were told to go there. We got to sleep in beds with quilts—what a great feeling. And running water! The house had two women and the father of the Burgermeister. As we were in the best shape of most of the other prisoners, we became the procurers of food.

Before leaving, the German commandant gave Col. Fuller a notice in writing that we were being abandoned. He advised the group to stay inside the schoolhouse as German soldiers were fleeing through the town. It wasn't long before I found out it was true. I took it upon myself to scout the town. I had seen a bakery shop on a side street. I walked into the bakery and said, *"Haben se brod?"* (That and *"Alles Kaputt"* and a couple of greetings was about the only German I knew).

The baker and his wife said they did. Now whether the word had gotten around town or not I didn't know but, without hesitation, loaves of black bread appeared. I loaded up. My arms were full when I departed from the bakery. No sooner than I had exited the bakery and stepped into the road I looked to my right and here came a German group of *soldats* trudging though the deep snow. Again, what do I do? Run back to the shop or try to run to the schoolhouse? I continued toward the Germans. They looked at me, me at them, they with their burp guns in their right arms, me with my arms full of bread. I walked right past them, to one I said, *"Guten Morgan."* He grunted and I continued on. I breathed with a loud exhaling sound when he didn't challenge me. As I reflect on the incident, I think the Germans may have heard there were POWs in the town.

I was a welcome sight when I took the bread to the troops in the schoolhouse. Every man got an ample supply of it.

My next tour was to the dairy barn. I found fresh milk and potatoes and took them back to the school. Our men were soon able to feed themselves. Some of our enlisted men who were our cooks at the Offlag had enough items to prepare the food we had brought to the school.

Col. Fuller, Maj. Burns, Lt. Campbell, the German Paul Hegl, and the interpreter Alex Bertin, stayed at the largest house in town, which became our headquarters. Higgins and I were watching out the window of our house when we saw Russian officers talking to Lt. Campbell and Alex Bertin. They went in and talked with Col. Fuller. Soon the Russians and an American group walked the town and went into the schoolhouse. We didn't know what they said, but they were out soon and came to our billet. They shook hands with us and left. As they walked back to their vehicles, they marked each place where POWs were staying, which was to be a notice to the Russian Army when they came into the town.

One thing that impressed me was the way the Russians dressed. They had real winter clothes on. They looked warm with all their parkas, wool hats, and boots.

Even though we were placed in a marked house, our presence helped only a little. One day I was in the front room of our quarters. Suddenly, one of the two women came in the room and yelled at me to come quick. She was very agitated, so I quickly followed her into the kitchen. There in the kitchen stood a brute of a man, a drunken Russian soldier, with his hat on, his great coat open, his pants dropped, and his penis standing at attention. He was tearing at a woman's clothes. She was screaming and saying, *Nein! Nein! Nein!*" I shouted, "No! No! No!"shaking my head in a negative motion. I yelled at Higgins to run to get the Russian officer who was billeted nearby. The drunken soldier reeled back, swaying with his body that must have been full of vodka. I could see he was wondering what the hell was going on. As he pulled back, he reached for his sidearm. Quite a sight: a drunken Russian soldier swaying back and forth, his eyes trying to focus on me and wondering what to do with his penis and at the same time wondering what to do about me. I had placed myself between him and the woman, and he gradually started backing out of the kitchen into the backyard. He slowly stuffed his penis back into his pants. His eyes were blinking trying to focus on me. He gradually raised his revolver and started to point it at me when, thankfully, a Russian officer came into the yard. The Russian officer yelled at the drunken soldier. We were all standing near a rain barrel full of water. The soldier dropped his gun to his side. The officer stood him at attention and berated him. The officer dipped his hands in the water and slapped the soldier. Over and over he repeated the operation and with each slap he would curse the soldier. After four or five slaps, he allowed the soldier to leave. He stumbled and staggered to his horse and cart. Calm came over the backyard. I had had quite a fright; I wondered what was going to be the outcome and whether or not I was about to be shot.

I thanked the Russian officer, "Thanks for coming to our rescue."

He looked at me and said, "You were lucky I was nearby. And I cannot blame the soldier. You see his women were raped when the Germans came through his village. To the soldier, he was only paying back for all the rapes that have happened in Russia." Alex Bertin, who came with the officer, said he couldn't understand why I would endanger myself by stopping the Russian. After all, he and others had suffered much at the hands of the Germans. My thoughts were that even though war is a terrible, terrible thing, even in war women, children, and any noncombatant should not be abused.

Alex couldn't understand why Col. Fuller was trying to save Hegl, the German, especially as he had spent a lot of time humiliating American and French officers by his interrogations—a man who didn't provide any comfort or help to us. Now to save him from the Russians! We also knew the Russians rarely took prisoners. We saw many Germans lying dead. I even discovered our German *Hauptman's* body on the outskirts of town, and I picked up his pipe. Now looking back, I understand why none of us ever uttered a word to the Russians. It rankled that Hegl had become a gentleman's gentleman. He served Fuller's every whim. Here he could speak the language, but the three of us, the providers who gathered food and found supplies, had to do it by sign language. Even so, by deduction and searching, we found plenty of food. Two days before we were to be trucked out of Wugarten, I was called to Col. Fuller's headquarters and found him griping about the lack of better food. At the very time he was bitching, Hegl was on his knees washing Fuller's feet. I saw red because I told him that maybe if he could spare Hegl for a time to have him go with us to talk to the civilians maybe we could find even more food and supplies. The truth must have hurt because the good colonel got red in the face and excused me. Later, I found out that Fuller told Maj. Burns and Lt. Campbell that they should court martial me when we got into American hands. Burns said they soothed the colonel and he forgot about it. But Burns added that what I had said was the truth, and Fuller realized it—that's what made him so mad.

A few days before we left the town, an infantry unit of the Russian Army entered Wugarten. By then we had taken over the town. The first thing they did was to call out the mayor. As he walked up to the Russians, one of them pulled out his pistol and killed him. At first they didn't realize we were Americans. The situation was touch and go for a few minutes. They finally saw the signs the previous Russians had left, so they eased their attitude a bit. But before that their tanks and infantry were ready to mow us down. By yelling, "Americanski" and through Alex Bertin talking to them, they finally understood who we were. When they had been advised we were allies, we asked why they had shot the mayor. The reply was, "We always kill the Burgermeister when we come into a town." Again the Russians wanted to celebrate with us, the vodka flowed. Most of our men couldn't drink much as we were too far gone physically, but they tried to celebrate with many hugs and laughter. The Russians were happy to share in our liberation.

Town of Wugarten

After that there were no more killings or rapes around us. An interesting situation occurred among our group. Our enlisted men bunked separately from the officers. We had six enlisted men, several of whom told me they had found billets with some young women of the town. The girls had asked the men, literally, to breed them. They said they would rather have an American baby than a Russian baby; they knew when we left the town, they would soon be forced to have sex with the Russians. They said the affairs with our men took place away from the girls' homes.

The men were getting restless; in fact, we food procurers, Higgins, Tate and I, began to get a little help. A group of our officers were well enough to find, kill, and dress a couple of sheep. So we had fresh mutton, fresh eggs, chicken, a great menu with fresh-baked black bread. Soon we started hearing gripes and grousing, which was a good sign that the men were getting stronger.

The day after the episode of my rescuing the woman from being raped, we were sitting in our room when the woman brought me a large cake with frosting. To me that was a great tribute and showed that she was thankful. I did wonder where the sugar came from.

(It was about this time that Molly in Lancaster received a letter from Mrs. C. Reedy, who had been her practitioner in Oxnard, postmarked Feb 20, 1945:

My dearest Amelia

I am sorry I have waited so long to answer your letter. I could have dozens of excuses, but I do not. I am a very sorry letter writer, can think of a lot of things until I go to put it on paper & then I have to hunt words to write. I have been awfully busy, in fact too much so.

I was sorry to hear Bob was missing but that doesn't mean he won't return. We must know God's Ideas are not separated from him. He lives & moves & has his being in God. Where nothing but good can touch him. You must make an effort to keep your thought above the clouds & that will not only help you, but will help him also.

When I heard it I worked all afternoon. We are not supposed to work without being asked but as I have worked for him at different times, I felt I wanted to.

If I were you I would get some good practitioner to do some work on it if you feel the least upset about it. Some way I feel he is in God's care & all is well.

Give my love to the family & yourself & baby. Lots of love,

Your friend

According to Burns and Campbell, Col. Fuller kept asking when we were to be liberated to the U.S. The answer was always the same, "When we win the war we will send you back." But Col. Fuller continued to pressure our liaison officer.

We kept wondering how we would be handled by the Russians, but we were left alone in our town. We started doing things to keep busy—and to keep our sanity. Higgins found some cheesecloth and by experimenting learned how to make cheese. I found some baking soda and a bag of flour and by trial and error, I learned how to make soda biscuits. My only clue was remembering how Mom did it, and especially my Aunt Leo who used to make "soader" biscuits almost every day when I visited in Goshen. The first batch came out well so we had "soader" biscuits daily.

One morning we were told to be ready to move out. It was about 1000 in the morning when the trucks arrived. Higgins, Tate, and I said goodbye to the ladies of our house. They had tears in their eyes and gave us a good hug and a handshake. I have wondered many times about the women and whether they survived.

We proceeded to Poznan, Poland. From the back of a truck a person doesn't see much of the scenery, so I can't recall much of the surroundings. My only remembrance was that it was a dark, commercial city that had a railroad. And we wanted a train to get us somewhere. As we loaded into the freight cars, we were told that we were going to Odessa on the Black Sea.

What I remember about Wugarten was a cake, a cup, and a pipe. The cup I still have on my dresser to remind me of the times of hunger and to be thankful today. On the bottom of the cup is the eagle with a swastika and the date 1940. The cake reminds me of the beautiful cake that the German lady made for me after her episode with the drunken Russian soldier. And the *Hauptman's* pipe: that I kept to remind me of being under the control of a German officer.

I learned several things during that experience as a POW, but primarily the importance of personal values: love, respect, and concern for my family and friends; doing what is right in responding to a variety of events and incidents as they occur; seeing what has to be done and then doing it without any fanfare; and keeping a strong belief that God will take care of everything.

We were loaded into boxcars again. This was my fourth trip in a boxcar. The two in Germany were bad, so it was with some reservations when we again began riding the rails. This one turned out to be interesting and almost comfortable. We only had about twenty men in each car, and our rations were ample. Each car had a Russian soldier as our guide and protector. Our train was also served by a Russian woman doctor who treated the sick. By this time most of those down with ailments had made remarkable recoveries, so she didn't have too much to do.

The train wasn't fast, but we were not unhappy as we could open the doors and watch the country go by. Most of it seemed flat. The weather was very nice so we felt we were on a tour. Once while the train was stopped, the Russian soldier jumped off and went into a field, obviously to relieve himself. I turned to Major Burns and said, "I'll bet you a package of cigarettes that he won't wipe." Burns took the bet—and paid off when we got to Odessa.

Our guide couldn't speak English. We couldn't speak Russian so we accomplished communication by sign language and teaching each other some words of our languages. I learned quite a bit during the three-day trip from Posen to Odessa. I was impressed by the land. I had heard that Russians love their land, and it is understandable.

Most of the laborers seen along the railroad were women—big husky women—swinging picks, using shovels, pushing brooms, toting rails, and anything else that needed to be done. Much war damage was visible in the towns we passed through. I wondered what stories there were about how the Germans treated the civilians. From all reports there had been killings of civilians, raping of women, and pillaging of the towns. By then I understood more about my encounters with the Russians.

Odessa

We arrived in Odessa early one morning. The city had a beautiful setting on the banks of the Black Sea. Where we detrained was above the harbor, so we could see ships waiting for loading and unloading. I was becoming excited as I knew we were almost in American hands.

They marched us through part of the town to a large school building that was no longer occupied. There we were to be greeted by an attaché of the United States of America.

On the way to the school, as we were walking down the street, I saw an American sailor. I knew he was American by his clothes and manner. "Hey, Mac!" I called out. "Got a cigarette?"

He came over and asked who we were and where we were going. As we told him our story, he took out a package of Chesterfields and gave me the package. He held his lighter for me, and I smoked the cigarette and savored every puff. On our trip through Russia, we had been given Russian cigarettes. They were terrible. I passed out the rest of the package to my friends, and saved one more for me. I wish I had gotten "Mac's" name.

We arrived at the large complex. The building had showers, toilets, and a kitchen. Cots were ready; we had little baggage so we settled in quickly. Soon we were greeted by a group from the U.S. Embassy bringing goodies. Each person got a full box of Hershey bars, a carton of American cigarettes, and other needed items. The best news was that we could write letters home, and the embassy people would mail the messages for us. I sat down immediately and wrote to Molly and Mom.

March 31, 1945

Dearest Molly,

Well, Darling, you have been in my mind constantly. By this time you no doubt know it has been impossible to write. How I've wondered and wondered how you and Tomilyn were and are? How Mom and all the families are and what they're doing? Wondering if you had given me up but hoping your faith in God wouldn't let you give up hope. I know it was a shock to get a telegram stating I was M.I.A. but I always knew you would have known before you got the letter something was wrong because of the sudden stoppage of my letters.

Well, to relieve your mind about my condition, I'm well as ever except for a slight case of frozen feet which are almost well. My weight is about normal again and I feel fine. The greatest tonic I got though was to get started towards the hands of our own troops. By the time you see me, I'll be in first class condition.

How I was captured is, I suppose, a military secret but this much I will say that we fought and held until everything around us caved in. My men were the bravest of brave and fought like demons. I still get a great feeling of comfort and satisfaction knowing they did their job so well. I cite you one of the feats of bravery.

Making the rounds of my men after the pressure had let up, I came across one of my gun crews. Ryan, a new boy, was looking a little peaked so I asked him the trouble. "Nothing wrong, Lieutenant, except we ran out of Jerries to shoot at," was his reply. Asking him again as he did look pretty white and sickly. "Well, Sir. I got nicked yesterday but didn't want you to send me back." He had helped stop three German counter attacks and been wounded for 24 hours and still wanted to stay. I ordered him back to the Aid Station and certainly felt bad about doing it, as he started crying. The only way he would go was for me to promise he could come back if the Doc said it was O.K. Well, Molly, that boy was back in action two hours later.

Well, Darling, I could go on and on telling you about feats of bravery, but the stories will all keep until I can tell you in person. My main thought is how much I'm in love with you and how I need to see you again or at least hear from you. When I get to mail this letter I don't know but I had to drop a line telling you how much I love you. You're my everything.

Your

Bob

Hello, Pumpkin, I sure hope you still remember your Dad

Molly had written to me on Prisoner of War Post on March 18th, addressed to Lt. Robert E. P. Moranda, Prisoner of War No. 316354 Camp Name and No. M-Stammlager IV B, Deutschland. It was returned by direction of the War Department and was postmarked June 18. In it she had written:

Dearest Bob

Here it is Sunday again, we are staying around the house and later we are going to take a walk. I saw Maye [my sister] & Forest Fuger and they were so happy about you and said to say hello. Buck and Johnny have both gone over. Tiny [her sister Rozeel] met this lady in Lancaster whose nephew is in your camp. His name is Capt. James H. Burns No. 316402. You might look him up if you can. He asked for a toothbrush on his card so I'll send you one too in case you need it. I had a letter from Lucy West. She was so happy about you and said Hugh talks about you all the time in his letters. Tiny sent me a map that the girl in the Red Cross gave her and it has all the camps on it. I know where yours is, the bulletin that came with it was very consoling and helped me a lot. You keep up your spirits and love us lots. Just think good things and dream of the future, that's what I do! Robin and I are so proud of our Daddy and love him so very, very much. The bulletin also stated that I can send a photograph or map to you by enclosing it in an envelope without a letter and you will get it, so I'll send a colored one soon. I write you every day, darling, but they may not get thru to you consecutively so don't worry, they are on the way! You write to us often darling, as often as you can, and remember, keep that sweet chin of yours up and be patient.

Love & Kisses, Molly & Robin.

The nonsmokers soon had trading material and traded for Hershey bars and other items. Most of the nonsmokers gave the cigarettes to a smoker. My friend Lt. Boyd, my bunk buddy in the Stalag, gave me his, so I was able to share with others. This is one of the jokes going around at that time:

First soldier: "How many Hershey Bars did you eat the first day?"

Answer: "I ate them all."

First soldier: "What did you do with the wrapper?"

Answer: "What wrapper?"

The men were fast recovering from the ordeal of being prisoners of war. They were active and even looked for games to play. That was a good sign; they had made it, and so had I.

One day as we were outside the building, we heard a beautiful chorus of male singers. It came from a company of Russian soldiers doing marching drills. As they trooped along, they sang a Russian song. The blend of the voice tones was beautiful.

Since we were able to send messages home via the Embassy, I wrote quite a few letters which was a great relief to me. While away from Molly and the baby, whenever it was possible, I would write. But for a long time I had not been able to, so I know the only communication she had possibly received was the message that I sent through the Red Cross from the prison camp.

At night when I was on my bunk, I would try to visualize my family and by mental telepathy send word to them that I was okay. The time spent thinking about all of my family kept me sane. A man must have an anchor. I knew all of Molly's prayers that she said every day, so I would say the prayer, sing or hum a song, and usually with my final prayer would say the 23rd Psalm—"The Lord is my shepherd, I shall not want." I said that prayer every time I had to do anything that was possibly dangerous. The 23rd Psalm was and remains to this day my personal prayer.

The day came when the embassy people told us to be ready to sail the next morning. We were ready! The morning came, and we marched down to the harbor and boarded an English passenger vessel. The ship had been converted from civilian use to service by the Armed Forces. We had individual bunks, a lounge, a complete dining room, and service *par excellence*. We were on our way back. And what a great way to go!

Return to the United States

The Black Sea was calm. We enjoyed watching the scenes from the deck. We sat and read, played cards, or talked. Alex Bertin and I were partners in bridge. He was an excellent player and showed me the correct way to bid and play the game. We took on all challengers and did quite well. As none of us had any money, the stakes were whatever we had: cigarettes, candy, anything, or nothing.

On the second or third day, we passed Constantinople—what a sight to behold. The day we sailed through the Dardanelles and entered the Mediterranean Sea, every one of the passengers became seasick—that is, everyone but me. When I went into the dining area for lunch, not a soul was there. The motion of the ship was caused by two sea currents coming together, so the ship wrenched one way and then the other making people sick. Later, as we approached Naples, Italy, we stood by the ship's rails enjoying the view of the coastline and of Mt. Etna in the distance.

From the time we left Wugarten and during the trip, no one saw either Col. Fuller or Hegl. On shipboard, they stayed in Col. Fuller's cabin. We wondered what the next step would be for Hegl. We soon found out. The ship docked, and we disembarked. We were back into the control of the U.S. Army. When we were in ranks for the first time, Col. Fuller and Hegl came front and center. Both saluted and Hegl then became a prisoner of war of the Americans. Many of us could not understand the situation, but as I now reflect on what happened, I realize that it took a lot of guts on Col. Fuller's part to save Hegl. I have often wondered whatever happened to him.

We were taken to a large resort where we had hot baths, a place to replace clothes, and friendly, more familiar surroundings which increased our feeling of security. I had a new outfit from head to foot. I saved my old boots and my muffler, items that are still with me. In fact, I used the same boots and shawl when I served in Korea a few years later.

On the third day, I decided to take a ride into Naples to see what was there. I rode into town in the back of an Army truck. On the way we were solicited by young boys for anything we could give them. One asked, "You want to make love to my sister? She is fourteen years old— very pretty." It made me think how bad the people were having it. I gave the kid some cigarettes. Those he could sell, and it was all I had.

We arrived at the USO. As I walked in I saw an old friend, Sgt. McFarland, a former classmate at OCS. He had failed in the last week. He had been a good friend, and we had shared many Saturday nights in Columbus, Georgia. We had a great time talking about what he was doing and where he was assigned. I found out he had been in Italy with a unit—a safe unit—so he was pleased. He remarked during our conversation: "Glad I failed OCS. If I had made it through and had become a 2nd lieutenant, I would probably be dead by now." How true! Lieutenants of the infantry didn't last long; many were the first ones killed or wounded in a battle. We said goodbye after a few minutes. I always wondered what happened to him at the OCS. I believe that he asked to be relieved from becoming an officer, but I hope he was washed out.

I also met a young lady from Santa Barbara, California, who was working for the USO. We talked about home, and she said she liked Naples as it reminded her of Santa Barbara. After the war when I got home and was back working in Santa Barbara, I called her folks and learned she was still in Italy. It was nice talking to her parents, and they were glad that their daughter was fine and happy. Later, when the daughter returned to California, she came into my service station many times.

I was in the USO in the morning for an hour or so. Then I left to see another part of the town and returned to the resort where they had us billeted. I later learned that on that same afternoon my brother

Ted came into the same USO. We found out our paths almost crossed. Wouldn't that have been great! Here it was in March, and I had been missing since December. No one from home knew where I was. To have run into my youngest brother would have been the greatest thing that could have happened to me in a long time. Ted was in the Air Transport Command of the Army Air Corps and flew all over the world delivering planes. He just happened to be in Italy on that date.

The night before we were to embark to go home, we were given a liquor ration. I received a bottle of scotch and a bottle of gin. Our little group proceeded to drink. But first we made a pact: we promised we would help each other board the Queen Mary the next day. Our group included Maj. Burns and Lts Duffy and Kazarian. Snockered we got, and we finally went to bed. In my lifetime I have only been drunk twice. The first time was on my first encounter with hard liquor when a youngster; the second was on the occasion of our being returned to the control of our forces.

The next day we helped each other pack our duffel bags. We went by truck to the harbor and boarded the Queen Mary. We were comfortable on board but less so than on the ship that brought us from Odessa to Naples. I missed my friend Alex Bertin, but I spent time with Maj. Jimmy Burns and his three friends.

On the second day out we were sitting on the top deck sunning ourselves when suddenly there was a loud blast from the ship's horn. The horn was only a few feet above us. The group started to look for their foxholes. What a scare! The ship lurched and cornered sharply. We found out the ship made forty-five degree turns every so often to avoid being trapped by a U-boat.

During the trip home, I was watching a group playing poker. The stakes were high. The table had six players, and I was sitting behind one of the players. I will always remember one of the hands I watched. Across the table a man opened. The play came around to the man I was sitting behind. He rose heavily. The opener rose again. All players but the two dropped out of the game. The pot was large by then.

The dealer asked, "How many cards?"

The opener said, "One."

The man I was watching picked up his hand to a position where I could see—three jacks and a pair of aces. Without much hesitation the man threw away the pair of aces and said, "I'll have two cards please."

The opening bet was high, and the raises were even higher. Finally the call was made. The opener had four tens.

Slowly the other man turned over his cards and exposed four jacks! Then he said to the man who opened, "You forced me to throw away my full house. No one would bet as you did with two pair or an almost flush or straight. Had I played a pat hand, you would have won."

I don't remember how many days it took to cross the ocean, but I think it was six. I was disappointed that we wouldn't see the Statue of Liberty as we were heading for Boston. As we sailed into Boston harbor, there on the docks waiting for us was a large crowd complete with a military band—the USO people, Red Cross representatives, and a group of young girls from a nearby college. We disembarked and went into a large warehouse where we were served coffee, doughnuts, and other food.

A few of us were singled out for interviews. I was introduced to a young lady who asked me about my experiences. There wasn't much to say. How do you tell a young lady how cruel and confining it was? How do you tell a lady that you questioned your own actions? Why didn't I go out fighting and take a couple of Germans with me? But then what do you do when a machine gun is to your front aiming at your chest and a squad of German *soldats* behind you with their guns also aimed at you? Survival is the prime factor. At any rate I mumbled something inconsequential.

And the question came, "Do you hate the Germans?" Without a thought I said, "Yes!" At this time I hated all German soldiers but not all Germans. I remembered a couple of incidents: the *hausfrau* in Wugarten and the lady in Germany who was a part of the jeering crowd as we marched through their town, and who came forward and squeezed a silver coin into my hand. As the coin entered my hand, she blessed me.

Later the reporter sent me a copy of *The Wheaton News*, Wheaton College, Norton, Massachusetts, dated, April 28, 1945. An article on the front-page had the heading "News Interviews Ex-PWs at Standish." The byline was Eleanor Johnson:

> "If you could get it over to your people what it means to hear of absenteeism, sit-down strikes and laxness..." Capt. Donald Gilinsky spoke quietly at Camp Miles Standish, and nervously played with the bar on his cap as he talked of his experiences in a German prison camp. Lieut. Robert Moranda, who had lost 54 pounds during his internment, and Lieut. Ross Gehring, a young Oklahoma boy, silently agreed.
>
> Captured by the Germans after the Battle of the Bulge in December when Von Rundstedt had driven back the Allies, they, along with other American, British, French, Polish, Yugoslavian, and Serbian prisoners of war, were marched across Germany into Poland. The Germans forced them to do an about face, however, when the Russians began to get too near in the east. Finally the Russians surrounded the town in which they were encamped; the Germans fled and the boys marched on again this time with the Russians to Odessa on the Black Sea, and then went by ship to Naples and the American Army....
>
> If it hadn't been for the Red Cross packages, the prisoners would have starved," blond Lieut. Moranda from California spoke. "Many times the Germans would hold out the packages, though, and refuse to give them to the prisoners. There were at least 500 boxes stacked up that hadn't been distributed." He paused, shook his head thoughtfully in remembrance and praised the Red Cross again. "Why, I could make you a wonderful pie with potatoes and chocolate from the Red Cross packages. All the Germans gave us the 11 days we were in the camp were six potatoes, one bowl of soup, a spoonful of molasses thrown in our hands and some hard tack."
>
> "You were lucky; we didn't even get that," the captain retorted...
>
> "The Russians certainly are a wonderful people to have as allies," laughed Lieut. Moranda crinkling his eyes as the subject of their liberators was introduced.

"You've never been kissed until you've been kissed by a Russian officer," Lieut. Gehring added, rubbing his cheek in remembrance...

Returning to the food situation, they told of being hungry and spending the night in a cow barn where a "city-bred boy tried to milk an ox" as he saw his companions getting results from the cows.

Talking to Wheaton reporters they, along with many khaki clad boys, were awaiting phone calls in the small Army building. The three of them expected to be home within a week, after having been from 12 to 18 months in Europe. Lieut. Moranda unconsciously described himself and his friends when he said, "No matter what happens, the American soldier never loses his sense of humor."

Soon we were bussed to the railroad siding and boarded an old Pullman car. Each man was assigned a berth. We even had a porter, a black man who took marvelous care of us.

For the next few days, we traveled the U.S.A. The route we took was via Chicago, through South Dakota, then swinging southward, and finally arriving at Los Angeles. At every stop where I could, I sent a telegram to Molly, telling her how much I loved her and how I was going to express that love when I arrived. I think my mother got a big kick out of the telegrams. She saved them all in one of her scrapbooks.

Home

We detrained in Los Angeles, and I started the long walk from the train, first along side of the train saying goodbye to the fellow officers, then through the entrance to the station, and finally up the long incline into the station. As I made the final curve, I looked up and there stood Molly, Tomilyn, my mother, Aunt Marie and Uncle Bill Cummings. Molly was prancing and waving and calling out to me, "Hurry, hurry, please hurry." I did. I was kissed and hugged by all. What a wonderful warm feeling! To hold my baby was something, for now my family was three again. All of a sudden I heard a gasp from Molly. "You've been wounded. You have the Purple Heart. Where were you wounded? Is it bad? Does it hurt? Why didn't you tell me?" Finally I quieted her down, showed her my scars on my face, a few marks on my nose and lips, and raised my pant legs and showed my scars there. None of them serious, just where shell fragments had hit me while in the St. Vith forest. A tree burst got me as I was in a foxhole.

Uncle Bill had driven the family to Los Angeles from Oxnard. Uncle Bill and dear Aunt Marie were always there for the Morandas. How wonderful it was to hear the voices at home, to be embraced by my mom, and to get the caresses and squeezes from Molly.

Mother, Molly, Loraine (Tommy Swain's wife), and brother Bill's wife, Jeannette, were all living together in Oxnard on B Street, where we soon settled in. One incident made what happened to the people at home clear to me. We who were away were memories, pictures, and letters. I was sitting in the front room the first night home and I saw, looking around the room, pictures of all the people of our families—my five brothers, my sister, and my brother-in-law—who all were in the armed forces. Nightly, before Tomi was put to bed, she would go around the room saying goodnight to the pictures. "Goodnight Uncle Tom. Goodnight Uncle Earl. Goodnight Uncle Bill, Uncle George, Uncle Paul, Uncle Ted, and Aunt Maye." She said to my picture, "Goodnight Daddy." Then she turned to Molly and asked, pointing at me, "Where did we get him?"

I was paraded around town by the family and saw many friends. My orders stated I was to be home for two weeks, and then Molly and I were to have a week at the Momarte Hotel in Santa Barbara. There we would be again analyzed, healed, and questioned to find out if we were able to continue in the Army.

While at the hotel the wives and families went to an "information enlightening" class conducted by the doctors. They wanted to let the women and families of the ex-POWs know that the next few months, and possibly years for some, they would have a hard time adjusting to a peacetime life. All they told the wives to do was to love them and try to understand and soon all would return to normal. Molly didn't need that advice for she already told me "Let us go back to where we were before you were drafted. We still love each other and we have to resume our life as it was." And that's what it took—a loving wife and daughter and our families not expecting too much. Later, as I looked back on my reactions during the war, I came to realize I was changed in many ways. I had learned to better control my thoughts and actions and had developed a strong dependence on prayer and a strong feeling that God is always with me and had been, seeing me through the battlefield and POW experiences I had gone through.

Something that never changed in all of our married life was that each time I arrived home, I'd reach out and hug Molly and say, "How about a dance, Babe?" Then start to sway and Molly invariably replied, "Some day I will dance with you."

Everywhere I walked around the towns of Hueneme and Oxnard I received greetings from friends such as "Glad to see you back, Bob." I was glad to see most of the people. But I was somewhat bitter and wondered how in hell some got to stay home and the government got all the Morandas—something I probably will never understand.

One day we drove to Lancaster to see Molly's folks and her sister Rozeel Gabbert. They operated a turkey ranch. Rozeel's husband Eddie was still a flight instructor for aviation cadets. While there we attended the graduation ceremony for Molly's youngest sister Shirley. The auditorium was filled with parents and friends. We were all so proud of Shirley, and her family occupied two rows of seats along one side. In front of me were Molly, Tomilyn, and Molly's parents Henry and Isabel, while I sat behind them with Eddie and Rozeel and their baby Patty.

The ceremony was going well, but during a quiet part of the procedure, Tomilyn broke wind very loudly. Everyone around us was snickering, but that wasn't enough—Tomilyn turned around and in a loud voice blurted out "Daddy, I pooped." It was embarrassing, but the family got a good laugh out of it.

While there, along with a few others, I was honored with a review of the troops. I was presented with the Silver Star for "Gallantry in Action." I wondered then if others had been rewarded. The citation read:

> Second Lt. Robert E. P. Moranda (01326108) Infantry, while serving with the Army of the United States, distinguished himself by gallantry in action in connection with military operations against the enemy from 17 December, 1944 to 21 December, 1944 in the area of St. Vith, Belgium. With the full force of the German Winter counteroffensive striking our lines, 2nd Lt. Moranda's machine gun platoon again and again repelled fierce enemy assaults. Inspired by his great courage and able leadership, the men poured devastating volleys into the ranks of the attackers, many times waiting until hostile troops were within fifty yards of our lines in order to gain maximum fire effect. Through the days and nights of bitter action, Lt. Moranda braved heavy fire to move from foxhole to foxhole checking the positions and encouraging the troops to hold their ground. When units on the flanks withdrew, Lt. Moranda remained in position, taking a heavy toll of dead and wounded even when completely surrounded and cut off. 2nd Lt. Moranda and the men he led are reported missing in action,

but by their determined stand against heavy odds they helped slow the armored spearheads of the enemy, giving us time to mass our forces and halt the drive...

When the War Department sent a telegram to Molly stating that I was "Missing in Action," she screamed and fainted. Mom would not allow that. She pulled Molly to her feet and told Molly that her son was alive and she knew that he would come home. She was steadfast in her belief all through the war that her family was all going to come home safely. She must have had an inside track to God. All of her children did come home safely. She never wavered in her belief.

One humorous incident happened also. At the bottom of the telegram there were two words which said that the telegram was "Sans Origin." Mom was telling her friend Mrs. Jim Lykins about the telegram. When they compared notes, Mrs. Lykins had also received a telegram with the "Sans Origin" at the bottom of a telegram telling something about her son Gerald "Shorty" Lykins. So the two dear ladies started to look in the atlas to see if their two sons were at the same place. The ladies were looking for an island or town somewhere in the world. Then someone told them that it was the way the War Department signed their telegrams, as they did not want to give the location that the telegram was sent from.

When we went to Santa Barbara, Molly and I had left Tomilyn with her mother, so we were like honeymooners. We had great food, good friends, time to visit, and were having fun. We spent most of the time with Jim Burns and his men from the 28th Division and their wives. Jim was single and eligible. In fact at one of the events, he met "Diz," his wife-to-be.

I attended a few sessions with Army Intelligence personnel trying to piece together the war. There was not much I could tell them. Even the F.B.I. interviewed me. Later I found out they had also questioned each returning POW officer perhaps to see if we were Americans and to find out what we saw that could aid them in understanding Russian warfare. They seemed to be especially interested in weapons. I am sure my testimony was of little value.

For a few days, I was lost in my memories of the past months. I wanted to forget. At the same time, I wanted to talk, but not to civilians nor to anyone in the service who was not in the infantry. My old friends were gone. The men I served with were not around, only those people who didn't want to hear and couldn't appreciate what it was like, even though they implied that they could. How close were we who served together? I can't answer that easily except to say there was a tightly-knit bond among those of us who served together and had shared experiences. With regard to relationships with the men in my platoon, that closeness was tempered, because I always felt I needed to keep a distance between my men and myself. For how could I become close and then order them into dangerous places or to perform risky jobs? Yet they were my eyes and ears, for without them I would be lost. Since I was required to read all their outgoing mail, I thought I knew their families and some of their innermost thoughts. But they didn't know mine. They didn't ask for anything but to get back home. And they were my protectors.

Soon it was time to return home and to the Army. When I got home and was visiting with one of my brothers, he saw that I had received the Silver Star. His comment was, "Who got the Gold?"

It was also a time to learn some of the things that had gone on during my absence. When the first card that I had written from the prison camp arrived, advising Molly and the folks at home that I was alive and was a prisoner of war, the card came into the post office in Port Hueneme. The postmaster Art Haycock didn't waste any time in getting the notice to Mom. He got in his car and hand-delivered the message to Mother. He also announced the news to most of the people in the township. Art and his wife Ann were good friends of the family so they had a special interest in what was going on in our family. Mom then called Molly, who was in Lancaster at the time.

I had my orders assigning me to Fort Ord, California. When I had arrived in Santa Barbara, I was promoted to 1st Lieutenant. The promotion was long in coming. It should have come when I was in Europe, but because I had been POW, the promotion was held up until I was liberated and returned to U.S. control.

Molly and I returned to Oxnard. I enjoyed the people there, but I was bitter about the whole affair which caused me, at times, to react rudely to a few people in the town. Some did rub me the wrong way and I told them off.

Brothers George, Bob, and Paul

When an able-bodied man said to me he had done his part in the war effort by buying War Bonds, it was the fuse for a minor explosion on my part. Yes, they were patriotic and wealthy. They had been promoted to positions over the men who had gone away to serve in the Armed Forces. It wasn't their fault; it was the luck of the draw. It did take some time for me to come to grips with myself, through a lot of understanding on Molly's part and my great family. They accepted me for what I was and treated me in the same manner as they always had.

While in Lancaster, Jimmy Burns, my buddy from the prisoner-of-war camp, came out to the house to meet the Swains and the Gabberts. Eddie Gabbert was an Air Corps Aviation Trainer so he arranged with a friend to take the two of us on a flight, and they tried to wring us out. They were playing dog fighting and were doing all the maneuvers to make us sick. But as Eddie told Rozeel when we got home, "There we were trying to scare those nutty infantry officers. On one of my loops I looked back and there were Bob and Jimmy pretending they were firing machine guns. I was almost passing out, and they were having fun. So I came down."

We stayed in Lancaster for about a week and enjoyed getting reacquainted with the families. The war was rapidly winding down in Europe. Some of us wondered whether we would be sent to the Far East to fight the Japanese.

It was time for me to go back to the Army. Molly and the baby stayed with her family, and I departed for Fort Ord where I was assigned to the Casual Battalion and given a job to brief the incoming soldiers on what was going to happen to them in the few days they would be in Fort Ord before getting their assignments. I gave a canned speech that the commander of the battalion had composed. He sat in the audience and listened to make sure I gave it as he had written. It was easy to do.

My other job was to be the mess officer. I had to supervise three mess halls where they served about 5,000 men every day. On my first day, I went into one of the mess halls to have lunch. As I started through the line, the mess sergeant came up to me and asked me to follow him. He said I didn't have to go through the mess line and took me to the large refrigerators and opened the door of each one. There were hundreds of choice cuts of beef. The sergeant said, "This is what we in the mess eat." I asked, "Why?" I didn't like the reply he gave, so I ordered the choice cuts be served to the incoming troops as soon as possible and in the future the mess personnel would eat the same food as the troops.

Soon Molly and the baby came north and joined me. For a time while we looked for a house, we lived with my brother George and his wife Nancy, who were stationed and had quarters at the Presidio of Monterey. Molly found a house in Pacific Grove. At that time, George was assigned as adjutant of the Civil Affairs Staging Area. Molly and I were treated well by them, but it was not in their best interest that we overstay our welcome. In addition, the Army didn't approve of having two service families living in one set of their quarters—another one of those curious rules. Here stood a large house that could hold two families, but rules are rules.

After we moved into the place that Molly found, we were very happy. One of the things that made me even happier was the day my former runner, now Corp. Maurice Connover, saw me walking around the company area and yelled out, "Hey, Lieutenant Moranda, wait up." We both ran to each other and there on the company area we gave each other a big hug—no salute—a hug right there on the grounds at Fort Ord. We questioned each other for a time. I told him where we were living and made arrangements for him and his wife to come to our house. They came that evening, Maurice and his wife Ellie, and we had a great time together. I remember when he read my Silver Star citation, he commented, "Hell, if I had known how bad it really was, I would have been scared." He was stationed at Fort Ord for the rest of his tour of duty. He then returned to his farm in Broadview, Montana, where they renewed their life of raising wheat.

One of the great things about living in that area and being a returned veteran was the famous golf courses. They allowed and encouraged us to golf during the week for fifty cents a round. What a challenge they were, and what a privilege. I golfed at Pebble Beach, Del Monte, Pacific Grove, Monterey Peninsula, and Cypress Point. Many afternoons, when we could, a few of us would take off and go to one of the courses and play. Brother George and I played once at Cypress. He hit his ball into one of the trees, and the ball didn't come down. He shinnied up the tree, shook one of the branches, and golf balls came raining down. We picked up a dozen balls. As golf balls were expensive and hard to get, we were happy to receive the bonanza.

[On May 2, 1945, the collapse of the German forces was complete, and fighting was brought to a conclusion when a surrender document, signed on April 29, came into effect.]

Lt. Bob being awarded Silver Star after his return to California, 1945

I was on duty on VE Day. It was quiet in the camp. I was almost alone in our area. It gave me plenty of time to wander and wonder. How many men were lost in winning that part of the war? I wondered how many more lives would it take to win the remaining war in the Pacific and about the inequities in the war, who serves and where. I know, too, that the foot sloggers, the infantrymen, know there are only a few ways to get out of the front lines: win the war, become a casualty of some kind, or come home in a bag. But there are benefits, too. With pride the infantryman could say, "I was there and where in the hell were you."

The time spent at Fort Ord was uneventful and routine. The weather was typical of the coastal area around Monterey Bay that summer—morning fog followed by bright sunshine, so we had plenty of outside activity.

My brother Earle and his wife Becky came from Washington, D.C. to Monterey to stay with George's family for a few days, for he was soon to ship out to the Pacific to enter the war against the Japanese. We had quite a reunion in Monterey. I brought Maye over from her nurse's station at the Army Hospital in Modesto. We had a good day catching up with each other before I took her back to Modesto that night. I got lost on the way home and finally got back in time to go to work at Fort Ord. But it was worth the lost sleep to have been together with at least several of the family.

[On August 10, 1945, the Japanese government issued a statement substantially agreeing to the terms enumerated in the Potsdam Declaration. Formal surrender ceremonies took place on the Battleship Missouri on September 2. The occupation and control of Korea by Japan was terminated and after much squabbling between the democratic south and the communist north, a dividing line at the 38th parallel was established.]

In a few days, Earle went to San Francisco, where he boarded the ship that was to take him somewhere in the Pacific. The ship was loaded and had started to sail out of the bay of San Francisco when the orders came for the ship to come back to the harbor. The war was over, and when the point system was announced by the War Department, he found he had enough points to obtain separation from the service. He came back, picked up Becky, and they proceeded back east to a separation point where he returned to civilian life as a member of the Army Reserves.

Sometime later I received a certificate, which I appreciated, from:

The Kingdom of Belgium

(SEAL)

The Ministry of National Defense

Has the honor to inform

2nd Lieutenant Robert E. Moranda,

That, by Royal Decree, his Majesty Prince Regent, from 3 Jan, 1946, N. 1578,

He was nominated

KNIGHT OF THE ORDER OF THE CROWN WITH PALM

For the diligent and brilliant organization work and for the courageous spirit shown in such a remarkable way by his bravery in the battles that have led to the complete liberation of Belgium in the hands of the common enemy. He is happy to be addressing his sincere congratulations in this nomination.

I continued to serve at Fort Ord. The war came to an end abruptly. As I had plenty of points to get out of the Army, I took advantage of the system. It wasn't long before we were home again. The circle had been closed. We were back home with family and work from which I had been separated for nearly three years. Brother Earle went from active duty to the Officer's Reserve Corps and returned to Washington, D.C. to take a job with the Central Intelligence Agency when it was created. Sister Maye went back to nursing at Los Angeles General Hospital. Bill was discharged from the Marines and went to work for the Sanitary District. Later when the town incorporated as Port Hueneme, Bill became its City Manager. George stayed in the Army for a while and then came back to Hueneme to try civilian life. Paul left the Navy and Ted the Army Air Corps, and both went back to college under the GI Bill. Things were never the same as before the war, but we were still a loving and caring family. And Mom took the ribbon with seven blue stars down from the window.

After World War II

Family Life

[During the war, the United States experienced a great dislocation of people with 15 million in the services, wives and sisters and parents working in various defense- related jobs including production lines for military materiel—an increase of nearly 7 million workers. The cost of living rose dramatically. Many factories had been converted to producing war materiel (6500 naval vessels, 296,400 airplanes, 86,330 tanks). The automobile industry had stopped manufacturing car to make tanks, jeeps, half-tracks, and other army vehicles. The war cost $321 billion. When production resumed, manufacturers allocated their products to dealers throughout the country. I remember months after the war ended our family needed a refrigerator. Art Haycox, who ran the hardware store in Hueneme, kindly put Mother on the list. When he got a refrigerator, he delivered it to her home, and she threw out the ice box. My wife Nancy's father, who bought a new Chevrolet every year before the war, bought a new Chevrolet and then gave us his old 1939 sedan. In 1946, after my separation from the military and our daughter Margaret's birth, I drove back to Hueneme.]

When I returned to California, I wanted to get back to work and wondered how I would be received by the company, so I called my old boss P. J. Sullivan at the division office of Standard Stations, Inc. in Pasadena. He asked where I was living. He remembered we had our baby shortly before I was drafted, so he asked about the two girls in my life. I told him they were with me at home, and I was ready to go to work. After returning home, I was sitting in the living room reading the newspaper and happened to look out the window and saw Mr. Sullivan walking up the sidewalk. The place was a shambles, but we quickly gathered baby stuff and clothes and threw them into a

261

bedroom so the place was somewhat presentable. My old station was not available, so he asked if I would consider going to Santa Barbara. I jumped at the chance with a quick, "Yes!" That's where Molly and I had been the happiest. He asked about some of my war experiences I had, so I told him and showed him the Silver Star Medal and citation. He asked to take them, for he wanted to place the story in the company quarterly magazine. He did so and then returned them to me. Mr. Sullivan was my sponsor within the company. He and I had a shared interest in baseball. He called me the "Hueneme Flash" after seeing me play in a game in Santa Barbara. On that night I hit a home run and a double—which he always remembered, and later arranged for me to play for his team in Pasadena.

The Standard Station was at Carrillo Street and Highway 101. I didn't care what size the station was, for it was great to be back in Santa Barbara where we had been so happy before the war. In a couple of days we drove there and met R. W. Smith. He greeted me with "Welcome back. Call me Ward." He had been transferred from the state of Washington and moved to Santa Barbara with his wife Jean and daughter. They did their best to make us feel welcome.

Next came the hard part—to find a place to live with the housing shortage. My typical day was to arrive early enough in the morning to look for a house before going to work or stay after work for a couple of hours and look some more. It was winter, and I had no heater in the car, a source of discomfort, but it was a lot warmer than I had been in Belgium, Russia, and Germany, especially during the time I was a POW tromping through the snow. I enjoyed the ride from Oxnard each day along the beautiful coast highway between the hills and ocean. On my days off, Molly and Tomilyn accompanied me as we searched for a house. When I came back, I was using the gutter language of army troops. This became apparent when we were going from one realtor to another asking about rentals. Molly and the baby were in the car while I was pleading our case to an agent. Suddenly, we heard a child's voice, "Daddy, you son of a bitch, come back. We want to go home." With that I hurried back to the car and vowed then to cut down my use of foul language.

One day at the station, one of my workers, Bud Mellolin, told me his sister and her husband knew there was going to be an upstairs apartment over them located at 224 Anapamu Street. I immediately drove there and talked to the landlords about renting it. They were somewhat reluctant about a child, but finally agreed. (As time went by, Tomilyn became the star of the neighborhood. I called Ward Smith and asked for a day off to move the family. He approved, and the next day we moved. We didn't have much because a fire had destroyed most of our belongings while I was in Europe. But we were happy. I loved to hear Molly's chatter. She sparkled like a diamond.

Shortly after, Ward and his wife hosted a party for returning servicemen and managers of service stations. There I met Cecil Perkins, who had returned from his service as a motor officer also with the 7th Armored Division. Many years later he was my boss when I served in Hawaii as Retail Manager for the islands of Oahu, Molokai, and Lanai. But we never talked about our service in the same division in Europe.

Everything was going great. I was on a baseball team and met a young man, Ray Emery who impressed me with his ability to get on base. Our two families became close. He was a city electrician and in charge of the street signals. Whenever I could, I drove at a prescribed speed limit from State Street to its end and reported the number of times I had to stop. In about three months, he had all the signals correctly timed. Of course, he accused me of making his life miserable.

Our friends also included Helen and Roy Raute. He was a ballplayer and a roofer by trade, and Helen worked in a clothing store. We played a lot of the card game Canasta, and we spent many Sunday afternoons trying to beat each other.

It was a happy time for us enjoying life. Molly was active in the school PTA and in her Christian Science church. When she became pregnant again, she was so happy for she wanted another girl. She found a new practitioner, and her daily readings kept her busy.

When the day came for the birth, I took Molly to the hospital, and then called the practitioner. Molly had problems, and the baby did not survive. She was devastated. We arranged for our baby to have a quick burial in the Santa Barbara cemetery. As she had to have a name as she went straight to heaven, we selected Christine Mary after Christ and his mother Mary. Molly was devastated at the loss, but, thankfully, we had Tomilyn, who was a godsend. Sympathy came from our families and the Rautes and Emerys. Ray and Ginnie came to the apartment the next day and gave me a check for $500—not as a loan, but a gift.

[When President Roosevelt died, Harry Truman succeeded him. Soon after the Soviets began aggressive moves in Greece, brought pressure on Turkey, and made other moves that indicated their intention to expand. They soon developed their atom bomb. President Truman issued what became known as the Truman Doctrine, which declared the U. S. policy "to support free peoples who are resisting attempted subjugation by armed minorities or by outside pressures." General Marshall was sent to China in December 1945 to try to prevent warfare between Nationalist and Communist forces and form a coalition government. That failed and by the end of 1949 the Nationalists retreated to Taiwan . This caused the U.S. to strengthen forces in Japan.]

We were unhappy with where we lived, so we had to do something. Ray, Roy, and I had discussed many times the idea of the three of us together building a house. Luckily, one of my customers mentioned that he was subdividing land in the Hope Ranch area. We knew we couldn't afford the area called the Park, but he said he had lots near there on Vista Clara and Modoc Road. Molly and I went out and selected one and agreed to pay a few dollars each month. There was no interest involved on the amount of purchase, so it didn't take long to pay the few hundred dollars. I then went to banks and lending agencies and the answer to my request for a loan was always the same, a big no. They wouldn't take the chance as we knew nothing about building. The third time, I went to the Santa Barbara Savings and Loan. The manager asked why I was so desperate to build a house. I told him of the recent tragedy of the baby's death and that Molly was having a very difficult time getting over it. He said, "Why didn't you tell me. I know what you are going through as my wife and I lost our baby." He then said he would approve the loan if we could find a contractor who would give us a contract of completion.

I was elated as one of my customers, Otto Dickscheidt, was a contractor. We had talked earlier about building and he had plans for a small house that he had completed. He said if I wanted one like that, he would give us a price. Molly and I drove out, saw it and liked it. I took the plans to the Savings and Loan, and they approved the loan. I called Ray and Roy, and each said he would help. So we started. The carpenter in charge was Dickscheidt's brother Bill—a large man and gruff. There was no nonsense about him. He ordered me around and seemed to enjoy his role as boss and I really didn't care. As soon as he laid out the plans for the foundation, he turned to me and said, "Now it's your turn." I had to dig the trenches for the footings after the lot was leveled. The ground was a dry adobe—almost like cement—which took a lot of digging and picking. So with a pick and shovel I started, but wasn't making much progress. When I finished one trench, my new neighbor came over and told me to soak the ground with water and it would be much easier. I borrowed four long hoses from neighbors and soaked the ground. What a blessing that was, for I then discarded the pick. I wished many times I had put in a slab instead. But I started to make some progress. Bill was much happier—he actually smiled. The lot was a third of an acre, fronting on Modoc Road. We decided to place the building on the back of the lot and leave the front part for fruit trees and a lawn.

The septic tank was next with its feeder lines. Again, I was lucky for the County was in the process of building a water line along Modoc Road. For $25.00, I hired the man in charge and in about one hour he had all the weeper lines dug. We were now able to start the house. Ray and Roy were a big help: Ray, the electrician and Roy the roofer. I was the grunt, fetching tools, material, and anything else they needed when they were on ladders or the roof. All went well. Molly spent a lot of her time on the site rather than stay in the apartment. She became the star for old Bill. He put in a lot of extra things in the house. The hell with me, I was just the husband. But Molly and Tomilyn were the stars.

The frame was next and then the roof. Brothers Bill and George came up one weekend and helped put on sheet rock. Molly's family came up and helped. Henry did most of the work building the fences. Once Molly's folks came up from Lancaster, and after we had been working for quite some time, I made some drinks—Moscow Mules. They were made with vodka and ginger beer—which Molly's mother liked. She asked for another. As I was mixing it, she headed for the bathroom, but didn't make it. Husband Henry got a big kick out of it, becoming one of the happy memories of the building project as "the day Mother Isabel was tipsy," and "the day she christened the house."

Molly's sister Rozeel came to be with Molly for the birth of her baby, and the house was full of love—three women ready to care for the new little one, Patsy Gabbert. After a day in the hospital, Rozeel came home. That activity helped Molly get over some of her sorrow.

The house was near completion, and we shopped for the least expensive furniture, except for the fixture in the den where we had the television. We had selected a nice copper overhead one for the den where it would be safe from our knocking it over. Ray came on a weekend to finish the wiring. As I was working on an outlet in the den, Ray suddenly hooked up the power, and it knocked me across the room. I landed on the one item of value we had obtained, the copper fixture. I wanted to cry, but we did some home repair so it could be used, and wasn't very noticeable.

The final job was painting. All the gang from the station came out along with my boss Ward Smith. They brought brushes and did the painting in one day. I painted the outside on a couple of weekends. And there it was, a bare house occupied with love. Molly was so busy with the project that she got over, to a degree, the great loss we had suffered.

My assistant manager, Harry Cook, raised pure-bred collies. When he asked me if we wanted one, I jumped at the offer. He only had the runt of the litter left. Lassie became an invaluable protector for Tomilyn

We kept improving the house, planted an orchard with oranges, plums, peaches, and nectarines. I also planted roses, and enjoyed our rose garden. Each day when I returned home from work, there greeting me in the yard were my two loves, with Tomilyn yelling, "Daddy's home, Daddy's home." I'm sure the neighbors also heard.

Brother Ted called one day and said he was going to marry a pretty girl from Selma, Dorothy Brough and asked if I would stand up for him. Paul was closest to him during his youth, but Paul was in Columbus, Ohio at the university working on his PhD and teaching to supplement his income. On the day before the wedding, Tomilyn threw a comb into the toilet and plugged it. We didn't know what she had done and discovered the problem when we used it. I tried the usual ways to clear it but they didn't work, so I decided to remove the toilet and take it outside to clear the problem. I must have been in the wrong position and got a sharp pain in my back. I crawled to find Molly and had her call Ray and Ginnie Emery. Ray came, removed the toilet, found the comb, and cleared the stoppage. I had to call Ted and tell him the problem and that there was no way I could make the wedding. Ted then arranged for Bill to take my place. Molly took me to see a friend, an osteopath who manipulated my back, and I was back to normal before too long.

Into the National Guard

After World War II, military service remained close to our lives. One day in 1950 a tall young man came into the station and introduced himself as Charles Ott, owner of Ott's Hardware, and Commander of the 981st Field Artillery Battalion of the 40th National Guard Division. He said that he was aware of my Army service and needed an officer to command his Service Battery. This meant taking care of the vehicles of the battalion, and he was certain he could get me promoted quickly. The offer was tempting. I had been in the Infantry Branch and was now in the Army Reserve, so I knew I was subject to recall. The National Guard service would mean getting some extra money and serving in a job similar to my civilian occupation, as well as being able to go home each night. Having one night a week for the drill plus two weeks of summer camp each year, and serving a total of twenty years (including my active service) would qualify for retirement pay.

A few days later, Col. Ott drove me to the 40th Division Headquarters where I met most of the staff and was interviewed by the Division Commander, Major General Daniel H Huddelson and some of his staff. I must have passed muster as I was sworn in, and on the following Monday I assumed command of the Service Battery. I was briefed on the divisions' World War II service in the Philippines, Japan, and Korea as part of the occupying forces. The Assistant Division Commander, Brigadier General Homer Eaton, was a school principal in the Los Angeles School District. Before leaving the headquarters, I was taken to Lennie Imburgia for uniforms.

On the first drill night after I assumed command, I introduced myself and decided to have some fun drilling the unit. I learned that it was a mistake. Col. Ott was observing and decided to reassign me to Headquarters Battery. So my civilian work background again no longer matched the job. But with some help from the battalion staff, I slowly learned the role of artillery.

On one of my days off, I went to the Armory with the supply sergeant and inventoried the supplies and equipment for which I assumed responsibility. Some of the items were old and outdated but had not been discarded. One item was a haversack, a World War I model. I asked why in hell that was still in the inventory, and was told that it would be eliminated on a Report of Survey. Several years later Major Flint came into my office to collect for a missing item, the WWI haversack. The loss occurred when I was Headquarters Battery Commander. I told him that item was supposed to have been taken off the inventory when I assumed command over a year ago. I also told him that if he could find a like haversack in any army supply depot, I would buy one. I never heard about it again.

By then Molly and I were out of debt, having paid off all of our bills. Some of the companies had carried us when we could not pay all our bills. Because of the way we had handled things when we couldn't make all of our payments, we had an excellent credit rating.

Our families came to visit often. The war was rapidly disappearing from our thoughts. Many former servicemen were going to school under the GI Bill. I signed up for a law course with LaSalle Correspondence, but dropped it because my instructor gave me a C on my first lesson and said I had not enlarged all the facets of a case in my first lesson, that there was no such thing and black and white, that everything was a shade of grey. It became apparent that I could not take the time to continue with it because of my work, family, and baseball obligations.

We bought a piano, a Lester, and started Tomilyn with lessons with Frank Engleman, who was organist at Molly's Christian Science church. I usually sat in the living room and listened. After an early lesson, I asked Frank to show me how to get past some difficult phrases of a piece that I was trying to learn. I played by ear and had not practiced a lot, and he helped me, too. Mom, George and Nancy, and children along with Maye and her boyfriend, Leonard Bailey, came on a visit to see the piano. George, Jr. brought his new toy, a medium-size metal wheelbarrow, which he proceeded to bump into furniture. I went over to the piano stool and fended off his attacks. Mom got a big kick out of my concern and said, "Now you know why we didn't have nice things at our home in Hueneme."

Our old Studebaker was acting up, and we decided to buy a Chevrolet. When a young man came into the station, I commented that it was a great looking car. He said he was on the way to the dealer to turn it in as he was in the Marine Reserve and was being recalled into service. He would transfer it to anyone who would take over the payments, totaling $1,000 remaining. I jumped at the chance and made the deal. It was reddish brown with tinted windows, fog lights, and a heater. Molly liked it as did the rest of the family, all of whom were impressed with our good fortune when we drove to Hueneme to show it.

A few days later, Col. Ott came by the station and asked if I would try to get my brother George to command Battery A in Oxnard. I told him that he was a major and a Battery Commander called only for a captain. Ott assured me that he would get him promoted as soon as he and General Huddelson could make it happen. He asked me to go with him to Oxnard and I told him I would not try to influence George one way or another. At the time, George was selling real estate in Camarillo. He listened to Col. Ott and said he would think it over. He drove to Santa Barbara a few days later and conferred with Col. Ott and accepted the offer, thus becoming a captain in the National Guard. Now there were two Morandas as Battery Commanders in the 981st Artillery Battalion.

Recruiting was one of our major responsibilities, I did not try to influence my workers and assistants at the station, but most of them joined. My station was going great. When Bob Price, John Reed, and Marvin Glover signed up, I knew the station would be severely depleted if we were called up for active service. But I also knew Standard Oil would survive. George took over a battery with 35 men, where the Guard Table of Organization called for 92, so he spent much time recruiting.

Molly and I became the friends with Tom Hidalgo and his wife. Tom was in the battalion Operations and Training (S3) section and taught me a lot about artillery operations which helped considerably in my assignment. A new law had been passed that prevented men in the National Guard from being drafted or individually recalled, which helped in our recruiting effort.

Some of the battalion officers were Lt. Col. Ott as Commanding Officer, Maj. Arthur Reed (Executive Officer), and Capt. Clark Howell, (S4 Supply Officer). Lts. Art Spring and Tom Hidalgo were in the S3 (Operations and Training) section. Capt. Burris was a liaison officer. Others were pilots handling the aircraft used mostly for spotting targets and adjusting artillery fire: the Rennie brothers, Lts. Fallon and Grant Hodges. Molly became acquainted with the wives of the officers. She became close to Betty Latham, the wife of the Commanding Officer of B Battery in Ventura. They became like sisters. The four of us got together frequently. Later Jim and Betty named their baby girl Molly.

Camp Cooke

[With the victory of the Communists in China in 1949 and the announcement of the Soviet atomic explosion, fear of Communist expansion and a determination to contain them became the dominant theme in U.S. foreign policy. President Truman directed the U.S. Atomic Energy Commission to proceed with the development of a hydrogen bomb that would be more powerful than the atomic bomb which ended World War II. On June 25, 1950 the North Korean army, supported by China and the Soviet Union, advanced south of the 38th parallel which separated the northern Communist state from the Republic of Korea. The United States presented the matter to the United Nations Security Council, and urged the UN military forces be sent to resist the Communist invasion. As the Soviet members had boycotted the meeting, the Security Council adopted a resolution for UN members to resist the invasion and support the U.S. Forces under General MacArthur who had moved his two divisions in Japan to Korea by landing in Inchon and cutting off the Chinese, who retreated to approximately the 38th parallel.]

The day we heard the news of the attack by North Korea, Molly was really upset. Her comment was "Not again." Many wives and children were disturbed when they heard the news. We knew we were vulnerable but didn't expect to be called up. There were a lot of National Guard units in the country, all of which would probably have to be trained for at least a year before being ready for deployment. I admit I was a bit concerned about my chances. Customers would talk about the war in Korea. Our unit was placed on alert. We listened to the radio and television not sure whether we would be called. Geographically, we were the closest division to Korea. Again, our country had a small active regular army, but we were slightly more ready than prior to WWII when the troops had to simulate tanks and other war equipment—and the men had to train with broom handles, pretending they were rifles.

Molly feared my going again. But when President Truman ordered the recall of 3500 company grade officers of various armed services from the Army Reserve, we knew that the decision I had made to transfer from the Reserve to the National Guard was the right one. I was much less exposed to the enemy in the Artillery Branch than in the Infantry. At that time the country's Army components were Regular Army, Active Reserve, Organized Reserve, training one weekend a month, and the Inactive Reserve, essentially a list to which I had been assigned when I separated from the service. Lastly, there was the National Guard. When I reviewed all of this with Molly, I told her that I was better situated now than I would be as an Infantry Officer in the Reserve. But deep down, I wondered if we would be called up. Molly and I discussed what she would do if I were called to duty. We were in our new home, back in my job with the oil company, and now faced with the possibility of being recalled. I talked with Molly's mother and father to discuss the possibility. They said they would take care of Molly.

[Fearing the possibility of Communist China entering the conflict, President Truman ordered four National Guard Divisions, called to active service and Congress gave permission to the President to extend the Draft for an additional 21 (later to 24) months. President Truman called to active duty, four Divisions: 28th (Pennsylvania), 40th (California), 43rd (Rhode Island and Connecticut) and 45th (Oklahoma).]

We were notified on September 1, 1950. The morning I received the message that I was to report to the Armory and assemble my troops I called my executive officer Clark Howell to notify the other officers to inform their troops. The men were given their physicals and inoculations. We spent the first few days getting ready for a move to Camp Cooke. We were allowed to go home every night but had to report for duty at 0600 each day. We packed equipment and loaded our trucks. Our cooks were not trained to prepare meals so we arranged for Manuel Melindez, chef at one of the best restaurants in Santa Barbara, to serve our men. Thankfully we could go home every night to be with our loved ones. The wives and families were very helpful with each other. Molly and Tomilyn were strong; they didn't want me to go, but were very brave. After all we had gone through during the last war, we were better prepared for this one.

[I had taken over Battery A with 35 men in it. Our weekly meetings were in the Oxnard Community Center, which had a baseball field that we used for most of our activities. I started a basic program of calisthenics and close order drill, followed by what is called the "cannoneers hop." But my biggest effort was recruiting, so I visited high schools and youth groups and gradually increased the strength of the unit. The State started a building program to construct an armory west of Oxnard High School. When it was completed, we moved into it. In late August I took the family to Huntington Lake, where we camped in tents. After two days there, the radio news came that the 40th Division was called up and for all personnel to report immediately to their units. We broke camp and headed home. We were told that the Division was to move to Camp Cooke, so I had to transfer all the armory property to a specified guardian—which kept me busy for a couple of weeks. The evening before we departed, the Battery was given a farewell party sponsored by the Oxnard Evening Press at which city officials attended as well as parents and friends—a gala ball. The next day we loaded into our vehicles and went to Camp Cooke. It wasn't long after we were settled in the camp and started our training program that I was reassigned to be the S4 (Supply) of the Division Artillery.]

Major Art Reed, the Executive Officer of the Battalion, worked for Union Oil Company. When we were called up, he was immediately sent off to school. His wife was left alone to get their house ready to sell. Molly and I and another couple spent several days painting their house, readying it for the market.

We were ordered to move to Camp Cooke, located on the coast north of Santa Barbara. We assembled at the Armory early in the morning. The trucks were loaded and convoyed to the Camp. The Division Band began to play as we moved out from the Armory with a couple of jeeps carrying flags and guidons followed by Headquarters Battery (my command). We were cheered by the citizens along the main street in Santa Barbara. When we passed my big Standard Station, a group of my employees gathered to cheer the marching men with great enthusiasm.

I shed a few tears and asked myself how this could happen to me twice in a lifetime. I felt lucky to be in the National Guard and not in the Reserve, for so many of them were being called up. Later I learned that a couple of lieutenants who had served with me in the Battle of the Bulge were called up from the Reserves. One was killed in action and never saw his infant daughter. He had been a platoon leader in the Bulge and was sent to Korea and killed in September 1951 at Heartbreak Ridge. The other one was lucky, became a staff officer, and served his time in Korea. Lt. Boyd, who had been in the same unit with me in Belgium, and my bunkmate when we were prisoners of war, had stayed in the Army as a career officer.

The Division had sent an advance party to Camp Cooke on September 1. The camp had not been used since WWII, and we knew it would not be up to the standards it should be. But that was where we were to train. The drive up the coast to Lompoc is about an hour's drive from Santa Barbara. Our advance party had unloaded the trucks by the time we got there. I took stock of the buildings and grounds as we drove in past the camp headquarters and down California Street to our barracks. Everything needed repair; the roads needed paving, and the buildings looked shabby. Looking back on the first time we rode into camp, I was reminded of an old western movie with the wind blowing dust down the streets. The only thing missing was Gary Cooper sauntering down the street looking for the bad guys.

After we unloaded, Clark Howell and the 1st Sergeant guided me to my office. From there I proceeded to the Division Artillery (Divarty) and reported in. Col. Ott had told me that I was to become the Divarty Headquarters Company Commander. I requested the 1st Sergeant from George's Battery A, Sgt. Berryhill. A day or so later, I reported into Divarty Headquarters, and who should be sitting at the G4 (Supply) but my brother George. He had been reassigned. Col. Ott had lived up to his promise and placed George in a major's slot.

My new command seemed to be lax in military courtesy. Because they were in a headquarters unit, they felt they didn't need normal Army courtesies. They addressed their officers by their last names with no rank named. I could see why Col. Ott had asked me to assume command of the unit. With Sgt. Berryhill, we went to a group who were lolling outside my headquarters and I told Berryhill, "Cancel all weekend passes for this group. Until these men understand military courtesy, they will stay in camp." With that, I turned and went back into my office with George. I was going home with him but asked him to stay around for an hour. I went to the barracks. When Sgt. Berryhill and I went in, I told the men to remember what I had been talking about. They responded with a loud "Yes sir." I turned to Sgt. Berryhill and said, "Issue the passes." From that day on, the headquarters unit was one of the best in following military courtesy. They marched the best, and the discipline around the headquarters was much improved.

We went home the next weekend. Molly and Tomilyn had stayed in our house, and I could go home almost every weekend. General Huddelson called the ride from Lompoc to Los Angeles the most dangerous one in the country. Several men were killed or injured trying to get to their homes too quickly. Every weekend the highways were packed with men from the 40th racing down the two lanes to their homes. General Huddelson said that they would have been better off stationed farther from Los Angeles.

I was happier being in the Artillery than having been recalled into the Infantry branch. But I didn't know anything about Artillery operations. That is typical of my assignments throughout of my military career. I was consistently placed in jobs for which I had limited experience. It wasn't long before I was reassigned to the Division G3 (Training the Operations) section. Shortly after reporting to that job, I observed a training session of the 224th Infantry. The troops were seated where they could hear artillery shells going over their heads from our artillery units. They had troops in the bleachers and made them sit there during the firing exercise. I told Lt. Col. Dean of the G3 that I had some critical remarks about the exercise. Not long after, the colonel commanding the 224th came into the G3 office. I heard him ask Col. Dean "Who in the hell is this Capt. Moranda and who is he to tell me how to train my troops?" I was surprised to hear Col. Dean respond "I know Capt. Moranda very well, and I can tell you that I agree with his report. He is a dedicated officer who has been through a lot of artillery fire in combat, and he knows of what he speaks." With that the colonel left.

A week later I was called into the G3 office and told to go to a nearby lagoon located near the ocean. The same outfit that I had given a poor report about the artillery firing was now testing their vehicles to see whether they had been waterproofed correctly. The trucks were to be driven into the deep water for the test. The officer in charge said that the lagoon caretaker would not let the trucks drive into it and was holding up the training. I drove out to the lagoon and asked the colonel about the man was in charge of the lagoon. He pointed to a nearby house. I drove over and knocked on the door and heard voices singing a hymn as it was Sunday and people were holding a service there. A man came to the door, and I explained what we were planning to do. He responded, "My boss, the Congressman from this district, told me no one was to go into the lagoon without his personal authorization." I told him that our 40th Division had been called up by the President of the United States to ready ourselves to fight the enemy in Korea and that he was holding up our training. We will go over your Congressman's head, but you might call him and tell him that Captain Moranda gave the orders and that if he has a problem with that he is to feel free to call President Truman for his advice. We never heard any more about the matter and continued with our training. As I was reporting to Col. Dean, the Commander of the 224th Infantry came into the office. It turned out that he was in charge of the lagoon dipping. He praised me and said that I had really helped. When he left, Col. Dean told me, "You will be in my section for the rest of the time that I am in charge of the G3 Section. I like the way you get things done."

A few weeks later George, who was in the Corps of Engineers during the last war, and I were told that we were to attend the Artillery School at Fort Sill. George took his family back to Arkansas where Nancy and the children were to stay with her parents, the Albert Dowels, in Little Rock. The rest of us were picked up at the airport, flown to San Francisco, and billeted at a hotel there. Captain Jim Latham and I went to a nearby bar to pass some time. As we were sitting there, I noticed a good-looking woman across from us and giving me "that" look. Hell, it had been a long time since anyone had given me "that" look. Soon she got up from her seat and came over and asked, "Would you do me the favor of introducing me to your good-looking friend next to you?"

Of course, Jim never left my side that night, but from then on I was known as Pappy Moranda.

I arrived at Fort Sill with the other officers. The next day George arrived in his car. We were assigned the same bedroom. The class was made up of officers from the 40th Division from California, the 45th Division from Oklahoma, and a group of officers from the National Guard in Connecticut. Because George had driven his car to Ft. Sill, we did not have to use public transportation and lived in high style.

School started, and I knew I was in trouble. I was not a math student in high school and that was twenty years before. Artillery is based on a lot of trigonometry and, hell, I had a difficult time with algebra. But George told me not to worry that he would get me through. He drew formulas on the wall where I could see it from my bunk. At first I questioned how things worked. Then George would question me about the drawing he had put on the wall. When I asked him why, his reply was always the same "Shut up and memorize it."

With Lts. Dick Rennie and Leroy Hare, George and I attended a few University of Oklahoma football games in Norman and had a great time seeing some good football. The ride to and from the stadium, with each of us telling of our life experiences, had us laughing. Rennie was particularly good at telling stories in a humorous way.

The school was different from what I went through as an enlisted man. I excelled in only one class. It was on machine guns and I "maxed" it. When they asked us to tell of the positioning of machine guns, I was in heaven. During one class in a large hall, the instructor described a particular problem and asked, "What do you think of that particular problem, Captain Moranda?" I answered, "Do you mean George Moranda?" The instructor replied, "Yes." I turned to George and said, "It's your turn." Everyone laughed, even the instructor. The other class that I passed, but not easily, was shooting the stars and translating their positions to the earth. I had no idea, so I made a couple of wild guesses and apparently I was correct. The instructor said, "I didn't expect anyone to pass the final examination," and to this day I don't know how I did. On his final review of our class, Major Crawford, stated that George should be a field commander and that I should be a good staff officer. That surprised me. I always thought that

I was a good field man, but, no wonder, as I was always confused the whole time I was in combat. And George had spent most of his career in the active army in staff work.

[General MacArthur's UN forces drove the North Koreans back to the 38th parallel and then pushed north to the Yalu River border of Manchuria, and the Chinese entered the war actively and forced the US troops into a costly retreat. President Truman declared a national emergency and planned to place the U.S. on a war basis.]

Christmas approached, and we talked about what we would do. George said he was going to Little Rock to be with Nancy and her family. I didn't have the time to go home, so George invited me to go to Little Rock with him, but I was reluctant to do so. Almost every night we would drive into Lawton to get away from camp and stop and eat at a small café. Our waitress was a tall, pretty lady. When she heard us talking about whether I should go with George to Little Rock or not, she said "Come to my house. I'm alone for the holidays." As soon as she left, I turned to George and whispered, "If you don't mind, I'll go to Little Rock with you."

The day before Christmas, we drove straight through to Little Rock during an ice storm and arrived about two in the morning. We knocked on the door, and there stood Nancy in a pretty blue negligee. She said in her southern drawl, "Well George honey, and Bob, I didn't know you were coming." She said "You two can sleep in our bed, and I will sleep on the couch in the front room." George whispered to me, "I'll kill you." With that threat, I told her I would be fine on the couch. I've had worse beds considering all the trenches and foxholes I've been in, but the couch was only five feet long; so I had quite a miserable night. The next morning I called our aunt, Annie Forney Newton, who invited me to her home.

On Christmas Day, George and Nancy picked me up at Aunt Annie Forney's house and drove us to Mabelvale where we had a dinner with Nancy's relatives. When dinner was served, the table groaned with the weight of turkey, chicken, beef and lamb and all the side dishes. We stuffed ourselves. Afterwards we went to our Aunt Annie Forney's. When we arrived at her house, she greeted me with "We've been waiting for you." There on her table, was all the turkey and trimmings that go with a Christmas meal. I quietly unbuttoned the top button of my pants and made it slowly through the evening. I enjoyed talking with cousins Anale and her husband Bill Yarbrough, and Alice and her mate Chaddie Gray.

Two days later, we returned to Fort Sill to attend classes again. One exercise was a two-day tactical problem, and we had to spend the night in freezing cold, with strong winds in the field. There were three of us in one tent. When we went through the chow line, everything was cold. George called the mess sergeant over and asked him for the recipe. The sergeant responded, "Yes, Sir. Did you like the meal?" Then George said "No. I want to get the recipe and have it duplicated so that when my troops screw up, I can serve it to them as punishment." With that, we marched over to the garbage cans and dumped our trays.

The people in Oklahoma must really like to eat, for one weekend we went to Drummond, Oklahoma, to visit our Uncle Bill's sister Mary and her husband, Chess. Uncle Bill still owned a part of the ranch and came back to Drummond every year to help with the harvest. As we driving there, I said, "I'll bet we'll have chicken for dinner." And we did—fried chicken and all the trimmings—a good old-fashioned southern Sunday dinner. That night they took us to Enid, to listen to the Barbershop Quartet National Championship.

Before finishing school at Fort Sill, we were given a demonstration on how to place the artillery in a combat situation. For some reason I was picked to be the commander. Having been in the Infantry before, all I had ever seen of artillery tactics was in combat. But somehow I was chosen to select gun positions. I looked at where I had placed the guns and picked an area about 50 feet in front of a row of trees so that the tree area could be used for the command post and ammunition storage. I vividly remember the many tree bursts at St. Vith, and I had scars to prove it. The Tactical Officer asked my reason for the placements, out in the open rather than under the trees. I told him my rationale. His reply was touché.

After the course ended, George had to take his family from Little Rock to California. I drove back with Lt. Fallon to Camp Cooke in California. During the trip, we stopped at a small motel and went to the motel office. A voice came down from the two-story house at the back of the motel and said "Hi, what do you want?" I told him we wanted a room for the night. He replied, "Fine, go into the office and sign the guest book, take a key from the rack, and pick out a room. Just leave $15.00 on the counter. It's too damn cold to come down." We never did see the owner of the motel, but when we left, I replaced the key to our room and noted that the money had been picked up.

We followed a truck through the snow, slipping and sliding for several hours over the icy roads. We stopped at a service station and asked what the road conditions were like ahead. He told us the best way to get to California, so we filled the gas tank and had chains put on the tires. In a few miles, the snow disappeared so we had to remove the chains. After two long days of driving, we arrived in Santa Barbara, where Molly and Tomilyn ran out to greet me. I spent the night and drove to Hueneme to see Mom and Bill and Jeannette. The next day Molly drove me to Lompoc. I went to the headquarters and signed in. During the time that I was at school, the Division received many more men, so we had a great deal of training to do with the new recruits.

Japan and Korea

[General MacArthur requested all four of the National Guard Divisions that had been called-up. The Joint Chiefs of Staff denied the request. He again made his request, pointing out that there were no Divisions in Japan and he needed them for the defense of Japan. At the end of January 1951, the Secretary of Defense approved the shipment of two Guard Divisions, the 40th and 45th, with the instructions that both divisions were to remain in Japan and not be sent to Korea. In early March 1951, the 40th and 45th Divisions were alerted for overseas shipment to Japan, with the 40th in the main island Honshu, and the 45th in the northern island of Hokkaido. In preparation, the divisions began intensive training. Neither Bob nor I thought we would be going there for anything but operations in Korea, after a training period, despite the restrictions placed on General MacArthur.]

Not long after I returned from Fort Sill I was told to report to General Huddelson's office. When I arrived, there were twenty officers in the room. General Eaton announced that the officers in this room were to go on a secret mission. It was to be the advance party of the 40th Division, which had been ordered to Japan. The advance party would arrange for the arrival of the remainder of the division that would follow by troop ship. No one was to know; not even family, friends, or fellow officers. Well, a person has to tell his wife and family, so I told Molly, who became very upset saying, "You have done your share, and now your daughter has only been with you three years of her life." I tried to assure her that this time my job would be different as I was on the Division Staff and would not be on the front lines. She calmed down and then went to the Christian Science practitioner for counseling. She planned to rent the house and found an elderly couple who wanted to rent it.

We had a wonderful twenty-four hours together before Molly had to drive me to Camp Cooke early the next day. We arrived at 5 a.m. at the front gate. We said our goodbyes bravely. Mom's diary entry for May 25, 1951, read: "The family is coming today and I am so excited. Bob arrived with a corsage for me to wear to church. The others arrived later, and we had such a wonderful visit together. It hurt me so much to kiss my boys goodbye. I did it quickly and they left. What a miserable ending of the day."

I reported to General Eaton and was briefed on what we were to do. After the meeting, I asked my boss Col. Dean why I had been chosen since I had been in the G3 Section such a short time. He smiled and replied, "You have never let me down."

On that day we were loaded onto a waiting plane and flown to Travis Air Base near Oakland. After a brief time, we boarded an old DC10. We were not allowed to check out, as we normally would, from Camp Cooke or Travis as it was a top secret mission. We flew to Hawaii and played cards all the way. As I was a stranger to most of the men, I spent time getting acquainted with them. General Eaton was very friendly and easy to talk to. All the others had been in the National Guard longer and lived in the Los Angeles area and thus had more in common, but we soon adjusted to each other. The first stop in Honolulu was only to allow a change of crew and for refueling. The next stop was Wake Island, which had nothing but an air strip, acres of sand and multitudes of gooney birds. From there we flew to Japan. We had had four box lunches on the entire trip which took close to 24 hours.

Upon arrival, we were loaded onto trucks and went to the headquarters building. The Japanese people along the route were waving and bowing to us. That was what they did each day as General McArthur traveled this road. He was apparently revered by the Japanese. We arrived at headquarters. Despite our disheveled appearance from all the travel, we went into a meeting room where there were more high-ranking officers than I had ever seen before. They didn't waste any time; they had everything arranged down to the last detail. General

McArthur greeted us and said that our mission was to replace the 24th Division, which had been ordered to Korea. We were to be his reserve and assume the mission of protecting Japan. Our division and the 45th Division would be in reserve for the Korean Operation. Another officer briefed us on the situation in Korea. We were served lunch in a nearby dining room and told to sit next to our counterparts for further briefing. We went into the dining room and looked for our counterparts who were sitting according to rank and all very senior officers. Except for General Easton, our group was nothing but captains and lieutenants, so we had no opportunity to sit next to our counterparts.

That night we stayed at the Fujita Hotel. Never in my life have I slept in such a beautiful bedroom—a far cry from the barracks and foxholes I had encountered. The next day we started our visits to all the camps assigned to the division. We were given a special train to shuttle from camp to camp. It was spring in Japan, and the scenery was beautiful. The ladies were in their kimonos of beautiful colors. We had been told that everything about our arrival was to be top secret. But someone must have leaked the information, for at every stop along the way we were met by dignitaries welcoming the 40th Division to Japan. The dignitaries wore their formal top hats and bowed, leaving General Eaton uncertain whether to salute or bow.

We went to Sendai and were greeted by the Mayor and his officials. We then proceeded to Camp Schimmelpfennig. We stopped at our new Division Headquarters and noted where we would place our staff sections. As I was standing, looking out the window of the G3 office, I noticed a wave of earth coming toward the building which rolled with the wave. Our guide said, "Get used to the earthquakes. We ride out the little waves of earth often." From then on when someone would see a wave coming, they would say "Hold on to your hats; another one's coming." For the next few days we traveled throughout Japan from the northern tip of Honshu to the volcano at Mt. Fuji.

To provide a defensive presence, our division was spread throughout Japan, an area of over 100 miles wide and 500 miles long. Division Headquarters and the 223rd Infantry Regiment (less one battalion), were assigned to Camp Schimmelpfennig near Sendai. Headquarters of the division artillery, the 625th and 981st field artillery battalions and

1ˢᵗ Battalion of the 223ʳᵈ Infantry Regiment were assigned to Camp Younghans near Yamagata. (This is where Brother George was located). The rest of the division was posted as follows:

- 160ᵗʰ Infantry Regiment, 143ʳᵈ Field Artillery Battalion, and 115 Medical Battalion at Camp Schimmelpfennig
- 224ᵗʰ Infantry Regiment at Camp Haugen near Mitsuichikawa
- 140ᵗʰ Tank Battalion at Camp McGill near Yokohama
- 578ᵗʰ Engineer Battalion at Camp Matsushima near Shiogama
- 224ᵗʰ Infantry Regiment and 980ᵗʰ Field Artillery Battalion at Camp Zama, near Yokohama (224ᵗʰ moved to Camp McNair on the slopes of Mt. Fuji near Yoshida in July 1951.)
- 140ᵗʰ antiaircraft battalion at Camp Whittington, former Japanese Air Base near Yokohama

When we met the remainder of the division to help them get aboard connecting trains to their various locations, I was surprised to hear someone yelling out a car window, "Hey, Pappy Moranda, do me a favor. Call a friend of mine and tell him I'm in Japan. His name is Joe Stanowitz, Joe the Pole." Capt. George Benson had joined the 40ᵗʰ Division from his assignment from ROTC duty in California. Someone must have told him my nickname, for that was when I first met George Benson. We became the best of friends. Benson and Joe, the Pole, were classmates at West Point. Joe was assigned to a unit in Japan. Benson and I were assigned to the same staff section at Division Headquarters.

The 40ᵗʰ Division needed replacements as rapidly as possible, and men were assigned to it almost every day during the early part of our tour in Japan. Many of the personnel in the 40ᵗʰ who had arrived in Japan applied for and received separation from the service because of hardship conditions or essential jobs in their civilian work. Extensive training was necessary to bring the division to combat readiness. Our mission was first to defend the islands of Japan, and to ready ourselves for combat duty in Korea. So our section in G-3 of the headquarters (Operations and Training) had much work to do.

Maj. Peterson, Capt. Ross, Col. Dean, Lt. Johnson, Col. Tietgen (Chaplain), Capt. Sullivan (center), lt. Nichols, Bob, Maj. Fox, Capt. Benson, and Capt. Wilson. This was the G-3 Section except for the chaplain. Other members of our section were Maj. Robert Elder, Capts. Robert Coultas and Tom Brown (the movie actor) and Lts. Sait and Johnson.

[At Divarty headquarters, I served under Col. Ott as SI. I had a warrant Officer as assistant who was very efficient, but he was picked up by military police while on a trip to Tokyo for engaging in sexual activity with another soldier. I gave him the option of resigning and leaving the service or a charge under the Uniformed Code of Military Justice. He resigned and was sent back to the U.S. Our Divarty commander was reassigned and we received Col. Slack. When Bob and I were in his office being introduced, he looked at us and said, "I'm surprised you are brothers. You don't look anything alike." Both of us raised our arms and said, "Under our arms we do." Fortunately, he laughed as he dismissed us.]

George surprised me one day by suddenly appearing at the Division Headquarters. He had been assigned as the assistant G-1 (Personnel) under Lt. Col. Wilkins, who soon left for a home emergency and was replaced by Lt. Col. Tom Lawson. I introduced George to the staff. Benson and I invited him to live with us: Benson, Bob Coultas, Maj. Whiteside, and I. Coultas planned to leave for home soon because his wife was ill. I purchased from him a bedroll and a camera. He had a model train and tracks that he had set up throughout the house, so we could order drinks from the kitchen and have them delivered to our respective bedrooms. When he left, he took the train and tracks with him, so we had to walk to the kitchen afterwards.

With the units scattered throughout Japan, we did a lot of traveling. We flew to most of the places in the small L19 plane which was tossed around like feathers in any significant winds. On one flight, we met some rough weather, and the pilot lost control of the light plane. As we were tossing around he announced, quite seriously and quite loudly "And what the hell do I do now?" I responded, "If you don't know, I guess we're in real trouble." We made it back to camp, but I made sure that future flights were with a different pilot.

At our medical detachment party in Japan: Front row: Maj. Eubanks (George's roommate), Lt Worthington (pilot), WO Conover, Maj. Morrision (communications officer). Middle Row: Chaplain Horrell, Col Slack, Col Ott, Capt George Moranda. Back Row: Capt Hethcote (training), Capt Gibbons (physician), Capt Mecham (pilot), Lt Clark (medical detachment).

The first winter in Japan our troops had not received appropriate clothing or equipment. We were visited by a Los Angeles television reporter named Clete Roberts, who nosed around the Division Headquarters for a day or two and sent stories back to his newspaper about how most men missed their families. He was invited to most of our functions, which included going to the Officer's Club at Tagajo. One day he left for the northern part of Honshu and wrote about the lack of winter equipment and how suddenly the weather had changed. He stated that there were several cases of frost bite, so men had to be taken to the hospital for treatment. The way Roberts reported the story suggested that the regimental commander had orchestrated the exercise to toughen up the men. When I saw the article, I knew the people back home would become upset. The next day I was called into General Huddleston's office. He told me he was disturbed about the Roberts' report suggesting that the colonel in charge forced the men to train under those conditions and that he had not supplied them with winter equipment. He ordered our G-3 Section to go to investigate.

The next day I went by train to their camp and caught a ride to headquarters of the 224th Infantry Regiment. I reported to the commanding officer, Col. Jim Richardson, and told him what I had been ordered to do. He calmly turned to his staff and said. "Gentlemen, provide Captain Moranda all the support you can." For a couple of days, I interviewed officers and enlisted men to find out what orders Col. Richardson had given. At the Officers Club that night, I asked several staff officers what the colonel had said that morning about weather conditions. Their response was that he had told them that they should include in the exercise all their winter clothes and supplies. They said that some of the unit commanders thought the colonel was mistaken as the weather was much too nice to be bothered by carrying extra equipment. I went to Col. Richardson's office and asked him if he had his briefing notes. He looked in his desk and came up with some papers and handed them to me. I scanned them and found that he had, in fact, included a warning to his subordinate commanders about the possibility of a weather change, and that they should be prepared for it. This took Col. Richardson off the hook.

The division was serious about conditioning the troops, both physically and mentally, for combat. The troops had daily speed marches. The Japanese people were impressed by the dedication of the troops and officers to get and stay in good condition. While I had to travel often to the various camps, my favorite was a camp located at the base of Mt. Fuji. Because of the concentrated population in Japan, one of the main problems was finding a place to fire our artillery and mortar weapons. Weapons firing had to be coordinated with the local Japanese officials. They asked us to complete our firing by 1700 hours daily so people could work their land.

We had a training exercise jointly with the Navy to practice a landing exercise. That convinced me that we would be ordered to make a landing in Korea. During the exercise, the general kept asking about the details and called Lt. England, our liaison officer from our G-2 section, to find out what the current status was. Lt. England's answer was always the same, "Like it was a couple of hours ago: the troops were aboard the vessels and would be coming ashore soon." Lt. England got so exasperated with the repeated calls that I had to calm him down and say that the top command was insistent on keeping fully abreast of the situation. When the landing occurred, the generals and others of the staff attended the exercise. I kept thinking of the difference in landing with no opposition to that which the American forces endured on D-day during WWII.

Korean peninsula

Earl Warren, the Governor of California, was one of the top officials to visit us. He came to see his California troops. Later it was announced that Mrs. Anna Rosenberg, an Assistant Secretary of Defense, would visit the division. This caused the commanding general to order a practice. Benson and I were assigned the mission to plan and conduct the exercise. After arranging for the division band to play, we rehearsed to make sure that everything would run smoothly. When we reported to our boss, Col. Dean, he informed us that nothing goes out of the G-3 Section without a written plan, "So you two go and finish your job and prepare the orders for my and the General's signatures." We had tried to take the easy way, but it was a lesson well learned. When the written plan was finished, Col. Dean hand-carried it to the General, who decided he would rehearse the troops as he wanted to make a favorable impression on the visiting Secretary. We alerted the troops and the band. When the General was ready, we proceeded to the parade grounds to the reviewing stand. The General gave the order to start the music, and the band music floated about a quarter of a mile away All went well for the first few minutes, but because the delay by a few seconds of the sound of the music to the leading troops, it appeared as though the troops were marching out of sync. The General turned to Capt. Benson and me and said, "Stop the parade! The troops are out of step with the music."

In an aside to me, Capt. Benson said, "What the hell is the command: Stop the parade!" We started toward the troops while trying to get the band to cease playing, but the General was not waiting. He got off the reviewing stand and started half running toward the troops. As he moved, pumped his arm up and down with the beat of the music and called out, "Left, left, left." His aide, Benson, and I followed closely behind. When we were about 50 yards from the leading troops, he noted that the troops were in step with the music and he stopped bellowing, "Left, left, left, right, left." He then returned to the stand. We followed and overheard him saying to his aide, "Well, I got them in the right step."

One Sunday, I was given another unusual assignment. I was Duty Officer at the headquarters. I had written letters home and was reading when an L19 plane landed in front of the headquarters. A courier came into the office and handed me a package addressed to the Commanding General with a return address of the Pentagon. It contained an allegation from a mother who had written her congressman that the Army charged her son $5.00 for postage stamp. I was sent to investigate and went by train down to the 160th Infantry at the base of Mount Fuji. The weather was cold and miserable with a few flurries of snow mixed with the sleet and rain. We checked in with the colonel who denied such a charge. He called his Executive Officer and a few others, and we all traipsed over to the soldiers' unit and his quarters where the soldier jumped to attention seeing all the brass approaching him—wondering if he was going to be strung up. I approached him and told him that his mother had reported to her congressmen that the army charged him $5.00 to mail a letter to her. The soldier paled, gulped a few times and with an upward sweep of his hand said, "Oh, my God! I wrote my mother a couple of months ago. The weather was bad and after I finished and sealed the letter, my buddy came in from buying stamps, so I asked him for one of them. He replied that he had frozen his butt off so the price of one stamp is $5.00. He didn't charge me that much, but I wrote Mother that she should really appreciate the letter as it cost $5.00 for the stamp."

That letter was much more costly than the alleged $5.00 considering the time and effort by the representative and senator and their staffs, the Army staff at the Pentagon, General MacArthur's staff (each stop required an endorsement to the letter), the pilot and plane to deliver the complaint, the four officers and myself traveling to the camp, and the four days it took us.

One Sunday George Benson and Bob Coultas were going to attend Mass at the Chapel and invited me to go with them. I told them I wasn't a Catholic, but they said to come anyway. I did and met Fran Fracino, the General's aide, and Al Holtzgang the Division Finance Officer, and walked in with them. All of us went to one of the front pews which we filled completely. I was sitting at one end and Benson was at the other end. When it came time to kneel, I sat in the pew and watched. In a loud stage whisper, I heard Benson say "Tell that Protestant to kneel." I did, but vowed to get even some day. That day came a couple of weeks later when I attended Father Duggans' service with Benson one Sunday. His sermon was how the Catholic Church hierarchy was similar in organization to the Army. About a month later one of the Catholic chaplains came to the headquarters and asked Benson if he would serve as Master of Ceremony at the Christmas Celebration. I asked what the MC does and was told he leads the priest from station to station at the altar. I told him, "I'm going to watch your performance during the service. Every time you lead the priest past the altar, I am going to get up and say, "Way to go, George," and then applaud. He said "You wouldn't!" I then reminded him of the time he told this Protestant to kneel, and I wanted revenge. When the day of the Christmas service came, I sat in the front pew. George looked at me and shook his head, mouthing the words, "Don't do it," and I nodded. When George led the priest, I straightened up as though I was going to rise. George looked and when I didn't stand, he smiled. But I had my revenge.

Bob and Capt. Coultas

Benson, Brother George, and I had a pleasant trip to Tokyo. We took Lt. Pierce from the G-2 (Intelligence Section) because he had been to the Army Language School to learn Japanese. We thought it would be great to have someone help us get around. Well, every time he addressed a Japanese person, the answer was always in English. Pierce explained then that the Japanese pride themselves on their ability to speak our language and welcome the chance to talk to an American. We stayed at the Fujita Hotel, one of the plushest I've ever seen. While there we decided to get a massage at the hotel spa. We bathed in very hot water. Afterwards, the masseur put us on a table, and we were massaged by two old men. It was very relaxing and when finished, George looked over at me and said, "If he could cook, I'd marry him."

[In April 1951, the United States and Japan signed a Peace Treaty in San Francisco which provided that U.S. troops could be stationed in Japan for an indefinite period. That same month and year General MacArthur was recalled and was replaced by General Matthew Ridgeway.]

When we returned to the base, we were called into General Eaton's office and told that we were again going on the advance party to Korea. We were to relieve the 24th Infantry Division and were scheduled to leave in two days. I was told the weather was freezing in Korea. Knowing it would be cold there, I gathered all the cold weather clothing I could.

We loaded into a plane at Haneda airport, took off, had engine trouble, and returned to the airport. It was Christmas, and we spent the night at the airport. The next day we were loaded onto a cargo plane and spent a miserable trip across in bucket seats. We arrived at the Seoul airport in Korea. General Eaton was met by a high-ranking officer, but the rest of us were herded into jeeps and drove through ice and snow to the command post of the 24th Division. Along the way, we saw sad-looking Christmas trees decorated with whatever the people had available— colored string, bits of tinsel made from packages, and empty k-ration boxes. We checked in with our 24th Division counterparts, toured the areas they were operating in, and met their key personnel. After making the decisions for our incoming troops and units, we planned the distribution of 40th units and the method of replacing the 24th Division troops in their front line positions. When our units arrived, we supervised their placement. We were never briefed, so we started to work in the tent that housed the G-2 and G-3 sections. The 24th Division personnel we met were most anxious to leave and quickly gave us all necessary information for us to do our jobs.

[I was sent to Korea to be oriented on location of units, and took a flight over the front in one of our L19 aircraft. After crossing the enemy lines, we started to receive antiaircraft fire. The pilot apparently knew the range of the enemy guns and stayed just above the bursts, but it was an uneasy feeling until we got back to the division airstrip. I also went to each of the two regiments to check their dispositions by talking to some of the men. Looking toward the enemy area, I couldn't see much movement. Upon returning, we readied ourselves for the division movement over to Korea, which followed on transports to Inchon.]

Lt. Col. Robert Elder described the movement of his Advance Party, 223d Infantry Regiment: "We went by ship to Inchon...the troops went over the side down nets into small landing craft which took us to shore....Walked a few hundred yards to a train to the vicinity of Chunchon, got off in the middle of the night, climbed aboard trucks and traveled north in blackout until we got to a tent camp the 24th Division had put up for the arriving 40th Division where most of the troops stopped, but we went further north until we arrived at the 5th

Regimental Combat team Command Post before daylight....it was 18 degrees below zero."

[Not long after, my section flew over to our assigned area. We left the airport in Japan in 70 degree weather and when we landed in Korea, it was minus 30 degrees. I went to my tent and started a fire in the pot-bellied stove and set up my sleeping bag. I had a one-person tent outside of which was a four-inch pipe driven into the ground which was my urinal. (This was convenient, but when the thaw came later and the pipe was removed it left a yellow pillar).]

Things were relatively quiet. We made a few company-size attacks. The North Koreans also made a few concerted attacks, which were repulsed. However, the North Koreans mostly used forays by small units that probed our lines almost every night, causing a few casualties in our front line units—usually by sneaking up on their bellies and dropping a grenade in a foxhole. Hardly a day passed without a few casualties to our troops.

[Several of us at Division headquarters had to stay up each night. I did because President Truman ordered a report of casualties be on his desk when he got to his office each morning, and it was my responsibility to prepare the Division report and phone it to Eighth Army Headquarters by midnight each day. Others were up each night for various reasons so we formed a bridge game group and played almost every night. Bob joined us several times. When I finally got to bed, I quickly became accustomed to and slept through the harassing artillery fire that passed overhead from our artillery units.]

George and I had a rule—never travel, especially by air, together for obvious reasons. We also avoided sharing a tent even when there was room. One night a bomb hit our headquarters area but missed any of the tents. We learned it was one of our Navy pilots off a carrier who made the mistake. He was given orders to come to the Division and apologize, which he did with hat in hands. I hadn't had one that close since the Bulge.

[Each of the Divisions was assigned 1500 South Korean soldiers. We received about 500 who were distributed to each of our regiments. I was

impressed with the severity of discipline imposed on any of their soldiers who made some mistake. The miscreant was slapped or ordered to do 100 pushups over a three- foot ditch.

Bob and George Benson hamming it up

George Moranda and buddies

Because of the possibility that nuclear weapons would be used, the essential staff units and the messes were dug in, covered with dirt, and sandbags placed around trailers and tents. After Col. Lawson departed and I became the Division G1, I was assigned to a trailer near the G1 tent—I thought what a way to fight a war. I had to give a daily briefing, as did each of the staff heads, in the command tent. I also had to give special briefings when visiting officials came—such as General Ridgeway after he assumed command of Eighth Army, and later to General Van Fleet.]

George Benson and I had been almost inseparable in our work in the G3 section. His greatest wish was to get the Combat Infantryman's Badge. So he pressured Col. Dean to get him assigned to one of the forward regiments, and his boss released him to the 160th Infantry. After six months, he received the coveted award at Division headquarters where some of the division artists made a 2 x 4 foot plaque with the words on it, and we hung it around his neck with much fanfare.

Again Back Home

[In June 1951, negotiations began between the UN and the Communist commanders at Panmunjon. The North Koreans insisted on a dividing line at the 38th parallel and the UN stand was that it be the existing front lines. The United States was reluctant to accede to the Communist demand that the 171,000 prisoners we held be released (50,000 of whom were reluctant to go back), so the talks stalled.]

At the end of WWII, a system of rotation for the troops was installed by the Army to provide an orderly and equitable procedure. That system was also installed for the Korean conflict. When one acquired 36 points for service, he was eligible for rotation back to the States. Four points in front line regimental areas, three points from regimental area to rear areas, two points for overseas rear areas, and one point for noncombatant service. I was in the first group eligible. We were sent to the Replacement Center to await transportation home. While at the center, one of the staff officers in the tent area with me and others started to clean his .45 caliber automatic and dropped it on the floor. I wanted to kill him—to go through two wars and have a nitwit endanger me and the others about to go home was unreal.

We loaded ship out of Inchon and took a slow boat to Seattle. I flew to the San Fernando Airport where Molly and Tomilyn met me. It was so great to be home again.

[After Bob left the Division, I stayed on. When Col Lawson rotated, I was made the Division G.1. Because most of the division personnel were gradually being rotated back to the U.S as they acquired sufficient points, the biggest job I had was supervising the assignment of replacements, and

meeting and escorting the senior officers to their units when they arrived. When the Division was pulled back into reserve, it was my responsibility to assign the areas for the headquarters elements to locate. It wasn't long after the Division moved from the front lines to a reserve position that I reached the magic number of points for rotation back to the States. I left from Inchon. The tide was out so we had to take small boats out to the transport. I spent one night in southern Japan and then was on a troop ship back to Seattle, a train to Oxnard to spend a couple of days with Mother, Maye, Bob and Molly, and friends, then again by train to Little Rock to Nancy and the children. My orders were to report to the Pentagon for duty with the Assistant Chief of Staff for Personnel.]

At home, I made contact immediately with my Standard Oil bosses. They asked me to take over the southern sector with office in El Centro. After I found a house, they arranged for a moving company. We stayed for a few days in a motel and became good friends with the two women who owned and operated it. After getting settled in our home, I began visiting dealers throughout the territory. My boss Harry Hogl invited me to dinner and to spend the night when I got to Indio. First, I went to Westmoreland, then on to Niland and Mecca, where I met Adda B Ruth, an elderly lady who ran the inside of the station and her husband Steve Ragsdale, the outside—both in their late sixties. The town consisted of a few houses, a library, a bunk house, and a Standard Station. Steve's ex-wife got about half the town where she and her son built and operated a Texaco station on the other side of town and went into competition with Steve. After ordering items Adda B needed, I went to Desert Center, taking a short cut through Bouquet Canyon with spare items, such a fan belt, spare tire, and water in case of a breakdown en route in the canyon.

In Desert Center, I met the station manager's wife, Mrs. Bobay, who had a parakeet on her shoulder and told me a story about the area. About thirty miles from Desert Center is a town called Hell which consisted of a few houses, a service station, and a restaurant operated by a young couple. She ran the café and the station. One hot day while visiting with the lady in her restaurant, she saw a new Buick came roaring down the highway. In front of the café, the driver lost control, crashed, and rolled over. Mrs. Bobay ran out and pulled a man from the car. While holding his head in her lap to shade him from the hot sun, he opened his eyes and asked, "Where am I." She said she didn't have the heart to tell him.

For the next several days, I toured my area of responsibility and met the owners, dealers, and operators. I went home each night and was greeted by both Molly and Tomilyn. Molly seemed healthier than she ever was and full of spirit. She worked for a clothing store for about four hours each day when Tomilyn was in school. We often went down to the El Noh Motel to visit with the two owners, and Tomilyn and I would swim in their large pool. It seemed as though Molly felt much better there in the desert and had fewer breathing problems. We played ping-pong and walked almost every evening, and she seemed to breathe more easily.

One day I got a call from my buddy George Benson. He was out of the Army and, with his wife Barbara, was on the way to San Diego. It was great renewing our friendship and reminiscing about our time in Japan and Korea. We all went to Mary and Zoe's Motel and had a swim in their pool. I said there wasn't much to show him in El Centro, to which he responded, "It beats the hell out of Korea," They left the next day. It was wonderful seeing them and recalling some of our experiences. He had taken a language course in Indonesian and later served in the Vietnam conflict. He had three tours in Indonesia as the Military Advisor and had a close relationship with that country's leaders for years after he retired from the Army

I was doing well in the job. My dealers were all my friends and seemed to look forward to my visits, which I did about once a month. I had the winning dealer in the company's sales contest almost every year. My bosses seemed impressed with the annual sales meeting we held each year. Every dealer came (some by driving over 200 miles) except Desert Center Steve Ragsdale and Adda B. Ruth, but both sent representatives.

I was told by the Division office that I should get the account of Desert Center cleared up as it was delinquent in both its retail and wholesale business, and the company was getting concerned. I made contact with the manager Floyd and arranged see the owner Mr. Ragsdale, better known as Desert Steve. He advised me to come early and be prepared for a long session. I left El Centro at 4:00 a.m. and made the long trip to Desert Center, getting there in time for a cup of coffee in his café—where he had a large sign over the door: "No Dogs or Drunks Allowed. We Prefer Dogs." I then went to Desert Steve's small cabin. A middle-aged woman greeted me and asked me in. The walls were covered with printed messages. One stood out: "Get Rid of Bad People. They Are Like Apples. One Bad Apple Will Spoil the Barrel." We were having a good conversation when Desert Steve Ragsdale came in. In one hand he had a cane and in the other a revolver. I assumed the weapon was part of his uniform. After listening to him for a couple of hours while he told me his life's story including his ownership of the station and most of the town and the top of the mountain overlooking Palm Springs where he and his lady friend were going to spend the rest of the summer. By noon we had worked out a plan, had lunch together, and I left. I called my boss Harry Hogl and briefed him on the results. About two weeks later, I received a letter from Mr. Ragsdale offering me a job with the incentive of one-fourth of his business and an amount larger than I was currently being paid. I wrote back to him declining and thanked him for the offer.

Tomilyn and Molly decided that one way to get acquainted with the boys and girls in the new school was to have a party. We invited four boys and four girls. We decorated the backyard where they could dance to music from our record player. Well, they all came, nicely dressed, clean and sparkling. We waited for the boys and girls to talk to each other, but they stayed apart. We waited for them to start dancing—no way. Finally a couple of girls danced together, but the boys stayed aloof and ate and drank soft drinks and the dips, hamburgers and hot dogs. I thought the party was a bust. That night I told Molly how disappointed I was and she shushed me. The next night at dinner I brought up the party and Tomilyn said the kids were happy and hoped we would have another party soon.

I enjoyed my work and Tomilyn seemed happy with school and friends. I noticed that Molly was spending more time with her practitioner. I joined and enjoyed the Toastmaster's Club. After a few weeks, the club sent me to the State contest where the judges seemed to like my presentation and I received the most applause of all the contestants. I finished second—and I my assigned topic was a subject I knew nothing about.

I was sent, along with the Assistant Retail Manager, John LaRue to New York to visit the Atlas Test Facilities. We met up with "Pappy" Buel—the other Retail Merchandiser from our Division—and were taken by helicopter (not my favorite form of transportation) to New Jersey to the plant. Before I left, Molly and Tomilyn went to Port Hueneme to spend some time with her parents. I was impressed with the Atlas Lab, especially seeing all the testing tires went through before they went to our company's stations. We did a little sightseeing. When the week was over, I was glad to get on the plane for home.

Molly seemed quieter than usual, not as bubbly, but she never complained. She and Tomilyn said they had a great time with her friend Beverly who visited them during my absence. Molly had taken them to the El Noh motel almost everyday for a swim, and they were sad to see her leave. I was back in my routine, working everyday and at the National Guard meetings each weekend—usually with the local Guard unit—instead of in Los Angeles.

After a year, my job was upgraded to Retail Supervisor with an increase in pay. I especially enjoyed visiting the car dealers. One day I was in the Pontiac agency in El Centro and noticed a customer looking at a car. Mr. Colove, the agency owner, was busy, so I approached the man and invited him to sit in the car. I suggested that he drive it. He liked the car and when we got back to the dealership, Mr. Colove sold it to him. He was so pleased he offered me a job, with the promise to let me buy into his business. Of course, I refused, for I was happy with my job with the company—which had changed its name to Chevron Oil.

My counterpart in the northern part of Harry Hogl's territory was Butch Edgin. Soon after I arrived in the desert area, he was killed in a car accident. His replacement was Bill Bossard. Bill and his wife became good friends. They invited me to stay with them when I came to Indio.

The first Christmas in El Centro we decided not to go to Port Hueneme, so we decorated the house. Tomylin was assigned the tree. She purchased the tree and the decorations for it. Molly had the front and dining rooms. I got the job of the top of the tree, the buffet, and the front door. We had a lot of fun doing it, and we got our neighbor, John Muscudini, who was a professional window dresser, to judge our efforts. Since we were in the desert, I tried to create a desert scene—getting large tumbleweed and some rocks for the top of the buffet. Tomylin won first prize, and Molly the second. They didn't seem to appreciate my work. We celebrated with the judge and his wife at dinner in the El Centro hotel.

Atlas Tire Company came out with tubeless tires, and Chevron sent me back to New York and New Jersey to get acquainted with the procedures in selling and installing the new product. I went with John LaRue, the Assistant Division Manager of the San Diego district, and "Pappy" Buell, another retail representative in San Diego. While I was gone, Molly and Tomylin went to Port Hueneme to spend a week with her folks. Molly's mother was also a student of the Christian Science religion. Lately Molly had been much more active in her religion.

After we learned the procedures to repair the new tires, it was clear that Buell knew how better than Larue, the man instructing us, especially in using their new tire-changing machine. When we finished the session, we all went to lunch together and learned that this was the first team the instructor had to train. The restaurant was busy with a long line waiting. Larue disappeared for a few minutes and talked to the maitre de. When he came back we were seated immediately. I asked him how he did it and he said "You have to know the system to survive in New York."

I had begun to notice more and more change in Molly. She was a lot more active in her church and became very interested in teaching their religion, and spent a lot of time with her tutor. She was still the vivacious, sweet girl, she always had been, but she seemed to spend more time praying. She was a Sunday school teacher, and she also worked in a small dress shop from 10 a.m. to 2 p.m. She was always at home when Tomilyn came home from school. My friends always sent their love to her when I saw them.

When we returned home, Molly and Tomylin picked me up at the airport. During the trip home I noticed Molly was very upset about something, but she wouldn't talk about her problem until we got home. When we were alone, I learned that she had found a lump in her breast, but she would not go to a doctor. Despite my pleas, she refused and spent more time with her Christian Science practitioner as she was determined to stay with her. That was her strong belief, and I couldn't stand in her way. From that day on, I was on edge and prayed with her and read the lesson with her at least once every day. Daily she would spend at least two hours with her practitioner.

She kept getting worse, and I became more and more insistent that she try another way. The practitioner had the church send a nurse to our house—then I knew things were bad. Each day the nurse came and worked with Molly with prayer and reading the Bible and books of the Christian Science religion. But Molly was getting weaker and weaker.

One Sunday we were at home. Molly did not want to go to church as she was feeling too bad. I had taken up painting and was working on a desert scene when the phone rang. Molly's brother Tom was calling to say that Molly's father had had a serious heart attack. They had taken him to the hospital where he was treated, and after a few hours released to go home. I then told Tom I had been hesitant to call and tell them that Molly was not doing well. She did not want to tell her folks that she had a full-time Christian Science nurse who has suggested that Molly go to the Christian Science Hospital in San Diego. My plan was to take her there soon. I asked him not to tell my family as Molly was determined to fight the illness by herself with the help of her religion. I then asked Molly if she wanted to speak with her folks, but she shook her head.

The next day when I returned from a trip to Indio, I was greeted by Molly and the nurse, who told me that they had made arrangements for Molly to go to the hospital in San Diego. The following day, I dismissed the nurse and took her to the bus station. Before departing the nurse said that she had never encountered or knew of a better Christian Scientist than Molly.

That afternoon I took Tomilyn to the El Noh Motel to stay with our friends there. After a tearful goodbye, I drove Molly to the hospital in San Diego. On arrival, we were met by the director and head nurse. They lost no time in getting Molly into a room and then dismissing me as they wanted to talk to Molly, make her comfortable, and examine her. I left and found a nearby motel.

The next morning I returned to the hospital and saw Molly, who smiled when I came into her room. She had spent a restful night. They had assigned a practitioner who had talked with her for over an hour. Molly was impressed with everything there. I visited with her until the nurse shooed me out. I went back to El Centro and called my boss, Harry Hogl, and asked him to bear with me as Molly was in the hospital. I told him that I would continue to make contact with the dealers in my area mostly by telephone, but would go back to San Diego each afternoon. He agreed and, on my request, promised to tell his boss.

The next few days were hectic. I worked in the morning until noon, then picked up Tomilyn and took her to our friends at the motel until I returned in the evening. I don't remember how long this went on, but I vividly recall the Saturday I went to see Molly, and she was very upset. The nurse had made her get up and sit on the toilet until she relieved herself. She wanted to go home. I stayed with her until about 8 p.m., then went to a motel, checked in, went to a nearby restaurant and ate a burger, picked up a newspaper and went to bed. At 4:00 a.m. I was awakened out of a sound sleep—I could hear Molly calling to me, "Bob, Bob, I need you. I really need you." I got out of bed, dressed, and phoned the hospital, told them I was awakened from my sleep by Molly calling and asked if everything was all right. The nurse said, "Your wife has been calling you! Please come right away." I quickly dressed and rushed to the hospital, parked the car, and ran into Molly's room. The nurse was talking to her trying to calm her down. When I came into the room, she stopped turning and fighting, smiled and said, "You are not going to get your dance." This puzzled me for a few seconds until I remembered the many times she refused to dance with me saying, "Some day I'll dance with you." I kissed her and held her hand, and knew then that she was dying.

Over the intercom came the message of the day. As we listened, a voice spoke the Twenty-third Psalm:

The Lord is my Shepherd, I shall not want.

He makes me lie down in green pastures; he leads me beside still waters;

He restores my soul. He leads me in the paths of righteousness, for his name's sake.

Even though I walk through the shadow of death, I fear no evil,

For you are with me; your rod and your staff comfort me.

You prepare a table before me in the presence of my enemies.

You anoint my head with oil, my cup overflows.

Surely goodness and mercy shall follow me all the days of my life,

And I shall dwell in the house of the Lord forever.

As the final words came over the intercom, Molly leaned back on her pillow and uttered, "Oh, God."

She died with her eyes open. At that very moment there was a rush of air inside the room, and the curtains swayed as her spirit left. I leaned over and kissed her, rang the bell for the nurse. When she came I told her, "Molly went with the Lord."

I waited outside the room, waited and watched as they took my darling on the gurney. The hospital manager told me they had made arrangements with a local funeral home. The nurse then gave me the few things that Molly had taken from home. I went to the funeral parlor in downtown San Diego, made arrangements with the funeral director to prepare the body, and call Reardon's Funeral Parlor in Oxnard for them to handle arrangements for her burial there.

As I was driving home, I saw a fellow Chevron retail representative, Dick Carlson, ahead of me. I honked and he pulled over. I asked him to call our boss, Bill Bade, and tell him Molly had died and that I would be home in El Centro in a couple of hours. He said he would, and I went home, praying most of the way and rehearsing how I would tell Tomilyn and the families. I stopped before reaching the motel to rehearse how I would handle things. I went in and told Tomilyn and our friends at the motel, Zoe and Mary. I'll never forget the scene, all of us weeping bitterly. Finally, Tomilyn and I left and went home after thanking Zoe and Mary for taking care of Tomilyn. We hated to go in, for everything in the house said "Molly lived here." Neither of us slept much that night. I kept busy the next day calling the two families and telling them the sad news and plans for the burial.

The following day Paul and Colette and their children brought my mother down to help me, having decided that we should not be left alone. She helped us through those dark days. We drove to Oxnard the day of the funeral. There were lots of flowers and lots of love. The service was very appropriate, handled by Christian Scientists. As we left, we stopped and said goodbye to our love, so beautiful, so loving with the family, and so full of love for her Maker.

I sang our song—which we decided would be our song when we first started going together and had heard it in a musical in Hollywood:

> Just Molly and me, and baby makes three,
>
> We're happy in our blue heaven.
>
> A turn to the right, a little white light
>
> Will lead you to our Blue Heaven.
>
> I see a fireplace, a cozy room,
>
> A little nest that nestles best
>
> Where roses bloom.
>
> Just Molly and me, and baby makes three.
>
> You're welcome in our Blue Heaven.[1]

The company transferred me to the Los Angeles area for a few years, then to run the Retail Operations in Hawaii, and finally to head up the Los Angeles office as Retail Manager. Tomilyn passed away in 1989 and left two sons and a daughter, who are all raising families of their own. I am spending my remaining years on a hillside in Granada Hills overlooking the San Fernando Valley.

Based on my experiences, I think I am entitled to make a few observations in the twilight of my years. We have the greatest country in the world by God's will, and we can keep it so only if we follow what He has told us to do in His book—the Bible. We still have the chance to continue to lead all the nations today in the struggle for

---

1 "My Blue Heaven." Music by Walter Donaldson; lyrics by George Whiting. 1927

liberty, equality, and justice. That chance will be gone if we continue to condone the immorality, unequal treatment, and unethical conduct by leaders in our business, social, and political life. I say we have the chance to correct the ills of society because those who created our system provided the devices that allow us to do so—basically the power of the vote. To exercise that power properly requires an intelligent citizenry, and I'm not so sure we have that today—but we could have it.

Those of us who were the "kids who saved the world for democracy" and who are still around may be unable to do it again. But we can pass on our devotion to country and family by example and by helping the following generations to understand their importance and what this country is all about.

Capt. Bob Moranda when recalled to active service during the Korean War as Headquarter Company Commander, 981ˢᵗ Field Artillery, 40ᵗʰ Infantry Division

Bob and Sgt. Totoni at the 1997 Reunion of the 7ᵗʰ Armored Division

Conclusions

[2]On the day before Christmas in 1944, while General Patton's Third Army was slowly approaching Bastogne to relieve the surrounded 101st Airborne Division and its attached units, four war correspondents, Joseph Driscoll of the New York Herald Tribune, Norman Clark of the London News Chronicle, Walter Cronkite of the United Press, and Cornelius Ryan of the London News Daily Telegraph were following along on the road from Arlon to Bastogne, the route Patton's forces were using in their drive north. While freezing in the bitter cold and waiting for the route to open, because of the fighting that was going on in the area, they had run into Major General Maxwell Taylor en route to join his command, the 101st Airborne Division, after his return from the States. They soon followed his route when the road was less dangerous to travel. When they reached the encircled troops, their reports amplified the Bastogne story—which by then had captured the public's imagination. Public Relations Officers at all levels from the Pentagon on down had a great story and the media played and expanded it so that the public perception of the 101st Division's stand became almost the entire story about the Battle of the Bulge.

The fact is there was a terrible breakdown of the American intelligence system in their failure to recognize the threat, their disregard of historical data, and their disregard of reports from the front line troops of enemy activities, as well as the signal intercepts by army signal intelligence groups that reported significant surrounded 101st Airborne Division

---

2 As mentioned in the Introduction, George Moranda included explanatory, historical notes printed in italics throughout the text. George Moranda also wrote this chapter, "Conclusions."

and its attached units, four war correspondents, Joseph Driscoll of the New York Herald Tribune, Norman Clark of the London News Chronicle, Walter Cronkite of the United Press, and Cornelius Ryan of the London Daily Telegraph were following along on the road from Arlon to Bastogne, the route Patton's forces were using in their drive north. While freezing in the bitter cold and waiting for the route to open wider, because of the fighting that was going on in the area, they had run into Major General Maxwell D. Taylor en route to rejoin his command, the 101st Airborne Division, after his return from the States, and soon followed his route when the road was less dangerous to travel. When they reached the 101st Airborne Division's encircled troops, their reports amplified the Bastogne story—which by then had captured the public's imagination. Public Relations Officers at all levels from the Pentagon down had a great story and the media played and expanded it so that the public perception of the 101st Division's stand became almost the entire story about the Battle of the Bulge.

It is small wonder that veterans who served with the 1st, 2nd, 28th, and 99th Infantry Divisions, the 7th and 9th Armored Divisions, the 14th Cavalry Group, and many other units during that battle have feelings of resentment for not having been recognized for their vitally important services, some heroic, especially the 7th Armored. It was these units and smaller groups who made the Germans stumble, delaying them long enough for the Allied High Command finally to recognize the situation in progress, their errors of judgment, and the need to provide forces to counter the Nazi drive. After the war, General Manteuffel, Fifth Panzer Army commander, in an interview stated that he needed, wanted, and intended to take the vital communications center of St. Vith by December 17 in order to have a means to logistically support the main German effort, his Fifth Panzer Army, and the Sixth Panzer Army to his north. Prevented from doing so by stubborn defenders, his plans were disrupted which caused much shifting of troops intended for other missions, some that were to assist and support the major thrust to the Meuse River along the avenues opened both north and south of St. Vith and clogged to routes for their supply trains. And Bastogne, which was not a first priority target in the German attack and was ordered by Hitler to be bypassed if defended, became important to the German effort only after St. Vith could not be captured and that essential communications hub was destroyed by artillery and, later, by Allied air attacks after the withdrawal of the 7th Armored units to a more cohesive line immediately west of St. Vith. Hitler didn't order Bastogne to be taken until St. Vith was unusable to provide the logistical support to the two Panzer Armies. This by no means diminishes their valiant performance, but there is more to the story of this campaign than what is now generally known in the public's knowledge.

During World War II, four critical events significantly altered the course of that war, and they all involved the element of surprise: the German invasion of Russia in 1941; the Japanese attack at Pearl Harbor on December 7, 1941; the Ardennes Campaign, popularly known as the Battle of the Bulge, in December and January, 1944-1945; and the atomic bombing of Hiroshima and Nagasaki. The first event split the German-Russian alliance and brought the USSR, with its tremendous source of manpower, into the Allied camp. The second event brought the United States, with its industrial and military and naval might, into the war. The third marked the demise of the German war machine and the collapse of the Nazi regime. And, of course, the last caused the sudden end to the Japanese conflict.

By the fall of 1944, the Germans were beset on all fronts. The Allied Forces were pressing on all of them, shrinking the German lines. On the Eastern Front the Russian army had pushed through a major offensive that overran most of Eastern Poland. In Italy the American Fifth and British Eighth armies had shoved the Germans northward beyond the Po River. On the Western Front, two German armies had been destroyed by British, Canadian, French, and American forces after their breakout from the Normandy beaches. With pressure on the Germans along the entire western front, too many of the Allied leaders had a sense that the German collapse was not only inevitable but also imminent. After all, the German homeland had been reached and the Allied generals were talking about their troops being home for Christmas—and even betting that they would.

Complacency or false anticipation was beginning to creep in. On the home front, plans were being discussed about when to implement programs to convert the industrial might back to civilian products.

Consideration was being given to the matter of which units to transfer to the Pacific to bring that part of the war to a conclusion. The Allied Command was continuing its efforts of constant pressure throughout the entire western front and preparing to maintain it. The military leadership was well developed and the top leaders winnowed into an effective command structure. Their fighting forces were "blooded" and had reached the level of a seasoned fighting machine. Logistics seemed well organized and supply lines were humming with activity. Air was under the control of Allied Air Forces and had almost driven the Luftwaffe from the skies. The personnel replacement system was sending streams of new soldiers to fill the ranks of those units with losses. All seemed to be going smoothly. Major plans were being made for schedules to attack the Roer River dams in the north and, in the southern sector, to reduce the Colmar Pocket. The only threat to the Allied positions was considered to be a counterattack to delay or prevent an attack on the Roer River dams and the approach to the Ruhr. So with such a positive and rosy outlook, why not put a newly arrived Infantry Division (106th), which had come from the States on December 10, with a Cavalry Group attached, and a badly mauled, under-strength, veteran infantry division (28th) pulled back after a bitter fight in the Hurtgen Forest to recuperate and receive replacements, to cover the Ardennes forest area—about sixty air miles across, several more in ground miles. And not worry or be too concerned over the fact that it was a route used by the Germans twice before: to implement the Schlieffen Plan at the start of World War I which brought the Germans to within sight of Paris, and in 1940 for the invasion of Belgium and France, which resulted in the conquest of those countries.

About the same time that General Eisenhower was holding his conference with Allied leaders on December 7 at Maastricht to discuss and settle some difficulties concerning the top command structure and differences in strategic plans, Hitler's armies were assembling for the execution of what he called *Wacht Am Rhein*: the Ardennes Campaign. General Eisenhower felt it was necessary to get his top field *commanders* together to arrive at a meeting of the minds about which strategy to follow. So there were many presentations in which individual opinions were expressed about whether the Ruhr or Saar basins, or both, should be the main effort. Mentioned, but not seriously, was the thinly spread defenses in the Ardennes area. The Ardennes and the Eifel were not considered as avenues of approach in their consideration of objectives, rather they were deemed to be obstacles for the enemy. General Eisenhower in his command post had remarked about the thinness of American forces there, and General Bradley even made a visit to consult with his VIII Corps commander, General Troy Middleton, who had also expressed concern about the frontage he had to cover. General Bradley calmed him by telling Middleton not to worry, "They won't come through here."

General Bradley's Intelligence Officer (G-2), Brigadier General Edwin Sibert, wrote his analysis of the situation in Bradley's 12th Army Group's area in his weekly summary of December 12: "It is now certain that attrition is steadily sapping the strength of German forces on the Western Front and that the crust of defenses is thinner, more brittle, and more vulnerable than it appears on our G-2 maps, or to the troops in the line... The enemy divisions...have been cut by at least fifty percent . . . The German breaking point may develop suddenly and without warning." General Bradley backed his G-2 over the intelligence estimate of Major General Kenneth Strong, SHAEF's Intelligence Officer, who suggested the increasing German reserve buildup, which had been detected, might be used to disrupt the overstretched American VIII Corps. (But Strong in November had made note of the German losses and that they were shifting their meager resources to meet various threats, like a "dwindling fire brigade.") Bradley's rather flippant retort was, "Let them come." Field Marshall Montgomery's Intelligence Officer, Brigadier E. T. Williams, at that time declared the Germans were in a bad way and could not mount a major offensive.

Some recognized the possibility of a German offensive. First Army's G-2, Col. Benjamin "Monk" Dickson, and his Third Army counterpart, Col. Oscar Koch, both identified the Ardennes front as being vulnerable and likely to be attacked. Col. Dickson must not have felt too strongly about it, or he became piqued at General Sibert's conclusions, and went on a long delayed four-day leave to Paris on December 12. On the other hand, Col. Koch's estimate fell on more receptive ears with General Patton, who put his staff to work to develop three alternate plans for such a contingency. After the German attack started, and General Eisenhower hurriedly called his Army Group and

Army commanders to a war council in Verdun on December 19 to deal with what had finally been recognized as a major effort by the Germans, he asked General Patton how soon he could shift his forces to counter the German breakthrough. General Patton replied that he could do it immediately, which was met with considerable skepticism and laughter, for no one believed he could swing his army around on a ninety degree angle over snowbound roads after disengaging from his ongoing battle. He was confident about doing so because he had accepted the Koch estimate and ordered his staff to develop plans for just such a contingency. He left the conference with orders to move, made a phone call to his Command Post to execute the plan, and was able to begin attacking by December 22 and not later than December 23, as General Eisenhower had directed.

The intelligence system in the U.S. Army was one with too many road blocks. Reports from the front line troops of sightings, patrol activities, interrogations of enemy prisoners, and other bits and pieces of information had to be funneled through inexperienced, untrained battalion and regimental S-2 or brigade G-2s, divisional G-2s, corps G-2s, Army G-2s and Army Group G-2s (S-2 and G-2 are designations for the staff intelligence officer) before they reached the top command structure. And at each level they were given interpretations or otherwise influenced by officers who did not have the training or experience to adequately evaluate the material. It is small wonder that patrols reporting tank movements at the front would have some S-2 or G-2 down-play the information to "trucks with chains" in their analyses sent up the chain of command, if it was passed on at all.

On December 15, General Eisenhower received his promotion to General of the Army, with five stars, putting him equal in grade to that of Field Marshal in other armies. That same day Field Marshal Montgomery requested and received permission from General Eisenhower to "hop over to England" to celebrate the approaching Christmas holiday with his son. At the same time he asked Ike to pay him the five pounds they had bet that the war would end by Christmas, which Ike refused to pay until that date arrived. At dawn the next day the German attack commenced in General Bradley's area of responsibility, and Field Marshall Montgomery was called off the golf course at Eindhoven

The fact is there was a terrible breakdown of the American intelligence system in their failure to recognize the threat, their disregard of historical data, and their disregard of reports from the front line troops of enemy activities. They failed to use the signal intercepts by army signal groups that reported significant enemy movement. It was costly in the number of casualties. In this battle, the largest of the war, American losses numbered about 100,000 soldiers, of which 15,000 were captured and over 19,000 killed—the equivalent of approximately six infantry divisions. The losses of equipment and weapons were monumental.

When Patton's Third Army commenced its attack against the southern shoulder to relieve the surrounded troops at Bastogne, the 7th Armored Division had delayed the German advance through St. Vith by six days. That bitter, magnificent defense, along with other delaying actions, gave the Allied Command the time to shift forces to contain the German drive, disrupt their timetable, cause them to shift the attack's center of gravity from that of General Dietrich's 6th Panzer Army to General Manteuffel's 5th Panzer Army, and put some starch back into the retreating American forces.

The three German panzer armies began their attack on the morning of December 16. Reports came in during the day to the VIII Corps, First Army, and 12th Army Group to relieve the surrounded troops at Bastogne, the 7th headquarters; it was clear that something had to be done. That evening General Bradley decided to shift the 7th Armored Division, then in Ninth Army reserve, to the VIII Corps, an order that proved to be one of the most important given during the battle. But what the 7th Armored ran into on the forced march from their positions in Holland to St. Vith was almost impossible to describe. Bitter cold, icy roads, snow, uncertainty, and rumors about enemy forces (spearheaded by Lt. Col. Jochen Peiper's leading troops of the Sixth Panzer Army) passing through the 7th's eastern march route. They also faced obstacles created by displacing artillery units and supply and support units, as well as fleeing soldiers of all ranks causing almost impenetrable traffic jams. Communications were bad; orders were late in reaching intended commanders—if they were received at all. Information was anything but timely or accurate.

Upon arrival in St. Vith, Brigadier General Bruce C. Clarke, CCB commander, found the 106th Infantry Division's Commanding General and staff in a state of shock and bewilderment. Told to take charge, General Clarke, even though junior in rank to the 106th Infantry Division commander Major General Jones, began to funnel units piecemeal as they arrived to build a line east of St. Vith using as a base a small engineer aggregation under Lt. Col. Riggs as a base. Elements of the 38th Armored Infantry Battalion, including its Headquarters Company commanded by Capt. Rusty Mattocks, were among the first to report and were sent into the line. They were gradually supplemented with a few additional units of the 38th Armored Infantry Battalion, parts of the 87th Cavalry Squadron, 23d Armored Infantry Battalion, and 31st Tank Battalion when they arrived in the area. All this was done while heavy fighting was in progress. Gradually the entire 7th Armored Division was deployed to defend northward, eastward, and southeastward in what has come to be called the "Fortified goose egg"— actually a horseshoe shaped defense with a large gap to the south. But the only reason that build-up could occur was the group of units under Lt. Col. Tom Riggs, and later Major Don Boyer, defending bitterly and gallantly about a mile east of St. Vith across the Prumerberg road.

On December 17, everything was fluid and vague. The German 6th Panzer Army was moving west rapidly after it was unable to break through the American 1st, 2nd, and 99th Infantry Divisions at Elsenborn, and was heading for Stavelot beyond Malmedy. On their southern flank, the German 5th Panzer Army was making progress westward north of St. Vith and was pushing westward toward Andler and Recht. The latter was also through Bleialf heading for Winterspelt to the southeast of St. Vith, after having completed the encirclement and the surrender of two regiments of the 106th Infantry Division and badly mauling the veteran 28th Infantry Division. As they progressed westward during the next four days, the two Panzer Armies moved both north and south of St. Vith and created what appeared to be a long finger, pointed toward Germany, with the nail of the finger being east of St. Vith. Within that finger was the 7th Armored Division with a miscellaneous group of attached units under the command of Brigadier General Robert W. Hasbrouck, who had established his headquarters in Vielsam. The tip of the nail was Major Boyer's Task Force a mile east of St. Vith across the Plummerville road.

The chains of command had been disrupted throughout the entire battle area. Corps, divisions, regiments, and battalions were being shifted around in an attempt to provide some cohesiveness, with some success and some failure. On December 20, Montgomery's 21st British Army Group was given responsibility for the northern sector and the U.S. First Army (less the VIII Corps which was to become part of Third Army) and Ninth Armies were assigned to him from General Bradley's 12th Army Group, leaving Bradley with the Third Army and that part of First Army south of the German penetration. Corps was reassigned as indicated above with the VIIIth transferred from the First to the Third Army. The XVIII Airborne Corps under Major General Matthew Ridgeway, which had been in reserve in France, was moved in and assigned the area from Malmedy to Houffalize, linking up with the VIIth Corps at Malmedy and with the VIIIth Corps to the south and southeast and the Third Army when they got there.

These changes resulted in the 106th Infantry Division and the 7th Armored Division being placed under the XVIIIth Airborne Corps along with the 82d Airborne Division, 3rd Armored Division, and the 30th Infantry Division. The latter three were en route to the Werbomont-Stavelot area from the west and north. While all this was going on, neither Hasbrouck in the 7th Armored nor Jones in the 106th Infantry were aware of the changes because they were out of communication with VIIIth Corps. By that time, the 112th Infantry Regiment of the 28th Infantry Division, which had fought a brilliant delaying action, about half of the 424th Infantry Regiment—all that remained of the 106th Infantry Division after its other two regiments had earlier surrendered—and CCB of the 9th Armored Division were all under the control of General Hasbrouck of the 7th Armored—a Brigadier General (Major General Jones was little more than a spectator). With the fighting troops, Lt. Col. Riggs, who had established the original line east of St.Vith with elements of his 81st Engineer Battalion of the 106th Division, relinquished command to Lt. Col. Fuller when the 38th Armored Infantry arrived on the scene. Then when Fuller decided to leave, his Operations Officer Major Don Boyer became the de facto commander of the troops. So there was a great deal of shifting of responsibilities, and command lines were anything but clear—but they were, in most part, worked out on the ground.

Another example of the disruption of command occurred in the 14th Cavalry Group, which had been decimated during the breakthrough at Losheim Gap and had lost over half of the group on December 17. Col. Devine had issued orders to his northern unit, the 32d Squadron which was under heavy attack, to withdraw to a line from Born to Wallerode, when he received orders from the 106th Infantry Division headquarters to hold his present line. That was impossible, and the 14th Cavalry Group continued its withdrawal through St. Vith to Poteau and Vielsam running into the tremendous traffic jam on the Vielsam road. Col. Devine met some Germans near Recht and his party was shot up but escaped on foot. When he got to Poteau, Col. Devine was so shaken he turned over command to Lt. Col. William F. Damon, commander of the 18th Squadron. Damon was ordered shortly afterwards to VIIIth Corps headquarters and Lt. Col. Ridge of the 32d Squadron took over. Then Lt. Col. Augustine Dugan, the Group's executive officer, arrived and he assumed command as senior officer present. So in a period of four hours the Group had four different commanders.

Most of the command relationships were amicably and cooperatively settled, although some with great reluctance. It became a little touchy when General Ridgeway arrived on the scene at Werbomont to set up the XVIIIth Airborne Corps headquarters. On December 21, Ridgeway sent a message to General Hasbrouck telling him that the 106th was no longer attached to the 7th Armored and that the two divisions henceforth were to cooperate in carrying our XVIII Corps orders. At the same time General Hoge, Commander of CCB of the 9th Armored Division, who had worked out an informal but effective working relationship with General Hasbrouck, was told that his Combat Command was no longer attached to the 7th Armored. These orders destroyed a clear, if unorthodox, relationship. Later General Ridgeway sent a plan calling for the perimeter defense of the St. Vith-Vielsam area and had sent a message to the 7th Armored to hold their present positions. When Generals Clarke and Hasbrouck decided to shorten the lines and withdraw to a more tenable position west of St. Vith on December 21, anticipating a strong assault by the Germans the next day, apparently General Ridgeway got his nose out of joint. Generals

Clarke and Hasbrouck wanted no part of General Ridgeway's scheme and probably recognized it as something typical for airborne units and not for armored forces which depend on ground supply lines rather than airborne droppings. Ridgeway's orders were confusing; at one point he placed General Jones (being senior to Hasbrouck) in command of the 7th Armored Division and then told General Hasbrouck to make the decision and inform General Jones. Talk about double-speak! What words were passed is not known, but it has been reported that neither Bruce Clarke nor Matthew Ridgeway ever spoke to each other again for the remainder of their careers—both of whom wound up with four stars before retiring from the Army. It's probably a good thing that the front line troops didn't know of such confusion and rancor. They continued to slog it out with the attacking enemy.

On December 22, after being briefed on the situation at St. Vith, Field Marshall Montgomery, then in command of that sector, overruled General Ridgeway by concluding that there was nothing more to be gained by holding the St. Vith salient and directed that the troops in it be withdrawn behind the 82d Airborne Division. Both he and General Eisenhower then sent congratulatory messages to General Hasbrouck for the magnificent stand of the 7th Armored Division and the units attached to it during the critical time they held off the German assaulting forces.

On December 22, General Clarke withdrew the CCB west of St. Vith. General Jones alerted General Hoge of CCB, 9th Armored Division, and Col. Reid, commander of the 424th Infantry Regiment, to shorten their lines for the contraction of the salient. What happened then to the Task Force under Major Boyer? Were they forgotten? Did the division plan to leave them as a covering force? Did communications again fail? Whatever the situation, it is small wonder that Don Boyer, Bob Moranda, and the others up there would feel that they were "sacrificed."

There were many, many heroic and daring deeds during this battle in the Ardennes during that bitter winter. The two Lt. Cols. William F. Slayden and Earle Williams delayed the German advance three hours (every minute causing the Germans to fall behind their schedule was extremely important) around Schonberg by successively establishing positions with small groups of various soldiers they could find and then calling for artillery fire on advancing enemy troop and tanks which caused the attackers to deploy their troops; the tough, begrudging withdrawals, fighting as they withdrew, all the way back to the St. Vith horseshoe, by the 112th Infantry Regiment of the 28th Infantry Division and the remnants of the 424th Regiment of the 106th Division; the great defense by the divisions holding the northern shoulder at Elsenborn, especially the 2d and 99th Infantry Divisions; the tree cutting, sawmill-operating 51st Engineer Battalion which had been producing lumber each day for the First Army winterization program about ten miles west of Trois Point, who were ordered to blow up the three bridges at the confluence of the Ambleve and Salm Rivers, got there, prepared the bridges for demolition, then with a 57mm antitank gun and crew they found wandering around, stopped the leading tanks of Jochen Peiper's assault troops with rifle and machine gun fire, bazookas (firing to give the impression of artillery), and by wrapping chains around the tires of a truck, running it up and down the road west of the bridges to simulate the sound of tanks, which convinced Peiper that he had to find an alternate route and caused him to turn north where he was stopped; and yes, the bravery pf the surrounded troops at Bastogne. These are a small representation of the many exemplary deeds done by those fighting men of the American army.

The failures and poor performances were notable. Accurate and timely communications was a large problem which was only overcome by the initiative, training, and experience of the troops. The intelligence function belied its name: traffic control was extremely poor. Planner made inadequate provision for road conditions, weather, numbers of military police, and possible withdrawals. Individuals, officers, and enlisted men who were unable to withstand the pressures of combat and "bugged out" complicated command lines and added to the horrendous traffic problems.

The German attack was contained, but it was a costly operation to squeeze the Bulge as the Allied forces did, for it permitted a good portion of the German army to escape. Both Generals George Patton and J. Lawton Collins had recommended the counterattacks should be at both of the shoulders of the bulge to pinch off the invaders, but they were overruled at the Verdun War Council by General Eisenhower.

Such a strategy would have cut off any escape by the Germans and undoubtedly would have shortened the war and prevented many casualties.

How many lives were lost in the Ardennes Campaign? A 1953 statistic reported 19,246 American soldiers were killed in action, 62,489 received nonfatal wounds, and 23,554 were taken prisoner—making it the heaviest battle toll in U.S. history. That report did not count the British, Canadian, or Germans. It has been estimated that the German losses were one-third greater. Prime Minister Winston Churchill told the House of Commons that sixty to eighty Americans were killed for every British casualty—which he felt justified calling it the greatest American battle of the war and a total American victory.

There is no question that the Germans had already lost the war by the time the Ardennes campaign occurred. Had the Germans not squandered their manpower and supplies and used them more sparingly in slowing the Allied advances, they could have extended the war until late summer or early fall of 1945. By conducting the campaign as they did, the war was considerably shortened.

The men of the 7th Armored Division can stand tall in the company of those throughout history who have performed magnificently, gallantly, and heroically in our country's service. The Germans called the 7th Armored Division "the Ghost Division" for they never knew where it would show up against their armies. After the war, recommendations for the Presidential Unit Citation were submitted, approved by both the Commanding Generals of the First U.S. Army and the European Theater, but rejected by the Department of the Army on November 26, 1947, saying that there would be no more awards to divisions, but only for smaller units. It seems reasonable to question the War Department's decision upon investigating the valorous stand of the entire division under some of the most difficult conditions that existed during the entire war. They had met an entire German Army corps, encouraged with an easy victorious breakthrough, and they halted it in its tracks for several critical days. They had choked the main enemy line of communication and supply and forced a crucial delay on the enemy's westward movement of troops, guns, tanks, and supplies needed by two German armies. They had given the XVIII Airborne

Corps badly needed time to gather and get organized and acquainted with the situation to conduct an effective defense. And they had carried out a successful withdrawal under most difficult conditions. Along with others, they bought the time needed for Eisenhower to get forces into action to foil Hitler's plan. If the Germans had been more successful at St. Vith, they almost certainly would have reached the Meuse River and perhaps farther, American casualties would have been much greater, and recovery by Allied Forces would have been greatly delayed. Field Marshal Keitel and Colonel-General Jodl of the German High Command both ascribed the main reason for the failure of their offensive was, "Tougher resistance then expected of, in themselves, weak U. S. troops especially at St. Vith." In his Biennial Report to the Secretary of the Army covering the period July 1, 1943 to June 30, 1945, General George C. Marshall wrote: "The Ardennes battle deserves a prominent place in the history of the U. S. Army. The splendid stand of the 7th Armored Division at St. Vith, the tenacity of the 101st Airborne Division and elements of the 10th Armored at Bastogne, . . .were in the finest American tradition."

The units of the 7th Armored that were cited and received the award were: the 17th and 31st Tank Battalions; 23d and 38th Armored Infantry Battalions; 434th Armored Field Artillery Battalion; 87th Cavalry Reconnaissance Squadron; Company B, 33d Armored Engineer Battalion; Company A, 814th Tank Destroyer Battalion; and Headquarters Company, Combat Command B.

The critical remarks I have made, of course, are hindsight and are based on the many studies and writings about this historic campaign. We must never forget that the American Army was victorious. It won the battle. It was a tremendous victory, and it was the American Army that did it as no other elements of the Allied Forces were involved in the actual fighting. All who served honorably in that fray deserve our undying gratitude.

Furthermore, I became greatly impressed with the tremendous accomplishments of the 7th Armored Division during that battle and am convinced that they were not adequately recognized, for whatever reasons. My research led me to discover the many mistakes, some of which I have enumerated, that were made before, during, and after that battle. If you disagree with these comments, your argument is with me—not Bob.

Our service in the Korean War was not nearly as perilous as that Bob experienced in Europe. But it does show how lives were disrupted not too many years after World War II. The adjustments we made again from civilian life to that of soldiers in training and combat, as experienced by many thousands, demonstrates the impact on our society. Yet such is necessary when our country calls for our citizens to respond to support our national interest s, as demonstrated in the Korean War when four National Guard Divisions and many Reservists were called to active service. Countless millions in our country have left homes and families to serve in our armed forces when called as the needs arise   After every war in which the United States participated, our armed forces have been reduced to levels which are then required to expand rapidly when emergencies come—which makes Reserve and National Guard an essential part of our National Defense, as has been demonstrated with the call-up of the personnel and units in Iraq and Afghanistan.

Unfortunately, our leaders have forgotten, or never knew, that ground forces are essential to control land areas. Naval and Air cannot. They are essential elements in modern war, but must be considered as support for the forces on the ground.

About the Authors

Robert E. P. "Bob" Moranda spent most of his work life with Chevron Oil Company, starting as a service station attendant and retired from the company as Retail Manager of the Los Angeles Area. His work with Chevron was interrupted twice: first, when he was drafted into the U. S. Army during World War II and served until the war ended, after which he joined the California National Guard's 40th Infantry Division; and second, when that division was ordered to active service and sent into combat during the Korean War. He lives in his home in Granada Hills, California.

George E. Moranda was drafted into the U. S. Army in July 1941. and assigned to the Corps of Engineers. He was commissioned at the Engineer Officer Candidate School and served in administrative and training positions during World War II. Following the war, he was in the Army Reserve and the California National Guard in an artillery battalion and served with his brother Bob with the 40th Infantry Division in Korea. He remained on active service and was commissioned into the Armor Branch of the Regular Army. George is a graduate of the Command and General Staff College and the Army War College, and holds Masters Degrees in Political Science from the University of Hawaii and the University of Wisconsin in Journalism. He retired from the Army in 1970. George E. Moranda passed away on January 4, 2009.

Bibliography

Books

Ambrose, Stephen E., *Citizen Soldier.* New York, Simon & Schuster, 1997.

_____, *The Victors: Eisenhower and His Boys: The Men of World War II.* New York, Simon & Schuster, 1998.

Astor, Gerald, *A Blood-Dimmed Tide: The Battle of the Bulge By the Men Who Fought It.* New York, Dell Publishing, 1992, reprinted 1994.

Baldwin, Hanson W., ed., *Command Decisions.* New York, Harcourt, Brace and Co., 1959.

Berebitsky, William, *A Very Long Weekend, The Army National Guard in Korea, 1950-1953.*

Boyd, Hugh K., *War's Journey: Memoirs of A World War II Prisoner of War in Germany.*

Bradley, Omar N., *A Soldier's Story.* New York, Henry Holt & Co., 1951.

Chapin, Neil (Ed), *The Seventh Armored Division: A Historical Overview, 1942-1945.* Dallas, Taylor Publishing Co., 1982.

Churchill, Winston S., *Triumph* and Tragedy. Boston, Houghton Mifflin Co., 1955.

Cole, Hugh M., The Ardennes: *The Battle of the Bulge.* Washington, Historical Division, Department of the Army, 1965.

Dupuy, Colonel R. Ernest, *St. Vith, Lion in the Way.* Washington, The Infantry Journal Press, 1949.

Dupuy, Trevor N., Bongard, David L., and Anderson, Richard C., *Hitler's Last Gamble; The Battle of the Bulge December 1944-January 1945.* Harper Perennial, Division of Harper Collins Publishers, 1994.

Eisenhower, John S.D., *The Bitter Woods: The Battle of the Bulge.* New York, Da Capo Press.

1995. Reprint of G. P. Putnam's Sons, 1969 edition, with a new introduction by Stephen E. Ambrose.

_____*Encyclopedia Britannica.*15th Edition, Encyclopedia Britannica, Inc.

Esposito, Colonel Vincent J., *The West Point Atlas of American Wars.* New York, Frederick A. Praeger, 1959.

Farago, Ladislas, *Patton: Ordeal and Triumph.* New York, Dell Publishing Co., 1965.

Gantter, Raymond, *Roll Me Over: An Infantryman's World War II.* New York, Ivy Books, 1997.

MacDonald, Charles B., *A Time For Trumpets: The Untold Story of the Battle of the Bulge.* New York, William Morrow and Co., 1985.

Merriam, Robert E., *Dark December: The Full Account of the Battle of the Bulge.* New York-Chicago, Ziff-Davis Publishing, 1947.

Parker, Danny S., *ed., Hitler's Ardennes Offensive: The German View of the Battle of the Bulge.* London, Greenhill Books, 1997. (From interviews with SS-Oberstgruppenfuhrer Josef "Sepp" Dietrich, General der Panzertruppen Hasso von Manteuffel, General der Panzertruppen Erich Brandenberger, and others.)

Toland, John, *Battle: The Story of the Bulge.* Lincoln, Neb. Bison Books, 1959 reprinted 1999.

Whiting, Charles, *Patton.* New York, Ballantine Books Inc., 1970.

Wilson, George, *If You Survive.* New York, Ivy Books, 1987.

William Berebitsky, *A Very Long Weekend: The Army National Guard in Korea, 1950-1953.*

Periodicals

MacDonald Charles, "The Neglected Ardennes," *Military Review*, (April, 1963).

Raymond, Captain Allen D. III, "The Battle of St. Vith," *Armor* (Nov.-Dec., 1964.

When are we Going, The Army National Guard and the Korean War, 1950-1953. Historical Services Division, Office of Public Affairs, National Guard Bureau.

Explanatory Notes

Recognizing that many readers might not be familiar with military terms used during World War II and the Korean War, the following might assist in understanding the organization, maps, and text used.

Both wars were fought by the U.S. Army with what was called the Triangular Division. It was organized from the bottom up with squads (9 to12 men), commanded by a sergeant. Three squads made up a platoon, commanded by a lieutenant. Companies or troops (a cavalry or armored designation) were commanded by a captain and consisted of three platoons. Battalions or squadrons (a cavalry term) were commanded by a lieutenant colonel with three companies. Regiments were commanded by a colonel and had three battalions. The infantry divisions, commanded by a major general with two assistant brigadier generals (one commanded the artillery), usually functioned with RCTs, or regimental combat teams. The RCTs were made up of a regiment, an artillery battalion, and combat support units such as signal, engineer, cavalry, and supply and maintenance units. (A brigade was a separate, non-divisional, large tactical unit usually formed of one or two infantry regiments with supporting artillery, armor, signal, and logistical units, and might have attached to it combat elements such as tank destroyers.) The size of an infantry division was approximately 14,500 personnel. As for equipment, these divisions contained 5 half-tracks, 13 armored cars, 18 assault guns (105 mm), 36 of 105 mm and 12 of 155 mm field artillery howitzers, 1371 motor vehicles, and 10 light aircraft.

Armored divisions had more organizational flexibility. The divisions were triangular and generally formed into combat commands, which were constructed of units for specific missions. The armored divisions were either light or heavy. Light divisions included about 10,500 men with 168 medium and 77 light tanks, 450 half-tracks, 54 self-propelled 105 mm howitzers, 35 assault guns (105 mm), 54 armored cars, 1031 motor vehicles and 8 light aircraft. Heavy divisions included 14,400 men, 232 medium and 158 light tanks, 54 self-propelled 105 mm howitzers, 18 of 105 mm and 14 of 75 mm assault guns, 54 armored cars, and 1242 motor vehicles.

A Task Force was any size grouping of units organized for a specific mission. A Corps was a tactical organization made up of two or more divisions.

Armies were both administrative and tactical with two or more corps plus attached combat, administrative, supply and maintenance units. Army Groups were essential tactical headquarter, having two or more armies.

At the time of the Ardennes Campaign, the Allied Forces were organized under the Supreme Commander, General Dwight D. Eisenhower. His headquarters was called SHAEF (Supreme Headquarters, Allied Expeditionary Forces). He commanded three Army Groups: the 12th U.S. Army Group, commanded by Lieutenant General Omar N. Bradley; the 21st British Army Group, commanded by Field Marshal Bernard Law Montgomery; and the 6th U.S. Army Group, commanded by Lieutenant General Jacob L. Devers.

12th U.S Army Group elements on December 16, 1944:

Ninth U.S. Army under Lieutenant General William H. Simpson

First U.S. Army under Lieutenant General Courtney Hodges

Third U.S Army under Lieutenant General George S. Patton

21st British Army Group element on December 16, 1944:

Second British Army under Lieutenant General Miles Dempsey

First Canadian Army under Lieutenant General H.D.H. Crerar

6th U.S. Army Groups elements on December 16, 1944:

7th U.S. Army under Lieutenant General Alexander M. Patch

First French Army under General J. de Lattre de Tassigny

Within the First U.S. Army were Corps:

V Corps under Major General Lenonard T. Gerow

VII Corps Under major General Lawton Collins

XVIII Airborne Corps under General Matthew B. Ridgeway

Within the Third U.S. Army were Corps:

VIII Corps under Major General Troy T. Middleton

III Corps under Major General John Millikin

XX Corps under Major General Walton H. Walker

XII Corps under Major General Manton S. Eddy

Within the Ninth U.S. Army were Corps:

XIII Corps under Major General Alvan C. Gillem

XIX Corps under Major General Raymond S. McLain

During the Ardennes Campaign, divisions, regiments, and battalions, and companies were shifted considerably to meet the requirements and conditions of battles, as described in this narrative.

In the Korean conflict, the 40th Division under Major General Daniel Huddleson moved to Korea and was assigned to relieve the U.S. 24th Division near Kumhwa as part of the IX Corps with the U.S. 7th Infantry Division on its east and RoK 6th Division on its west.